STEALING SAINT NICK

STEALING SAINT NICK

A LEGENDARY *corpse*,
A NOTORIOUS *theft*,
AND THE STORIES THAT
SHAPE THE *world*

by **M. T. ANDERSON**

DUTTON BOOKS

DUTTON BOOKS
An imprint of Penguin Random House LLC
1745 Broadway, New York, NY 10019
penguinrandomhouse.com

First published in the United States of America by Dutton Books,
an imprint of Penguin Random House LLC, 2026

LIBRARY OF CONGRESS CATALOGING-IN-PUBLICATION DATA

Names: Anderson, M. T. author | Title: Stealing Saint Nick : a legendary corpse, a notorious theft, and the stories that shape the world / by M. T. Anderson. | Description: New York, NY : Dutton Books, [2026] | Includes bibliographical references and index. | Audience term: Children | Audience: Ages 14 and up | Audience: Grades 10–12 | Summary: "M. T. Anderson recounts the life of a humble young man named Nicholas who became one of the world's most influential figures in religion, government, and commerce—whether you believe in him or not"—Provided by publisher. | Identifiers: LCCN 2025048998 (print) | LCCN 2025048999 (ebook) | ISBN 9780593699546 hardcover | ISBN 9780593699553 ebook | Subjects: LCSH: Nicholas, Saint, Bishop of Myra | Christian saints | LCGFT: Literature | Biographies | Classification: LCC BR1720.N46 A53 2026 (print) | LCC BR1720.N46 (ebook) | DDC 270.2092—dc23/eng/20260401 | LC record available at https://lccn.loc.gov/2025048998 | LC ebook record available at https://lccn.loc.gov/2025048999

ISBN 9780593699546

1st Printing

Manufactured in the United States of America

BVG

Design by Anna Booth
Text set in Dante MT Pro

The authorized representative in the EU for product safety and compliance is Penguin Random House Ireland, Morrison Chambers, 32 Nassau Street, Dublin D02 YH68, Ireland, https://eu-contact.penguin.ie.

To the miracle workers.

TABLE OF CONTENTS

This book deals with many different religions and the ways they change and evolve over time. It is not intended to promote or to criticize any particular religion, but simply to give a vivid sense of the role faith and belief play in human culture and identity.

—M. T. Anderson

STEALING SAINT NICK

PROLOGUE

Don't let anybody tell you Santa Claus isn't real. I've seen where they stashed his body. It's in Italy, under a basement floor.

Yes, it's true. Saint Nicholas—better known as Santa Claus—really lived and died. Centuries later, his corpse was stolen from a tomb in Turkey and taken to Bari, Italy, where it started riots. It was locked in a crypt, where it still sits in a cage a thousand years later.

Why was it stolen? Who would steal Santa Claus's dead body? How did they get away with it?

Picture an ancient church a thousand years ago. Domed, dusky in the evening. The floors are dazzling mosaics that glimmer in the candlelight.

Now imagine you are kneeling on that floor. You are a monk, and your whole life has been devoted to living in this place and protecting the body of Nicholas, a saint—called *thaumaturge*, wonder-worker—a being so powerful that even in death, his body itself is supposedly miraculous.

But that evening, you are not kneeling on the floor in prayer. You are kneeling there because a thief is holding a sword to your throat. He does not even bother to wear a mask. He tells you he has come for the corpse of Nicholas. Show him where it is hidden, or he will kill you.

He is not alone. Behind him, ranks of his companions bearing swords, spears, iron bars, hammers, recede into the twilit darkness of the church.

You know that if you give these men what they want, if you show them where Nicholas's body has been hidden for all these centuries, they will smash open his tomb and steal his sacred remains. You will betray your life's great mission, to protect the Blessed Nicholas.

If you refuse to tell this band of adventurers where the body is, they will kill you. But if you do tell them, when the people of your city discover that you've broken all your vows and given away the miraculous corpse of Nicholas, they will probably lynch you anyway.

Why have these strangers come from so far away to steal the remains of the wonder-worker, forcing you to face this impossible choice?

Because supposedly the corpse of Saint Nicholas, Santa Claus, drips an ooze that heals all wounds, all diseases. One of your duties is to scoop up the miraculous grease that flows from his bones and serve it in little glass bottles to believers.

Night is falling, and even the thieves are starting to get nervous as the sun sets. They have a long way to go before they are safely back on their ships, and they do not want to anger the ghost of the holy Nicholas, who flew through the air and fought demons and calmed storms.

Their voices shake with anxiety, but they make themselves clear: *Show us the body, or we will cut your throat in an instant.*

What would you do?

This is the story of that theft, and of the saint who was stolen.

In reality, Santa Claus did not live in the frozen north, among the snows, attended by reindeer and Claymation penguins. He lived in an arid city by the Mediterranean Sea, a city of ancient ruins and even more ancient tales, where the air on the spiky hills shimmers with heat and with the seething chant of cicadas. He was bishop of Myra, in the land of Lycia—in his lifetime, part of a vanished empire—now in southern Turkey. The earliest stories about Nicholas are actually far stranger than any of the cute myths we tell about him with our cotton-bearded-Santa booths and our animated Christmas specials.

The closest thing we have to an ancient biography of the "real" Saint Nicholas was written a few hundred years after his death and already describes him performing miracles, soaring above the sea, rescuing sailors. The stories are bizarre, fantastical, and sometimes grotesque. There are no elves, but we're told he fought a demon goddess. He did deliver presents, though under somewhat shocking circumstances. He was known for protecting children because he defeated a husband-and-wife serial killer team that was butchering schoolboys and serving them for dinner. The origins of many of these stories are lost, told for generations before people wrote them down.

Is anything in Saint Nicholas's legendary biography true? What can we learn about the real man who, over the course of seventeen centuries, has become Santa Claus? What can we learn from a biography that is so full of fantasy? Where is the truth? And where does his body now actually lie?

I have traveled to Patara, the city of his birth, and to Myra, where he died. I have seen the scene of the crime where his body was stolen in a bold heist a thousand years ago. And I have gone to Italy, to the city of Bari, where that body still rests in a tomb, and where pilgrims still come to buy the sacred fluid that drizzles off his bones. I have a bottle of it on my shelf.

Before we talk about that heist, the Santa Claus job, we will look at the impossible life of Saint Nicholas of Myra, weirder than any flying sled. The first third of this book tells the strange stories that collected around him after his death and asks what we can understand about the real history of the man himself when it has been transformed by centuries of myth, imagination, and longing. He was a new kind of hero in a changing world.

Once we've looked at the way he became legend, we'll investigate the theft of his body. Gangs of thieves from two Italian cities—Bari and Venice—raced across the sea to try to be the first to steal his corpse. These rival cities would stop at nothing to outdo each other. Both of them claimed a victory, in a turn of events stranger than fiction.

Finally, in the third section of the book, we will take a brief look at how, almost a millennium after his body was stolen, Nicholas, the bishop of Myra, became the figure we know as Santa Claus: chubby, jolly, red suit, a man from the North Pole.

The story of this ancient Santa is not just a wild tale of demons, saints, gods, monsters, and holy spells. It is also a story of politics: empires falling—cities fighting for mastery—merchants using a dead saint's body as a pawn in games of wealth and power. To understand his history, we have to hear from sultans and emperors, sailors and thieves, poets and pirates, princes and killers. We will watch the rise and fall of religions, the tumbling of nations.

And at the center of all this chaos and change, there are the fragments we will reassemble into Nicholas of Myra: stolen fragments of bone, fragments of ancient stories. How do any of us know each other, except by putting together fragments like these—hints and broken pieces—as carefully as we can, until we think we can see the outline of a person?

Historians and archaeologists are essentially detectives. They search for clues in archives and old manuscripts, in crypts and ruins. They assemble files of evidence. They try to judge the truthfulness of eyewitness testimony like someone questioning a suspect. They ask, *Why does this witness want this story to be told?* They try to fit scraps of information together to form a picture of the dead and their lives.

The word *history* comes from ancient Greek. It did not originally mean "the things that happened long ago"; it meant "*the investigation into* the things that happened long ago." History isn't a fixed set of events in the past. It's an inquiry into the vanished and unknown.

We'll be following the investigations of historians as they seek the truth about Saint Nicholas of Myra. We'll be looking at autopsy reports that examine the remains. We'll be casing the scene of the crime. We'll track down the accused by name on the docks and through the alleys of medieval Bari, Italy. We'll assemble a story, or a set of stories interlocked, stranger than a fantasy novel, a story of crime and redemption that spans seventeen hundred years.

I do not believe in the magic of Santa Claus. But as I've investigated the heist of his body, his story has convinced me that there are miracles flickering all around us. A glimpse of the strangeness of this world and its hidden beauties: These are the gifts Saint Nicholas's own story offers us all.

Let's start at the moment of his birth, back when the world was much younger, and yet still very old.

We begin in a land where gods were born.

Part
I

NIKOLAOS

300
AD

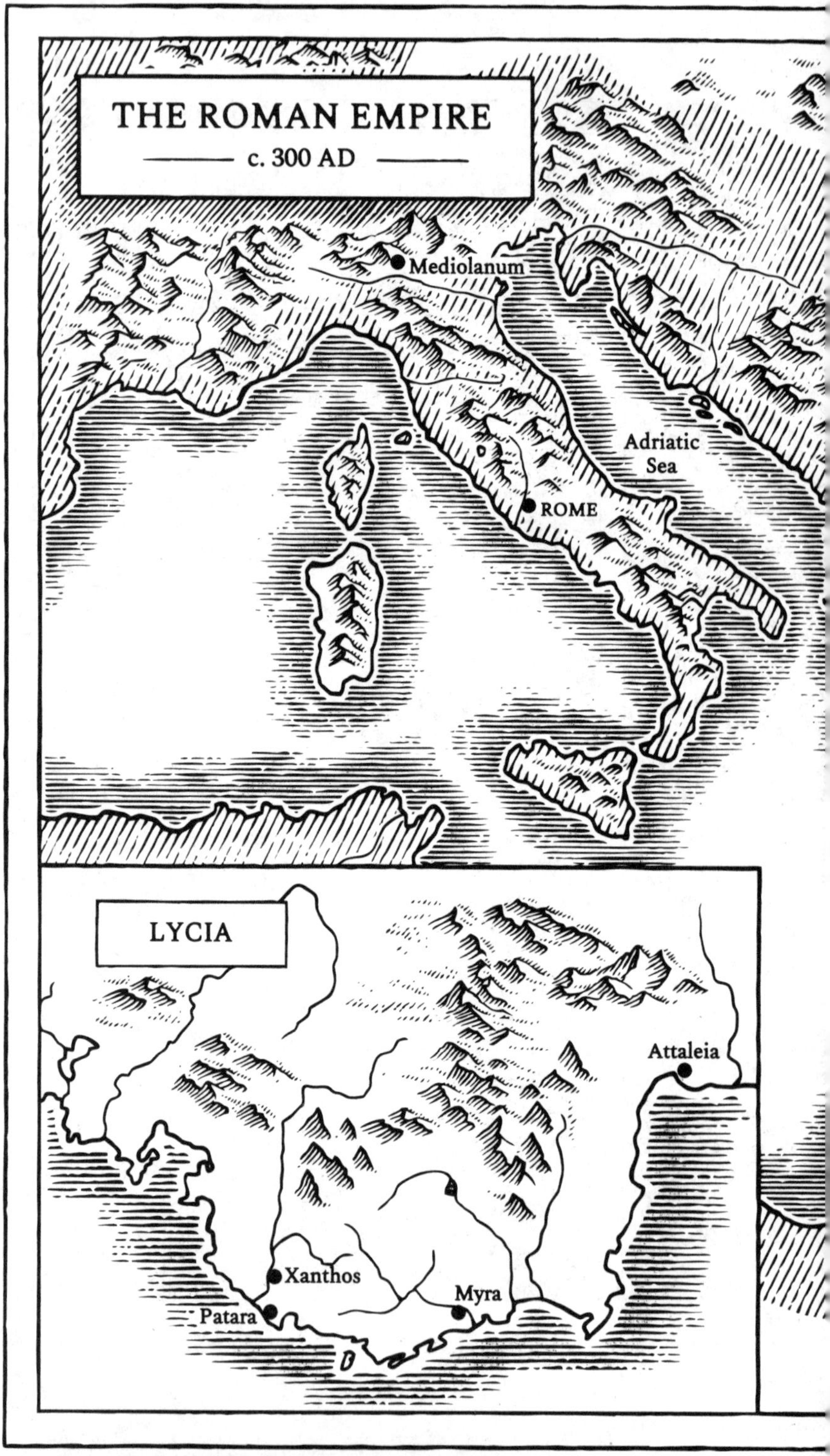
THE ROMAN EMPIRE
c. 300 AD
Mediolanum
Adriatic Sea
ROME
LYCIA
Attaleia
Xanthos
Patara
Myra

LEGEND
Roman empire
Cities
LYCIA
CONSTANTINOPLE
Nicomedia
Nicea
salonika
Aegean Sea
EPHESUS
TAURUS MOUNTAINS
LYCIA
Myra
RHODES
Tarsus
ANTIOCH
Mediterranean Sea
JERUSALEM
ALEXANDRIA

Nicholas was born into a landscape of legend.

The port city of Patara, his birthplace, sits in the province of Lycia on the edge of the Aegean and Mediterranean Seas. From Patara's ancient lighthouse, it was only a voyage of a day or two on a ship to the isle of Rhodes, where the Colossus, a gigantic statue, had once guarded the harbor. It was one of the Seven Wonders of the World, though by the time Nicholas was born, it had been through an earthquake and was only a couple of lower legs.

Inland from Patara rose the Taurus Mountains, sharp as fangs, where monsters were reputed to live. Far to the east lay the den of the fire-breathing chimera: a monstrous lion with an extra goat's head and a venomous serpent for a tail. As a child, Nicholas would have heard the stories of how the chimera had crawled down out of the mountains to terrorize Lycia. A hero had supposedly flown down from the sky on a winged horse, Pegasus, and fired arrows from the air at the creature until it was wounded and weakened. Then the hero had dived down and plunged a lance tipped with lead into the chimera's flaming mouth. The lead melted and burned the savage creature from the inside, killing it.

We may picture the boy Nicholas hearing this legend and staring, wide-eyed, up at the dark mountains where the beast had once hunted.

Here's the thing: The chimera was not entirely made up. Tourists in eastern Lycia can still visit it today. The chimera's "den" is a fissure in the hillside that releases burning gases. Geologists call this a *fumarole*. At some point, somebody must have decided to tell a story about the flames that burned night and day from that hole in the ground. And so the chimera was born, a story built around a geological peculiarity. As we will discover, it is rare that legends are explained so easily and so tidily.

At the time of Nicholas's birth, the Roman Empire spread wide across the continent, from what is now Spain all the way to the Middle East, from what is now France down to northern Africa. The Roman emperors ruled so much of the world that they were supposed to become gods when they died.

The coast where Nicholas was born was reputedly also the birthplace of two of the most powerful gods, twins: Artemis and Apollo. Their cults may have begun nearby. When Nicholas was young, one of the most famous temples of Apollo in the whole of the Roman Empire was right in his hometown, Patara. That was where Apollo supposedly spent his winters, having passed the summer on the breezy Aegean island of Delos. Even gods need a change of scene occasionally. In the winter, pilgrims would come to Patara from all over the Roman world and ask the priestesses of Apollo for guidance. These priestesses would fall asleep and then recount their dreams when they woke; the dreams were considered prophecies, sent by the god himself.

Artemis, Apollo's sister, was goddess of fertility, the moon, the countryside, and the hunt. Elsewhere in the empire, Artemis was depicted as an athletic young woman darting through the woods by moonlight, seeking her prey. Along the coast where Nicholas was born, however, her statues took a stranger form: She rears up, less a human than a supernatural entity, her body less like a human trunk and more like a column of flesh stocked with beehives, cattle, sheep, and other livestock, many of the animals probably sacrificed to her or that she provided for her worshippers. Most notably, her chest is ringed with dozens of breasts that hang almost like alien growths all around her.

At first glance, she may seem bizarre to us, like a being from another world. (Her followers said that in fact she *was* from another world, and that the most famous statue of her had fallen from the sky, for which reason some have speculated that the original statue contained a fragment of a meteor.) As odd as **"many-breasted Artemis"** might look to us, she was a beloved figure to her worshippers in Nicholas's homeland. To them, the many breasts signified fertility, maternity, and a promise that the land would provide for its people, just as a mother does for her children.

Artemis would play an important role in Nicholas's life: She would become the saint's most dangerous enemy.

Nicholas was born in Patara around the year 260 AD. We don't know much about Nicholas's parentage. Supposedly, his family was rich and well-respected in the city. The name they gave him,

---

You'll find many endnotes citing my sources at the back of this book. Occasionally, the endnotes contain a strange or unusual fact that some readers might find interesting. These are indicated by these little hands. Flip to the back and find the page number if you're interested in learning more.

Nicholas—Greek *Nikolaos*—means "Victory to the People." (The word *nike*, now familiar as the name of a shoe, actually is Greek for "victory.") It is a heroic name, and his parents, "eager to devote themselves to the work of justice," must have brought him up to fight for his community. Certainly, when he was older, he showed the qualities of true heroism: great bravery, fury at injustice, terrible ferocity when defending the innocent, and yet, at the same time, generosity, empathy, and humility.

His parents were not, however, followers of Apollo and Artemis. They belonged to a cult that the Roman emperors deeply distrusted, a cult that met at night in people's homes and in burial grounds. Romans writing about this cult described it as a dangerous superstition born in Palestine. The cultists worshipped an undead god-king, a condemned criminal who during his public execution vowed to break out of his tomb and someday rule the world. It was said that in their rites, they ate human flesh and drank blood.

They were, of course, Christians.

You are going to have to forget a lot of what you know about modern Christianity to understand the story of Nicholas's life. When he was born, Christianity was a small cult, just a couple of hundred years old, a recent offshoot of Judaism. Many citizens of the empire did not understand the beliefs and rites of this austere new religious movement, with its symbolic eating of bread and drinking of wine, a stand-in for ritual sacrifice. The Roman emperors generally distrusted Christians, who refused to sacrifice to the gods of Rome, gods like Jupiter, Janus, Mars, Venus, Neptune, and Apollo. Worst of all, the Christians would not slaughter animals on the altars of the previous Roman emperors, who had risen into the heavens and become gods after death. What did that mean about the loyalty of the Christians to the imperial throne? The Roman rulers didn't know, but it made Christians seem deeply untrustworthy—possible revolutionaries and terrorists. Right around the time of Nicholas's birth, a few prominent Christians in Patara were publicly executed by order of the emperor, dragged by horses over rough stone and then hurled into a pit. People like Nicholas's parents had to be careful. Their lives could be in danger.

We are told that Nicholas immediately showed himself to be a Christian, even as a newborn who couldn't understand human speech. On the days when Christians were supposed to fast (when they went without meat or without food altogether), the baby refused to suckle.

He was an only child. Nicholas's early biographies take this to be a sign of the Christian God's blessing: Nicholas was so perfect as a person, they say, that his mother was sterile from the day of his birth—there was no need for any brother or sister.

We have witnessed the birth of Nicholas near the birthplace of the goddess Artemis. Yet these two holy births could not be more different. They sum up perfectly the rising clash between these two powerful religions, early Christianity and the ancient gods of Olympus. On the one hand, "many-breasted Artemis," and on the other, Nicholas, who refused to breastfeed. The goddess of fertility versus a family that became infertile. One story stresses plenty, bounty, voluptuousness, the fruits of this world; the other emphasizes the value of self-control and the hope for a reward in another world.

Artemis would become Nicholas's archenemy, his nemesis. She was the old world. He was the new world. And soon they would be dead set on destroying each other.

We are told that as a boy, Nicholas had a good, solid Greek education, going to a school with other boys and reading classics like Homer's *Odyssey* and *Iliad*, the ancient epics that told of great adventures and bloodcurdling tragedy. Perhaps he looked out at the ocean from the bay of Patara, in the shadow of the lighthouse, and dreamed of the isles there in the blue Aegean Sea where the heroes of antiquity had struggled with gods and fought one-eyed giants and fled from sorceresses who could turn men into swine. Nicholas himself would become a very different kind of hero.

He would eventually become as famous as those ancient Greek heroes, Achilles and Odysseus, though it would take perhaps a thousand years. He would appear not in epics, but in books of saints' lives written by men who wouldn't be born for another five hundred or six hundred years after his death. Even later, he would be made into wrapping paper and inflatable lawn ornaments.

What does it mean to say *Nicholas thought this* or *Nicholas did that*? The sources that record his thoughts and deeds are from hundreds of years after his death. Moreover, they're filled with things that we now would generally regard as ridiculous impossibilities. Did Nicholas really fly with a cape spread out behind him, as one source tells us? Did he bring children murdered by a psychopath back to life, as another insists?

The Catholic Church, sponsor of saints, does not expect anyone to believe most of the stories of Nicholas's miracles anymore. The tales simply are too bizarre and recorded too many centuries after his death to be trusted absolutely. They are too encrusted with legend.

So why tell these stories at all? What use are they to the historian? How can we use them to get at any sort of truth?

We'll conduct our own investigation. I'll tell the tales as they have come down to us: impossibilities and all. After each little tale, we'll ask what it might mean or reveal about Nicholas and his world. Strange myth and stark reality often collide in surprising ways: Think about how we can look behind the legend of the fire-breathing chimera and find the physical reality, the fumarole, the fissure spewing burning gas.

Is there any reality to anything about Nicholas other than his beaten and pulverized bones?

If we picture him there on the shore, at childhood's end, not knowing what life will bring him, it is hard to imagine how that kid would react to the tale of his own future adventures. How did he begin here, a clever teen from a mildly successful family, wandering the streets of seaside Patara, and end somehow as a legend known throughout the world? And how, somewhere in between, did this boy's skeleton, now just growing to its full height, end up wrapped in someone's cloak, slung over a rogue priest's shoulder as thieves escaped with it toward the harbor in the dark of night?

THE TALE OF
THE THREE DAUGHTERS

The first story we'll tell about the young Nicholas is perhaps the most important story about him ever told. It's the story that established him as a secret gift giver. Its details, however, are surprising.

Sometime in his teenage years, Nicholas's parents died. They might have been killed by the plague that swept the empire in the middle of the third century. We simply don't know. We don't hear much about how he reacted to their deaths. Having no one left on the earth, we are told, he turned to his God.

He inherited his parents' money. He didn't want it for himself. He just gave it away to those who needed it.

Next door to Nicholas lived a family who had fallen into poverty. They'd lost everything in some financial disaster. One day, Nicholas was walking by their window when he heard the father tell the three daughters, "I'm sorry. We have nothing left. I can't even feed you." And then, grief-stricken, the father told his daughters that he was going to sell them into slavery at a brothel.

It is an unthinkable thing now, though, grimly, it still happens. It was also an unthinkable thing then.

Nicholas could not stand it. These girls were around his own age.

He wanted to give the family money, but he didn't know how to do it. He didn't want to humiliate them through his charity. Nicholas knew that there can be an ugly power in giving gifts.

So he put some of his parents' gold into a bag and waited until dark. Then he went to the alley between the houses and tossed the gold through his neighbors' window. He scrambled home to hide himself, afraid of being seen.

In the morning, the father got up and saw the bag. He opened it and couldn't believe his eyes. He rubbed the gold to make sure it wasn't fake. He bit it. It was real. He couldn't guess who'd given it to him, but he was overjoyed.

He gave it to his eldest daughter. With a small fortune like that, it was not hard for her to arrange a marriage. That very day, she was happily wed.

Nicholas saw what had happened. Success! So that night, he wrapped a second gift of gold for the middle daughter. He sneaked to the alley, tossed it through the window, and crept back to his own house.

The next morning, the father was even more shocked by the second gift. He couldn't speak, we're told. But he apparently fell to his knees and prayed silently: "Show me the angel among men who has just been so kind to us. Show me who this person is, who saved us . . ." That day the second daughter was engaged to be married.

That evening, Nicholas prepared to drop a third and final gift for the last and youngest daughter. He wrapped the gold. He readied himself to go out.

But at the same time, the father was prepared. He wanted to find out who his mysterious benefactor was. He waited inside, beneath the window.

Late at night, a third little bag of gold came sailing through the window and smacked onto the floor. The father ran out into the street to see who was responsible.

There was the boy from next door—Nicholas—darting away.

The father threw himself at the young man's feet. He sobbed his thanks. "We are in your debt," he cried. "We ought to give thanks to you all of our days, because you stretched out a hand to help us and lifted us up from the dunghill through your generous gift."

Nicholas was horrified—deeply embarrassed. He raised the old man up from the ground. Then he demanded that the father take an oath, a firm oath, that he would never tell anyone about the gifts or about his identity. Nicholas would not let the man go until the father swore that this act of kindness would remain a secret forever.

All three daughters were married. The father's cruel solution was avoided. Nicholas, however clumsily, was learning the lessons of compassion.

What do we think of this story? What part does it play in our investigation into the history of Saint Nicholas? It is one of the oldest surviving stories about him. It doesn't make sense entirely as a real event. **The three daughters, three bags of gold, three nights—these sound like the ancient patterns of a fairy tale.** And unfortunately, it is not a story that directly addresses the brutality of a system in which women are bought and sold.

It is just a small story, a story where only one family is saved. It does not involve magic, the supernatural, or any demonic force. It is simply about one person's ability to change the lives of a few others through compassion. And that, perhaps, is why it is one of the most important stories from Nicholas's life.

Historian Adam English writes:

> Here was a young man . . . performing a seemingly random act of kindness on behalf of three poor girls. There was no voice from heaven, no blinding light, nothing paranormal, nothing bloody or gruesome. The girls were not daughters of the emperor or some other celebrity; they were like anyone else caught in the trap of poverty and hunger, a trap that ensnared millions of faceless and nameless individuals in the ancient world. . . . This was a story to which ordinary people could relate.

As a result, this was one of the deeds of Nicholas that people remembered best through the centuries. It is why pawnshops, even now, often use three golden balls as their symbol—to represent Nicholas's three gifts of gold to the family next door.

More importantly, this story is probably why we imagine Saint Nicholas—Santa Claus—as a secret nocturnal gift giver, and why we blame him for the presents put under the tree.

THE TALE OF

HOW YOUNG NICHOLAS BECAME BISHOP OF MYRA

So Nicholas spent his youth, as one biographer wrote, "fattening those who were afflicted by hardships and comforting those who were afflicted by the thirst and heat of poverty."

One day, as he traveled along the coast of Lycia, Nicholas stopped in the city of Myra, a few days' journey to the east of Patara. He took a room at a little inn. Nicholas must have walked around the city that afternoon, seeing the sights.

Myra was a good-sized city set back a little from the sea. Like Patara, it profited from the huge Roman grain ships that plowed through the Mediterranean, supplying distant cities with food. Timber cut in the Taurus Mountains was dragged down to Myra's port and shipped to Egypt, where such wood was rare. In dark huts around the square by the docks, men cracked open shellfish to remove a delicate gland, which provided the imperial purple that dyed the clothes of the powerful. The city had a huge amphitheater built into the side of a rocky hill, a place where thousands gathered regularly to watch the plays of ancient Greece in which mortals slew each other with swords or poison. By the time Nicholas visited, the old theater was also being used for more brutal entertainments: Archaeological evidence suggests that the stage had been fitted to make way for gladiatorial combat. Enslaved men fought wild beasts or each other to the death. In the hills around the theater were ancient tombs stacked on top of one another, like apartments of the dead carved into the cliffs—tombs so old that their origins were long forgotten even by Nicholas's lifetime. Their silent chambers echoed with the shouts and screams of thousands of the living down below who watched the deaths onstage.

Like Patara, Myra had an important temple to Artemis's twin brother, Apollo, nearby, right across the mouth of the Myros River. Ancient authors tell us that it was famous for its fish oracle.

What is a fish oracle? It's a good example of how Roman religion worked. Believers who had a request for the god or a question about the future would lead an animal up to the temple of Apollo, where the priests would ritually slaughter it on the altar. Most of the meat would be eaten by the family or their followers or the priests themselves. Four of the best pieces of meat, however, would be skewered on wooden stakes. The priest and the family would then descend a long, winding stone staircase that led down the hill to the banks of a whirlpool where fresh water from the river collided with the salt water of the sea. The lagoon there constantly bubbled and churned in uneasy motion. The priest would sit on the shore and watch as the worshippers threw the meat skewers into the whirlpool. As the meat hit the water, the surface roiled even more: Giant fishes rose up from the depths and nipped and sucked at the sacrifice. An eyewitness tells us, "There are sea bass, bluefish, sometimes whales or sawfish and many never-before-seen and strange-looking fish." The oracle, seeing which fish seized the skewers, would make a prediction about the future, answer questions, and announce whether the god Apollo was pleased or displeased.

Myra also had a temple to Artemis herself, which was famous for its beauty. Down by the port, there was a Jewish synagogue. To this day, you can see a slab of the synagogue's floor with a menorah engraved upon it. It looks out over the ruins of the docks and storehouses. And Myra had a Christian church.

Nicholas may have been surprised at the church building. During this period, Christians often met in the secrecy of private homes, since the Roman authorities were suspicious of them and were prone to drag them off to prison. Christianity was an urban religion, though, that was rapidly spreading through routes of trade—and Myra was a bustling trade city. So he discovered that the town had its own church, freely declaring its religion.

Nicholas did not know what was going on inside that church as he walked past that day. The local bishop had just died. (A bishop in the Christian church is sort of a regional overseer of many priests.) All the priests and bishops from nearby cities were meeting there to try to decide who would become the next bishop of Myra.

The meeting had apparently reached a crisis point that afternoon. No one could agree on a candidate. The priests and bishops took a long break for prayer, perhaps also to cool down.

And that night, one of them had a dream. A glowing figure appeared before him and told him to go to the church the next morning at dawn. The first person to walk up the steps should be made bishop

MYRA AND ITS PORT, ANDRIAKE
c. 300 AD
TAURUS MOUNTAINS
Fortess
Theater
MYRA
SURA
Fish Oracle of Apollo
Church of Saint Nicholas
Andriake
port of Myra
MARE LYCIUM

of Myra. The name of this person, the spirit said, would be Nicholas.

It is a strange way to choose a high-ranking administrator, as uncertain as a fish oracle.

At dawn, young Nicholas left his inn and went to the church in Myra to pray. There was an old man standing awkwardly in the entrance hall, as if waiting for someone. As soon as Nicholas walked in, the man looked sharply at him and demanded, "What do people call you, my son?"

Nicholas was startled. Confused, he saw the man was dressed as a bishop. Why would a bishop be standing here alone at this hour, asking his name? The young Pataran answered, "Nicholas the sinner."

At this, the bishop smiled. "Follow me, son," he said. He led the young man into the church, and there, to his astonishment, Nicholas saw all the local Christian priests and bishops gathered in the dawn light, waiting silently, inspecting him carefully.

Nicholas had answered well by answering humbly. The assembly told him he was going to be the next bishop of Myra. At first, he refused: He didn't feel he had the right experience. He was far too young. He wasn't from Myra. He wasn't even a priest. His protests were ignored. Bewildered, Nicholas watched as people from the neighborhood flooded the church. Dazed, he heard the announcement being made to the crowd: "Accept this man as our shepherd. He has been made our leader not by human but by divine decision. He whom we have been longing for we now have; he whom we were seeking we now receive."

They led the young man to the bishop's throne. He climbed onto it unwillingly, caught up like someone in a dream, half horrified.

His destiny had found him.

THE TALE OF
THE BOILED BABY

The woman who had rented a room to Nicholas for the night was giving her baby a bath that same morning. She heated water in a clay pan over a fire, tested it carefully with her hand to make sure it wasn't too hot, then laid her infant down in the water to wash him.

She heard a commotion outside. She stuck her head out the door to see what was going on. A crowd was rushing to the church. She stepped out of the inn, curious about all the excitement. She crossed the town square and went into the church to get a peek.

There, up at the front of the church, was her guest, the young man Nicholas. He was looking shocked and bewildered. He sat in the bishop's chair, swamped in his new robes. Everyone was calling out his name.

Then she remembered: Her baby was still in the bathwater, sitting in the earthenware pan over the fire. By this point, the water would be boiling.

The mother realized this in horror. She screamed and pushed her way out through the crowd. She ran back to the inn, shrieking her infant son's name. She threw the door open and ran inside.

The pan of water had grown so hot it boiled, "and the child who was in it, whose body was tender and bare, was sitting in the boiling water."

But he was absolutely fine. The water hadn't scalded him a bit. He sat in the boiling bathwater, "playing with the bubbles and grabbing at them," gurgling as if it were the perfect temperature.

She swept him up into her arms and dried him off. She wrapped him in a blanket and carried him around, telling all her friends and neighbors what had happened.

They decided it was a sign: Nicholas, the new bishop of Myra, was destined for miracles.

SANTA CLAUS IN CHAINS

Virtue, at the moment, is not in style. We like our heroes with a hard edge. We like them to brood darkly, dangerously, heart-scarred. Nonetheless, Nicholas during his lifetime appears to have been an extraordinarily virtuous man. A man, for example, who would have hated being called extraordinarily virtuous.

We are told he worked hard for the people of Myra, making sure they were fed and protected. His manner toward those around him was humble and mild. "Who would not be amazed by your patience?" a bishop later asked Nicholas's departed ghost. "Who would not be struck with your gentle speech and mildness? With your peacefulness?"

Soon he would have to find deep within himself a new ferocity.

History was about to collapse on Bishop Nicholas's head.

Several hundred miles to the north of Myra, the Roman emperor Diocletian was getting worried. The empire was coming apart at the seams. It was utterly vast; it could easily take half a year to get a message from one end of the empire to the other and another half a year to get a reply back across mountains, forests, deserts, and seas. Diocletian tried to create co-emperors to divide up the huge, unwieldy territory and rule it together, but they all just turned on each other. They gathered armies and attacked one another. Meanwhile, peoples of other nations—peoples the Romans considered barbarians—were trying to force their way into Roman territory from all directions: the Franks and Alemanni from the northwest, Goths from the north, Vandals from the south, the Persian Empire from the east. The Roman emperor at the time of Nicholas's birth had actually been captured by the king of Persia and had been turned into a living human footstool. Then he'd been skinned, his skin had been dyed red, and it still hung on the wall of a Persian temple as a gentle reminder to Roman visitors of how weak their empire had become.

This did not make the next Roman emperors in line feel particularly secure.

When the emperor Diocletian asked his soothsayers to tell him about the future and whether he would succeed in fighting the Persians, they were too frightened to answer. They said they couldn't hear the gods at the moment. Something was interfering with their signal. Diocletian looked around his throne room for an explanation.

His eye fell upon his Christian courtiers. They had refused to participate in the ritual sacrifices to the old gods. The soothsayers were eager to point the finger and blame someone. Yes, indeed, they said, it was the Christians' fault. The gods no longer wanted to speak to the emperor because he was surrounded by Christians. His wife was a Christian. His daughter was a Christian.

Emperor Diocletian was furious that the gods were unhappy. And so began the decade of brutal imprisonment, torture, and massacre of early Christians later known as the Great Persecution.

The Romans did not, in general, care what gods you worshipped. The religion of Rome was *polytheistic*, involving many gods, which meant that they didn't worry too much about new gods they encountered in new lands. They tended to just assume that a local love goddess, for example, was actually the Roman Venus under another name; they assumed that the goddess Artemis, odd-looking as she might be, was really just their own goddess of the moon, fertility, and the hunt, Diana. They accepted the stories of foreign gods, gods from Greece or Egypt. In this way, they avoided a lot of religious conflict with the people they conquered. It was this flexibility, as much as the strength of their armies, that allowed them to keep control over fallen kingdoms from Egypt to Britain.

Everything was different, however, when it came to Judaism and its more recent offshoot, Christianity, both of which are *monotheistic* religions: visions of a world with only one god. This god was not a local city god who, when defeated, would join the Roman pantheon and sit at the feast of Olympus with the rest. The Judeo-Christian God specifically declared, "You shall not have other gods beside me. You shall not make for yourself an idol . . . you shall not bow down before them or serve them. For I, the Lord, your God, am a jealous God . . ."

This was awkward. For one thing, many Roman authorities

worried that if too many people in the empire stopped making their traditional sacrifices to the old gods, they'd anger the heavens, and the results would be catastrophic: floods, earthquakes, famines, fires.

The Christians not only refused to make those sacrifices—they also talked about their renegade god-king who would return to rule the world. They called him *Christos*, Greek for "the Anointed One." He'd been executed on suspicion of treason against the empire. His cult could possibly be a revolutionary movement, meeting in secret to try to overthrow the Roman government.

Diocletian decided he needed to move quickly against them. At first, he just wanted to kick the Christian cultists out of government and out of the army. He and his co-emperor stood on the roof of the palace in Nicomedia and watched as guardsmen hacked the local church to the ground. As the two rulers stood there, Diocletian's co-emperor argued that he was not being brutal enough. The Christians were a government hidden within the government; they had their own ranks and their own order. There were priests and bishops and archbishops, an international hierarchy. They were all in communication with each other. They were rebels. They deserved death.

A few days later, the emperor's palace caught on fire. We still don't know who lit the flames. But the Christians were blamed. That was all it took: At the end of February, 303 AD, orders went out from Emperor Diocletian that Christianity was no longer a legal cult. Not only were Christians expelled from the government and the army, now the houses and lands of Christians were seized by the Roman government and given away to loyal citizens. Christian writings and scriptures were confiscated and burned in the public marketplaces.

As the Great Persecution worsened, the decree went out that if the priests and bishops of the Christian cult didn't bow down and sacrifice to the gods—especially the spirits of the dead emperors—they should be arrested, tortured, and executed. It was only a matter of time until Nicholas, as bishop of Myra, would be targeted.

The decree spread slowly across the empire, which was already inflamed with revolts and rebellions, small-time puppet emperors trying to seize power, sloppy sociopaths slaughtering each other for the throne. The anti-Christian order was enforced unevenly, but with dire results for thousands.

Nicholas must have heard the stories as the noose drew tighter around his neck. The Romans were geniuses in the grim art of torture: They buried men alive, threw men into the sea with millstones around their necks, had men torn apart by bears in front of audiences. Christians were killed by leopards and bulls in public arenas as fans cheered. The bodies of other Christians who wouldn't relent were scraped with shells until they bled to death.

Diocletian's co-emperor in the east was merciful, by contrast, and wouldn't allow the Christians to be killed. Instead, he had their ears and nostrils slit, their hands and feet lopped off, and their eyes dug out of their sockets. Practices varied from place to place.

Since Christians were accused of starting the palace fire, they were burned alive. One eyewitness has described the Roman science of torture by fire in excruciating detail. It involved dripping water on the victims so they couldn't die too quickly as their limbs burned. "At length they did expire when, after many hours, the violent heat had consumed their skin and penetrated into their intestines. The dead carcasses were laid on a funeral pyre and wholly burned. Their bones were gathered, ground to powder, and thrown into the river or into the sea."

The remains had to be scattered—because, quickly, the Christians were developing the practice of collecting the bones of their dead and revering them. The term for someone who dies for their faith is a *martyr*. The Roman governors realized that martyrs, though dead, were still dangerous. They inspired people to fight, to resist, not to yield and make the required animal sacrifices. Instead, through their torture and death, they became the sacrifice themselves and acquired a holy status. The Roman executioners wanted to make sure there was nothing left of these insurrectionists after death—no skull or bone that could be worshipped. As we will see, the bones of the holy dead would become very important to Christians after this—important enough to steal.

Nicholas, in his church in Myra, would have heard that the bishop of Patara, his hometown, had been arrested and executed.

And then it was his turn. Roman magistrates came to his door and dragged him away. "Being subjected to blows and tortures by them, he was thrown into prison with other Christians." He was beaten and chained in prison for five years.

Local judges, who didn't necessarily want to execute Christians (after all, they made up about 10 percent of the population), were astounded by their stubbornness. The Christian cultists refused to do even the minimum to save themselves. They would not even touch the flesh of a sacrifice, though it would save their lives. The problem, the judges and governors realized, was that the Christian religion had changed the notion of death itself.

We are cursed to be an animal that understands that it will

someday die. We watch the hours pass, and the time of our death grows closer. We seek answers about what will happen next. Roman paganism didn't have much to say about what happened to most people after they died. Their picture of the afterlife was murky. Emperors were vaulted up into the heavens, where they feasted with the gods—but after death, the rest of us apparently wandered, dazed and bewildered, around a dim, gray underworld, drinking from the waters of forgetfulness that gradually erased even our own names from memory. It was not much to look forward to. Cults from the fringes of the empire offered more attractive solutions.

One reason for Christianity's steady spread through urban areas was its populist approach to the afterlife. Anyone could be saved from death and go to the Christian Heaven. You didn't have to be an emperor. Like Egyptian religion before it, Christianity associated death with justice. Those who had fought during their lives to act morally would go to Heaven; those who had harmed others, no matter how powerful they were, would go to Hell. That was important in the ancient world, where justice on earth was hard to come by. (It is often hard enough to come by here in the present.) It allowed the average person to feel a new kind of hope. As a result, many Christians during the Great Persecution apparently greeted their executions not only with bravery, but with joy. They were about to ascend into Heaven. This was an attitude that perplexed judges and magistrates.

It led to a whole genre of literature popular among Christians for the next millennium and a half or so, stories of the torture and death of saints during Diocletian's Great Persecution, stories of martyrdom. These stories end in hideous torture and violent death—but that's seen as a victory.

It's one thing to imagine the joy of martyrdom when you're a monk writing a martyr's biography five hundred years later. It's another thing to sit in prison waiting to be burned or fed to beasts.

As the empire roiled in rebellion and execution, it seemed likely that for humble Bishop Nicholas, chained in a cell, bloody martyrdom was next.

A LIGHT IN THE SKY

As we will see, in the mid–twentieth century, a forensic pathologist (someone who studies human remains) spent a long night with the bones of Saint Nicholas. He only had a few hours to examine them. He worked quickly, trying to be methodical, trying to determine if there was any proof that this skeleton, preserved for at least a thousand years under a cold stone floor, could really be Nicholas, the bishop of Myra. One of the things he found was that several of the vertebrae of the spine were fused. The man whose bones lay in front of him would have had chronic back pain. He'd had a condition called ankylosing spondylitis, which can run in the family, and can be made much more acute by conditions like damp and a lack of movement. The doctor noted, "We shouldn't wonder at this pathological finding, if we take into account that—according to what historical reports tell us about the life of the Saint—our Wonderworker, around the age of fifty, suffered the noxious influence of cold and damp for several years in unhealthy prisons."

This is hardly proof, one way or the other, of the identity of the skeleton—but it does give us some sense of what it might have been like for Nicholas in prison during the Great Persecution. Roman prisons were dark and dank, and those who stayed there too long often came out with arthritic aches and pains that never went away.

More brutally, it appears from healed fractures in his skull that in life his nose was broken by a powerful blow from the right side. This too could possibly be a sign of torture and interrogation. Someone beat him mercilessly.

As Nicholas crouched in a cell, chained up with other Christians, civil war raged across the Roman Empire. Co-emperors fought each other to be sole emperors in charge of the whole vast nation. They roved around the empire as if playing a game of chess, knocking each other off the board one by one. One of these men, Constantine the Great, would change not only Saint Nicholas's life, but the course of human history.

Constantine's story, as told by chroniclers at the time, sounds almost as strange and fanciful as Nicholas's. It reads less like history than like a fantasy novel. Constantine was the son of an innkeeper's daughter and one of the most powerful men in the empire. He'd spent his youth at the court of Diocletian in the early years of the Great Persecution. When his father died, Constantine declared himself a co-emperor in his father's place. Now he wanted to rule the entire empire.

His greatest rival was another co-emperor named Maxentius, who was in control of the city of Rome itself. The two were not on good terms. Maxentius's father had once tried to kill Constantine in his sleep. Now Maxentius sat behind the city of Rome's almost invulnerable walls, prepared for a siege, engaging powerful and venomous magical forces to protect himself. We are told by one historian of the time that Maxentius turned to ever more gruesome rituals to try to convince the gods to give him victory over Constantine and all other rivals. He called on priests to practice dark magical arts that shocked even the pagan population of Rome: They sacrificed lions on the altars of the gods. They sacrificed newborn human infants.

Meanwhile, to the north, as Constantine developed his plans, he started to wonder which gods he should pray to, which gods would hand him a victory over his rivals. Roman paganism was a highly *transactional* religion: You did not simply go to a temple and hope for a mystical experience. You chose a god to pray to based on their specialties, then you went and asked the god for specific, practical things: a healthy child, a successful business deal, a safe voyage, a marriage, triumph in battle. You bargained with the god. You promised to provide them with animal sacrifices or (for a big request) a new temple if they gave you what you wanted. You worked the system.

As he marched with his army, Constantine had a vision that changed the direction of world history forever. This is how he told the story:

> Constantine said that about noon, when the day was already beginning to decline, he saw with his own eyes a cross of light in the heavens, floating above the sun and bearing the inscription, *By this sign, you will conquer*. At this sight he himself was struck with amazement, and his whole army also, which had followed him on this expedition and witnessed the miracle.

Constantine was astounded. He didn't know what to think of the vision. Indeed, people have been arguing about it ever since, for seventeen hundred years.

If you need a scientific explanation for how a whole army could see a cross in the sky, there are some possibilities. Most interesting is the idea that Constantine may have seen a solar halo, an atmospheric refraction of light through ice crystals in the upper atmosphere, which would have created crosshairs surrounding the sun, forming a brilliant, encircled cross in the heavens. This would have been particularly powerful to Constantine, who was already an enthusiastic worshipper of the sun god Apollo.

He did not immediately become a Christian. But, like a good Roman polytheist, he agreed to work with this cross-bearing sun god who offered him victory.

Constantine gathered his army and started to march south to Rome to knock Maxentius off the game board.

As Constantine's army approached the city, Maxentius's fears got more and more wild. He asked the great Sybilline oracles to read their books of prophecy and tell him what he should do, whether he should stay safe within the walls of Rome or march out and confront Constantine directly. The oracle channeled the wisdom of the gods. Their prophecy announced, *On October 28, an enemy of the Roman people will die.* Maxentius took that as a very good sign that he would defeat Constantine.

As you can guess, he shouldn't have. Oracles notoriously spoke the truth but in riddles.

Constantine reached the fields that surrounded the city of Rome. His army was ready for battle. That night, he had a dream.

He was told by a shining presence that he should take the symbol he had seen drifting in the sky as his military insignia. Again, he saw the symbol floating before him: now not merely a cross, but a more elaborate figure that combined a cross and the first two letters of the Greek word *Christ*, and looked somewhat like an Egyptian ankh, a symbol of eternal life.

When he got up in the morning, he called his jewelers and goldsmiths to him and described the figure he had seen in the dream. He told them to make one for him out of gold. The army would march upon the city of Rome with this symbol held over them. They would have it painted on their shields.

On October 28, 312 AD, Maxentius and his army marched out across a hastily constructed pontoon bridge to meet Constantine's forces. (He had torn down all the bridges to Rome to protect the city from invasion.) The battle that followed was a disaster. Almost immediately, Constantine's cavalry drove Maxentius's army back toward the river and the walls of Rome. Their retreat was utter confusion. They clattered back across their makeshift bridge. But it wasn't made for that kind of weight and stress. There were too many of them mobbing it at once. It collapsed. Boards splintered. Hundreds of soldiers went plunging, fully armed, into the river and thrashed there as they sank. Maxentius fell from his horse and shot down into the depths. He was weighed down, trapped by his own gorgeous ceremonial armor. Far beneath the surface of the Tiber River, Maxentius drowned.

As the oracles had predicted, a great enemy of Rome had died. It just hadn't been the enemy Maxentius hoped it would be.

Constantine's army was left victorious on the shore. Above

them flapped banners with their new symbol on it: the symbol of the cross. Supposedly, as Constantine entered Rome, the people there greeted him with cheers as their liberator.

The god of the cross in the sky had given him victory. He was now the emperor of the Western Roman Empire. It was time to thank that god, who people told him was the one God of the Christians.

Now, keep in mind that most of these stories were told to us by Christians who wanted to dress Constantine up like a hero of their religion; one of them, Eusebius, was actually a friend of his. Can we really believe, therefore, that Maxentius was sacrificing infants in rituals of dark enchantment? It is hard to tell. Even the pagan historians suggest that there was something vaguely cursed about Maxentius. One of them, for example, says that as he rode out to battle through the gates of Rome, "an infinite number of owls," birds of ill-omen, soared over the walls of the city and settled there, eerily peering down at the humans preparing for slaughter below.

The victory was not just Constantine's that day. It was also a victory, in the long run, for the Christian God, who now had as an advocate one of the most powerful men on earth. Constantine prepared to fulfill his end of the bargain with this god.

In 313 AD, Constantine, Emperor of the West, and Licinius, Emperor of the East, came together in the city of Milan and announced that the Great Persecution of the Christian cult was over. They issued a statement of religious freedom and universal tolerance for the whole Roman Empire. It opened with these stirring words: "Perceiving long ago that religious liberty ought not to be denied, but that it ought to be granted to the judgment and desire of each individual to perform his religious duties according to his own choice, we give orders that every man, Christians as well as others, should preserve the faith of his own sect and religion."

This is a surprisingly modern statement—a statement we might even expect to see in the constitution of a modern nation, in a world where we expect government to be separate from religion.

The proclamation (now called the Edict of Milan), more specifically, demanded that Christians be set free from the prisons and the mines where they were being held. The property of Christians that had been seized by the government had to be returned. Christians were free to worship as they pleased. Constantine and Licinius were hedging their bets: They hoped that by giving all their citizens the right to worship, they'd please whatever gods there were—Roman, Christian, Jewish, Egyptian—so that "whatever Divinity lives in heaven may be generous to us and to all who live under our government."

The Great Persecution had lasted ten years and four months. And suddenly, Christians were released, as if by a miracle, to walk free.

Humans have an unfortunate habit, during moments of great fear and disruption, of blaming everything on a scapegoat group, people of another religion or ethnicity, in a frenzy of hysterical accusation. The accusations don't need to make sense: They just need to justify violence that feels good to the mob and the rulers who watch from their balconies. Diocletian and his co-emperors had convinced themselves that Christians, angering the gods, had brought about all the terror and instability of a decaying empire. Now there was a dazed restoration, and Christians hobbled out of hiding or out of their cells to take part in civic life again.

Unfortunately, in coming centuries, Christians would periodically behave exactly as their oppressors once had, blaming all a nation's sickness on particular religions or ethnicities—the Jews, especially—telling deranged stories of impossible conspiracies, and then indulging in acts of terrible violence. This is a human trait that spans cultures and eons.

But for the moment, there was simply gratitude that the horror was over.

Nicholas would have been released around this time, in 313. He returned to his flock, welcomed as a hero for what he'd suffered in prison. While he was not a martyr—that title was reserved for people who died for their faith—he was, technically, a *confessor*, someone who'd suffered for their faith and stood strong. He was home, ready to start helping his people once more. As one of his biographers wrote:

> When every land subject to his rule had received Constantine's decrees of toleration, all Christians and confessors returned to their own states. Thus the citizens of Myra received back their bishop Nicholas, an unbloodied Victor, though by nature and will a martyr. Strengthened by the gifts which God had granted him, he cured all the infirm from everywhere.

Nicholas returned to his flock, the Christians of Myra. But he had changed during his five years of imprisonment and torture. On the one hand, he may have returned with pains in his back and a broken nose mashed to the side. On the other hand, his sufferings had made him somewhat more than human. In the remaining stories about him, he acquires a kind of ghostly glow, as if he was at once living on the hard earth and yet was already part of another world. After that dark period in prison, he had a new strength; his invisible God began to grant him supernatural powers.

This is when his real miracles began.

THE TALE OF
THE THREE GRAIN SHIPS

In the same year as Constantine's Edict of Milan, ancient historians tell us, "The rains were less abundant than usual, and so unexpected famine hit the land. . . . Those who died in the cities were innumerable, and those who died in the country and villages were still more." The city of Myra was starving, even as grain ships regularly docked there on their way across the Mediterranean. Nicholas had a duty to his people. He had to find them food.

He went down to the docks of his city. There were three ships at anchor there, three ships filled with grain on their way to Constantine's new capital, Constantinople. Nicholas approached the captain of the fleet. He said he wanted to buy some grain for the citizens of Myra. The captain refused: These ships were sailing by order of the emperor. The grain had already been measured by the imperial authorities. It was government property.

Nicholas begged: Please unload a little from each ship, just a little measure, "in order that we may not perish from the famine." One of Nicholas's strengths as a leader was that he argued well for his people. The captain, seeing the awful starvation around him, melted. He agreed. They unloaded a hundred measures of grain from each ship and piled it high in the port's huge granary. Then the ships sailed away for Constantinople.

When the ships got to the capital, the captain explained to the treasury officials that he'd had to give away some of the grain to a starving city in Lycia. But when they checked, the ships were completely full—if anything, bulging more than they had been when they were first loaded.

It was a small miracle, a slight miracle—something that might even actually have happened. After all, in this version Nicholas cleverly suggests that they just take a little from each ship. It made a big difference to the citizens of Myra, but perhaps, because it was spread out across the whole grain fleet, it didn't look like much on any given ship.

If you prefer, however, there are other versions that dress the miracle up more. In a sixth-century retelling, Nicholas appears to a captain in a dream and tells him to stop in Myra. The dream vision hands the captain real cash, which remains hard and cold in his hand when he wakes.

If you want some solid fact associated with this story, the granary still stands there at Myra's abandoned port. It's huge. It was built by the emperor Hadrian in 129 AD. It has stood for almost two thousand years overlooking the mouth of the harbor, even as the harbor has silted up and become a swamp. Where the ships docked, now grasses grow. You can still see carvings of Emperor Hadrian and his wife, Sabina, on the granary's wall. Time has eaten their faces, though. They are barely recognizable as human.

It could be that this story was concocted precisely because a huge granary survived in the old port of Myra. Or it could be that it records a real event, when Nicholas, Victor for the People, managed to save his city from famine.

Before the end of this famine, however, we are told Nicholas performed a far greater miracle when he confronted a couple killing humans for meat.

THE TALE OF
THE THREE PICKLED BOYS

In those days, three boys, scholars, were wandering through the Lycian countryside. They'd been sent away from home during the famine. Maybe if they went to study in another city, they would find there was more food there. They stopped for the night at an inn.

The innkeeper made a room ready for them. Then he went down to talk to his wife. "They have a lot of money," he whispered. He looked at his knives. He hadn't used them to cut meat for a long time. He said, "That money could be ours. Are you in with me?"

The wife hesitated. But her eyes were sharp with hunger. "We have borne the burden of poverty, my husband, as long as we have lived; if we are willing to murder them, we can avoid that poverty."

And so they crept upstairs. They quietly opened the door to the bedroom. The boys slept hard, their breath rising and falling in the warm darkness. Perhaps they felt the woman's touch on their faces like a mother's before they realized she was holding them down. Then came the knife.

Blood splattered across the walls.

The innkeeper and his wife dragged the three bodies down the stairs, thumping. Then, we might assume, they mopped.

A day or two later, a pilgrim appeared at their door. He did not give his name but said only that he was a wanderer. It was Nicholas, of course, who was hiking between the country churches under his care, checking to see how people were doing during the famine.

The innkeeper and his wife welcomed him in. They had a room free, they said.

Saint Nicholas announced that he was hungry. (Wasn't everybody?) "If you by chance have some fresh meat out back, you might grant me a morsel . . . I ask you in God's name, do not hold back."

"I don't have anything," said the innkeeper.

Nicholas's eyes were fixed on his. "I think you do. I think you have fresh meat in the kitchen."

The innkeeper relented. "For a price," he said, "we have pies."

He went into the kitchen. His wife had suggested making the pies. The boys, as it turned out, hadn't had much money. She'd argued, "We can make more off their bodies than what they had in their pockets."

Nicholas followed the innkeeper. When the innkeeper tried to stop him with an arm, Nicholas thrust him aside. The bishop strode across the kitchen to where a pickling tub stood against the wall. He pried off the lid and threw it onto the floor.

There, drifting in the pickling brine, were the three boys, half butchered, their dead eyes peering through the green.

Nicholas held back a sob, half pity, half fury.

Behind him, the innkeeper and his wife were terrified at the discovery.

There is little record, oddly, of how Nicholas faced them down. Did he at that point call out, and others came? How did he avoid death himself, a meat cleaver or a poker in his balding head?

We don't know, because the stories all stress his compassion. He laid out the bodies of the three dead boys, the long bones. He placed the meat from the pies beside them. He prayed.

We do not know how the bodies reassembled themselves. You may picture the miracle of the reanimated gobbets. You can ask what had happened to those parts that had already been eaten. The plays and poems of the Middle Ages do not answer these questions.

They end instead with the boys sitting up, blinking, alive once again. They did not remember the murder. They had slept well.

When they heard they had been raised from the dead by the bishop of Myra, they sang a hymn for him.

The innkeeper and his wife, on their knees, begged for their lives.

This is where the stories end.

What are we to make of this story? Scholars who look at tales like this first ask, *What are the sources of the story?* In the case of this ghoulish little tale, the earliest version we can find is a play acted out by boys in a monastery around the year 1030. Shortly after, it was turned into a monastic opera, a kind of musical, a medieval *Sweeney Todd* sung by monks on Saint Nicholas's Day, December 6. It appears to have been a French and English story—none of the older Greek sources mention it. Since it doesn't appear until about seven hundred years after Nicholas's death, it's extremely unlikely that this was an ancient tradition that stretched back to his lifetime.

It's much more likely that this story was made up, essentially, for some kind of school play. Certainly it seems to have gained popularity among the young monks of western Europe because it told a deliciously creepy story they could act out—and it was about young students like themselves.

Modern scholars look at *variants*, all the different ways a story is told. I have smashed a bunch of variants into one for this retelling, but it's also important to sort out the differences between versions that survive. In some, the innkeeper's wife resists the killing. In others, it's her idea. In some versions, the boys are baked into pies. In others, they're served with a simmering brown sauce.

In the two early dramatic versions, the boys aren't pickled at all. A hundred years later, the boys are always pickled, and they appear, rising up out of their pickling barrel, in stained-glass windows, wooden carvings, and manuscript drawings.

One difference between medieval versions of this story and modern storytelling technique is clear: The story feels unfinished to us because there is not a final clash. Nicholas doesn't take on the cannibal couple and thrash them. No angels appear with flaming swords to drag them off to Hell.

There is a deep difference between medieval priorities and our own. Oddly enough, in this case, we are the ones who, trained by modern hero narratives in action movies and comics, long for a simple, morally clear resolution in satisfying violence: blasts of holy fire; the innkeeper melting. It is the medieval versions that don't seem to care about this. They emphasize forgiveness and redemption. Either the innkeeper and his wife simply fade out of the story once the boys are revived or they repent in a kind of holy terror, having seen the resurrection of the boys, and they are given a second chance to live better. The priorities of the medieval storytellers are clearly to prove that Nicholas was truly a wonder-worker, someone who was given the gift to raise the dead—and to express to an audience who all had their secret little crimes that there was no sin so great that it could not be forgiven by the Christian God.

Let's make no mistake: This story is trashy. Even in the Middle Ages, it was hard to take seriously. But it was also a crowd favorite. It was likely acted out each year in December, as well as the story of the three daughters and a few of the other miracles of Nicholas. But it didn't make it into the saint's biographies written by more serious churchmen. It is hard to tell to what extent people actually believed it.

For the moment, let's leave it here: Some religious traditions are handed down from above by authorities, by clerics or kings; others arise from folklore, percolating upward into the official doctrine. Regardless of the truth behind any given religion, the details of how a religion is practiced are a collaboration between all its believers. Religions evolve through an incredibly complicated process of conversation and ritual. What stories and ideas help people? What gives them a better understanding of the world around them? What thrills them? What changes them? What opens new spiritual realities to them? What makes them feel connected to others around them? What explains the world to them?

For some medieval Christians, this story was an embarrassment. For others, it was a perfect tale to create a shiver and a laugh on a cold winter's night.

THE TALE OF

THE DEMON IN THE TEMPLE

We are told that when Nicholas got out of prison, he also set about ridding Myra of demons. Apparently, the city was infested with "great broods" of them.

These demons were the old Roman gods. Nicholas would storm into the temples where they lurked and tear the buildings apart with his own hands. If his back was hurting, that still didn't stop him from demolition. As he pulled stone from stone, the demons, crouching in the shadows with their bat wings, would flee, launching themselves into the sky, shrieking as they skittered off like a murder of anxious crows.

The largest and most beautiful temple in Myra was the shrine of many-breasted Artemis. The Myrans were very proud of her: Their coins featured Artemis and her brother Apollo of Patara, hometown gods. Every year in the cities of Ephesus, Myra, and Patara, they held great festivals for Artemis. They would sacrifice bulls to her and pour offerings of wine near her altars. They would process through the streets in long parades, men holding statues of her aloft, girls walking before them, holding baskets of flowers and ceremonial knives. There would be sacred dances to the sound of the flute and loud fanfares on trumpets. Young men would beat their spears on their shields. The wealthy would hold great feasts and try to outdo each other, showing off their money and power through their devotion to the goddess. Those who paid for a bull to be killed in the goddess's name would be entered in a lottery. Because Artemis also helped sailors, people would go down to the seashore and offer the goddess meals of salt and celery.

From the point of view of the Christians, however, Artemis was not a goddess: She was a demon. And so Nicholas set out to destroy her cult and her temple in Myra. One chronicler wrote:

> **When Nicholas launched his attack against the temple,** he not only destroyed everything that towered aloft, and hurled that to earth, but he uprooted the whole from its very foundations. Indeed, what was highest, at the very pinnacle of the temple, was embedded in the earth, and what was in the earth was thrown into the air.

The devil Artemis howled with rage and, with a flurry of demonic followers, took off screeching into the air.

She hated Nicholas from then on. She prepared her revenge.

That's the story we are told. What do historians do with a story like this? Unless you are someone who believes that there might have been a demon queen named Artemis, there doesn't seem to be any *historical* use for this story.

But let's look at it as a historian might.

The emperor Constantine, having had his vision of the cross that had led to victory, gradually converted to Christianity over the next fifteen years of his reign. As the next few years passed, Christianity went from being seen as a dangerous cult to being the most important religion of the empire. Not too long after Constantine's death, the whole Roman Empire would officially become Christian. Around 330 AD, Constantine really did issue a law that allowed people to tear down temples to the old gods, as long as they didn't destroy the statues and the treasures held there—those had to be given to the Roman government.

Over the course of a single lifetime, the ancient religions were replaced. This story reflects one of the ways that Christians convinced people to convert, by painting the old gods as demons, tricky devils who were only trying to mislead you. Artemis became a monster haunting her temple. Her brother Apollo became the demon king Apollyon.

How well did these tactics actually work? There is some concrete evidence that the cult of Artemis was no longer quite as popular as it traditionally had been. In 262, around the year of Nicholas's birth, the great temple of Artemis in Ephesus had been destroyed through two awful events. First, a terrible earthquake shook all of Anatolia. "The sound of thunder was heard, but it was more as though the earth was roaring than like Jupiter thundering. And many buildings were swallowed up with their inhabitants, and many people died of fright." In the midst of this quake, the temple of Artemis at Ephesus, once one of the Seven Wonders of the World, caught fire and burned. A few months later, before the city could recover from the earthquake, the Goths invaded and sacked the temple again. It was not only a temple: It operated as a bank, holding on to treasures from all over the realm. The Goths grabbed all the wealth and took off, a masterful and brutal heist.

After that, no one rebuilt this temple of Artemis, once one of the Seven Wonders of the World. It was abandoned. It seems as if the people of Ephesus decided that the goddess could no longer protect them. She was clearly too weak. She couldn't even protect herself. Their old agreements with her didn't seem to work anymore; the customary bargains fell through. Apparently, the people of Ephesus abandoned her and sought new gods.

Christianity was ready to replace her. Its priests and bishops argued that the old gods hadn't been able to do anything they had promised anyway.

The description of Nicholas's attack on Artemis describes an incredible upheaval, a churning maelstrom of slabs being thrown up into the air and toppling down into the earth. (It's unclear exactly how we're supposed to imagine this sacred demolition—did he do it alone? Did he do it with words or with a crowbar?) The thing is, we can find real examples of this kind of thing happening right nearby.

Just north of Patara, where Nicholas was born, there is a sacred site called Letoon, after the goddess Leto, mother of Artemis and Apollo. Three huge temples used to stand side by side here, next to a swamp: one for Leto, one for Apollo, and one for Artemis.

The Roman poet Ovid tells us that after Leto gave birth to the twins, she was exhausted. She staggered through the dry hills, looking for a drink. She came across a pool here, at Letoon, and saw peasants leading their cattle to the water. She asked them for a drink, but for some reason, they refused. She was a stranger. When she asked again, they got mean. Out of pure spite, they started jumping up and down in the water, kicking at the grime on the mucky bottom, muddying the water so badly that no one could drink it.

Leto, irritable, reached out an arm and turned the Lycian peasants into frogs.

Now they could jump around in the water all they wanted. And so there, for centuries afterward, in the sacred swamp, they croaked sadly beneath the moon.

This site was very important to the Lycians. A long highway led from the nearest town, Xanthos, and on feast days, hundreds of people would process along that road. To either side of this sacred way rose statues of emperors and gods and the tombs of the dead (which still can be seen today, now lost in tomato plantations and pomegranate groves). The worshippers would enter near the sacred pool and come to the three mighty temples of their gods—gods who were local, but who were also worshipped all over the Roman empire. This was a source of great pride.

But then some great catastrophe befell Letoon. Archaeologists believe that at the same time the temple of Artemis in Ephesus was nearly destroyed, some disaster—either the same earthquake or perhaps the Goths—severely damaged the temples at Letoon, and no one ever bothered to repair them. Perhaps this catastrophe lost the gods some of their followers. After the empire converted to Christianity in the fourth century, the Lycians really did tear down the remains of Letoon's fallen temples. The stones were used to build houses and farms. People carved crosses and Christian graffiti on the ruins, perhaps to drive out any lingering pagan spirits. But most notably, in the sixth century, the stones of the temples of Artemis and Leto and Apollo were used to build a Christian church and a monastery right next door. Just as the passage about Nicholas suggests, the bottom became the top and the top the bottom. The altar in that church was the top of a pillar from one of the pagan temples.

Christians literally used bits and pieces of the pagan world to build their own new world. They didn't just repurpose stories of gods and make them into demons. They used the physical building blocks of temples for churches, houses, castles, barns—whatever was needed. In Constantine's new capital of Constantinople, the giant heads of ancient gods and monsters were used to hold up the sewer system.

This story about Bishop Nicholas knocking down the temple of Artemis was written about five hundred years after his death. What's interesting to historians, though, is what it preserves nonetheless: a memory of this period of conversion. It preserves the arguments Christians used to convince followers of the old gods to instead follow the single Christian God.

And as Nicholas replaced the old gods with his monotheistic One God, he started to take over the duties of the old gods, too.

THE TALE OF THE DROWNING SAILORS

A storm hit a ship at sea. The ship was battered by waves, which crashed over the sides and threatened to wash the sailors overboard.

They were on their way to Myra. Though they had never seen the bishop there, the famous Nicholas, they'd heard he helped everyone who begged him for assistance. And so, as the ship was flung from side to side, they called out his name, begging him to come save them from the storm.

And there he was, miraculously, standing upon the deck of the ship beside them, dressed in shining robes. "Behold, you have called me, and I am here to help you." With that, he began working with them to haul on ropes and unship the mast and steer the boat toward land. He worked beside them to brave the hurricane.

When the rocky coast near Myra was in sight, the figure evaporated. The storm calmed.

They reached Myra's harbor and grounded their ship for the night.

As soon as they could, they tumbled thankfully onto dry land. They made their way up the great steps to the wide public square and began asking where they could find Bishop Nicholas to thank him.

They found him at home in his study. They recognized him immediately. He was not dressed in shining robes, but in ordinary, drab clothes. He seemed surprised by their visit. They fell on their knees before him. He didn't understand. They explained what they'd just been through and told him that he'd appeared on the sea.

He said they shouldn't thank him—he hadn't done anything. He'd been at home. They should thank their God instead.

This story, and variations on it, became one of the most important stories told about Nicholas.

In one variation, a fisherman's boat is capsized during a storm, and he is hurled into the cold waters. As he fights to keep his head above water, he calls out Nicholas's name. Suddenly, he finds himself teleported. He is no longer struggling in the waves. He is standing on his own street, his clothes still drenched and dripping.

In another account, a drowning man whose ship was sinking called out to the bishop for help. Nicholas stalked across the sea and laid his brocade cloak on the water, which floated atop the waves and carried the drowning man to safety.

In various stories of rescue, Nicholas flies through the air or utters simple words to get the storm to cease. And yet, as these nautical miracles happen, he is still sitting in his home, in his study, unaware of the storms far out in the Mediterranean and the voices calling out to him.

He became the patron saint of sailors. For the next millennium and a half, Christian sailors from all over the world would pray before they set out on a voyage: "May Saint Nicholas guide our rudder."

Whenever sailors encountered a storm at sea, they'd pray to Nicholas, and if they lived through the storm, they'd tell their story when they got back to shore. (If they didn't make it, well, no one knew if they'd called out to him or not.) These stories reinforced the idea of Nicholas's power over the seas. One of the earliest biographies of Nicholas was written by the Patriarch of Constantinople, whose father had been saved from shipwreck by calling out the name of Nicholas as he sank. His son wrote a biography in thanks to the saint.

What we see here is Nicholas, as a Christian saint, starting to serve some of the same purposes the pagan gods had served in his youth. Sailors from Anatolia had previously called out to the sea god Poseidon or to Artemis herself for help. They'd made offerings at their temples before a voyage to beg for calm seas. After Nicholas's death, when he had become a saint, people would go to a church and pray to him instead. Wealthy men built churches named after him when their ships were saved, just as once they had offered to build temples or donate pricey statues to the gods in exchange for aid. In this way, oddly, having overthrown the old gods, Nicholas (and the other saints) started to act as their replacements.

This fact did not escape Christian writers at the time. Many religious thinkers resisted the idea of these saints, these dead and potent spirits, floating around performing magic as the gods had done before. "Under the cloak of religion we see really a heathen ceremony introduced into the churches," runs an angry letter from 404 AD. "While the sun is shining, heaps of candles are lighted and, everywhere, all sorts of paltry powder, wrapped in a costly cloth, is kissed and worshipped." People were presenting votive offerings to the saints as they'd once given them to the gods. Ironically, this irritable letter was written to a scholar named Jerome who, when dead, would become Saint Jerome, for whom people still light candles all over the world.

So Nicholas's fame spread—perhaps even during his life—as a wonder-worker who could save sailors.

An old Serbian carol tells a story that after Nicholas's death, he was at a party with all the other saints in Heaven. They were passing around the wine when Nicholas fell asleep in his seat and let the cup fall out of his hand. Saint Elias shook him awake. "Nicholas! Nicholas!"

"Oh, I beg the company's pardon," he said, "but I have been very busy and was absent from your festival. The sea was rough, and I had to give my help to three hundred ships that were in danger. Excuse me: That's why I'm so tired."

THE TALE OF

THE HELLFIRE JAR: OR, THE REVENGE OF ARTEMIS

Artemis was angry. Her temple lay in ruins, and now people prayed to Nicholas instead for grain and for safety on the waves. She decided to take her revenge.

A group of pilgrims was setting off on a ship to go see the famous Nicholas—perhaps getting his blessing before a longer sea voyage to the Middle East. The demon Artemis dressed herself as a nun and prepared a container full of the fires of Hell.

She rowed out in a little boat to the pilgrims' ship. She said she'd heard they were going to visit the good bishop Nicholas's church in Myra. She had a gift to give him. It was precious oil, scented with perfumes, to fill the lamps on the altar of Nicholas's church. They offered to take her along. She said she was too frail for a long sea voyage. Would they perhaps take her jar of oil and give it to him so he could light his sanctuary with it?

They reached down over the gunwales and took the deadly jar

from her. She smiled and waved. If they had watched, they might have noticed that she then simply faded away.

They sailed off toward Myra. That night, one of them dreamed of Nicholas, bishop of Myra. He was terse: "Rise at dawn and throw the strange jar you are carrying into the depths of the sea." The sun rose, and so did the sailor. He told the others of his dream.

They hurled the jar overboard.

The sea erupted.

Flames blasted out of the waves. Smoke billowed up and blackened the rising sun, the red waters of dawn. "The whole ship was being violently driven by the swell, and the pilgrims, driven out of their senses by invisible blasts of wind and by the fear of what they saw, gave no heed to the rudders and cables that steered the ship."

In the middle of this chaos, Nicholas appeared. He raised his hands, and the ship moved away from the burning of the sea. When they were safe, he disappeared.

Behind them, though, they could see that the flames upon the waters where they had thrown the jar still flickered for hours.

Artemis had planned to destroy Nicholas and his church the way he had destroyed her temple.

When the pilgrims got to Myra and met Nicholas, they were gobsmacked. "You really are he! You are the one who appeared to us out at sea and saved us from the snares of the Devil!"

As per usual, he had to be told what he'd done. The miracle lay not in him, but in his God. He was only the clay vessel through which the miraculous moved.

The *Lives* of Nicholas written a few hundred years later are very proud of his work converting Roman pagans. This was important work for a religion that, at the time of the Great Persecution, was an imperiled minority. They needed converts. Christians had just been through a terrifying purge where they had seen people they knew imprisoned and executed. Nicholas's zeal in destroying temples and converting worshippers of Artemis was therefore one of the things that made him heroic in the eyes of Christians.

In practice, though, conversion must have happened slowly, and it brought with it some very profound social and psychological changes.

Imagine that you're a believer in the gods of Greece and Rome. Your universe is fundamentally chaotic. No single being is in control—for the gods themselves squabble and bicker. They don't generally pay attention to you unless you visit their temples and speak to them, offering them some gift—or if you break one of their rules, go against the ancient customs, and anger them. They are not particularly moral.

The Greco-Roman gods cannot read human thoughts, unlike the Judeo-Christian God. Emperor Constantine recalled that in his pagan youth, he did not "think that the supernatural Power saw any of those things that I did in the secrecy of my heart." The Roman gods in the stories can slip invisibly between mortals and hear things that are said aloud (boasts, promises, profanities). But they can't tell what you're thinking. This is very different from the omniscient God of Christianity and Judaism, who is supposed to know every hidden thought and desire; who is all-knowing, in charge of each mortal's fate.

Let's think about this practically. If you are on a ship, for example, that is going down in a storm, a Roman pagan will cry out to a god for help (Poseidon or even Artemis). The god might help or might not, but you don't have to come up with a *reason* that the ship is sinking. The gods do not pay attention to all mortals, and often people are destroyed somewhat by accident.

Now imagine the shift to the Christian perspective: Instead of a chaotic universe of competing spiritual forces, there is one all-powerful, all-knowing God in charge of the entire cosmos. Every mortal fits into His plan. In one sense, this is comforting. It's one of the things that attracted the middle and lower classes to Christianity in this period: They matter to the God. In another sense, it complicates things. If you are drowning on a sinking ship, there must be a reason for it. As Christianity is more concerned with justice, ethics, and self-control than Greco-Roman religion, you have to start asking yourself some difficult questions as the water rises around you. *Why is this part of God's plan? Why is this happening to me? What did I do to deserve this?* The whole nature of cause and effect seems different.

This is a broadly simplistic portrait, of course, but it gives some sense of the conceptual revolution that went on as Christianity spread throughout the empire. Perhaps it's not surprising that many people found a middle way: They might switch religions, but they now prayed to the saints and the angels as they'd once prayed to the gods, making promises, trying to get some specific wish granted. In many ways, Christianity and paganism in this period both mirrored the structure of Roman society itself. The idea was that the hierarchies on earth—from peasants to wealthy men to regional governors up to councillors and kings—were mirrored in the hierarchies of Heaven. You took your request to an official who was lower on the ladder, and they appeared in the court of Heaven to argue on your behalf. In 1098, for example, a famous English churchman and writer, Anselm of Canterbury, went on pilgrimage to the tomb of Nicholas in Bari. He wrote a prayer to Nicholas, fearing that his sins were so great that the Christian God wouldn't even listen to him if Anselm didn't have a messenger to ask for mercy. "I will pray to one of the great friends of God and perhaps God will hear him on my behalf. I will call upon Nicholas, that great confessor, whose name is honored throughout the world. Nicholas!" he pleaded. "If only he will hear me! Great Nicholas!"

At that time, the hierarchies of power on earth seemed to extend up to God Himself.

Old ways change slowly. Oddly, when, a millennium and a half after Nicholas's death, he was transformed from Saint Nicholas into Santa Claus, the friendly, chimney-diving, stocking-stuffing elf combined aspects of both pagan gods and the Christian God. Think about this: On the one hand, as a supernatural figure, Santa is transactional. You go to him with a list of very specific material requests and make promises to try to convince him to give you things, just like you once would do at the temple of Artemis or Apollo. On the other hand, like a lo-res, tinny version of the Christian God, Santa is both omniscient and concerned with judging the moral action of his believers. He sees you when you're sleeping; he knows when you're awake. He knows if you've been bad or good—so be good, for goodness' sake. Santa Claus would become a figure suspended halfway between the gods of Olympus and the Christian Heaven.

The emperor Constantine, as he got older, became convinced that he had been bad. He was worried about the judgment on his eternal soul. Shortly before his death, he was finally baptized and fully became a Christian. Sarcastic pagans of the court said he only converted because he felt guilty he'd killed his own wife and son without reason—and the Christians offered him forgiveness.

He was probably not a model Christian by any account. For one thing, he was very proud, very vain. In Constantinople, the imperial capital he'd named after himself, he knocked the head off a giant statue of Apollo, the sun god he had once worshipped. Then he replaced it with his own head.

It took Nicholas of Myra to get Constantine to doubt himself.

THE TALE OF
THE THREE GENERALS

Three Roman generals on their way to put down a rebellion of the Goths stopped off at the port of Myra to provision their ships. There they met Bishop Nicholas, who invited them to dinner. They saw immediately that he was kind of a local celebrity, embraced by people on the street, notable for his humility, friendliness, and soft-spokenness.

They followed him up from the port into town. But before they could even get to his house to eat, a messenger ran up to Nicholas on the street, out of breath, and told him that several innocent men were about to be put to death by the governor for crimes they didn't commit. The three startled generals watched as Nicholas, seventy years old, excused himself and bolted off into the crowd.

Nicholas made it just in time. He found the executioner standing with his sword in hand. The prisoners were kneeling before him, their faces covered by linen cloths, about to be beheaded.

Nicholas pushed his way to the front of the mob. He "fearlessly grabbed the sword from the executioner and cast it to the ground. Loosening the men from their chains, he took them with him to the city." He marched to the governor of Lycia—who had just been appointed by Constantine—and accused him of taking bribes to execute innocent men.

The three generals were impressed. Here was a man not afraid to stand up for what was right.

The next day the generals went off in their ships and quashed the Gothic rebellion. When they were done, they sailed back to Constantinople, the capital. But there they discovered that someone had been whispering lies about them. Constantine's right-hand man, who went by the unfortunate name of Flavius Ablabius, had been paid a large sum of money to tell the emperor that these three generals were planning to overthrow the government. Ablabius coaxed Constantine to have them imprisoned and executed.

The generals were dragged off, shocked at the accusation. They'd just come back from fighting the emperor's enemies—and now they were going to be put to death by him. They sat helplessly in prison. They despaired. "What did we do, to be snuffed out so miserably?"

Then they remembered the holy man they'd met in Myra who had stood up for the innocent against the governor. They called out to him, though he was hundreds of miles away. "Just as you saved the men in Lycia who were wrongfully and shamefully condemned to death, please now save us!"

Constantine, at the time, was sleeping in his royal bedchamber. He suddenly awoke: There was someone with him in the room.

An old man. An angry old man. "Constantine, emperor," called the apparition, "free those three men who you have sent to prison, officers of the army, who have been condemned on hearsay. If you do not obey me, I will stir up an uncontrollable revolt against you—your corpse and innards will be thrown to wild beasts and devoured!"

The emperor demanded, "Who are you, and how did you get into my palace?"

The old man answered simply, "I am Nicholas, a sinner, bishop of Myra."

And with that, he vanished.

Then he appeared by Ablabius's bed. His eyes flashed with fury. "You fool!" he shouted. "You senseless man! Why have you arranged the murder of innocent men? Hurry now and set them free, or your body will be riddled with worms and your house will collapse in ruins!"

Ablabius cowered.

In the morning, Constantine woke up and he called for Ablabius. They both admitted they'd had strange dreams about an angry man from Lycia. They called the three prisoners. The disgraced generals were brought before the emperor's throne.

He interrogated them. "Tell me, what kind of magic do you do, that you can force dreams on us while we sleep?"

The men looked at each other in confusion. They had no idea what he was talking about. They denied they had anything to do with it.

The emperor asked, "Do you know anyone by the name of Nicholas?"

At this, the three men gasped. They said they did know a Nicholas—a bishop of Myra—who had intervened to save innocent men from execution. They told the emperor the story of what they had seen.

Constantine thought it over. It seemed like a miracle. This man had appeared right beside his bed in the middle of a palace protected by guards. No normal human could have done that. The prisoners were untied. The emperor told them, "Now understand this, it is not I who have granted you your life, but the man you called on, Nicholas."

They were free. They couldn't believe it. They shaved their heads and dressed as pilgrims. They sailed back to Myra, taking costly gifts to thank the miraculous bishop for saving their lives. They distributed gold and built a mile-long covered walkway from Nicholas's church into the center of town, lined with free new housing for the city's poorer citizens.

This became one of the most famous stories about Nicholas: how his insight and mercy saved innocent prisoners from wrongful death.

There are some interesting historical connections here.

There really was, believe it or not, a powerful man of Constantine's court named Flavius Ablabius; he actually was known for his skillful manipulation of the emperor. The three generals, who are mentioned by name, really did exist. (One of them, in fact, did later rebel against a different emperor, leading "a band of persons addicted to robbery and all kinds of debauchery.") The rebellion of the Goths that these men put down really did occur. This tale seems like it might describe events that happened in 331 AD, near the end of Constantine's reign.

Did Constantine have a dream of Nicholas that caused him to change his mind? It is not impossible.

The story also preserves another historical fact: In 318 AD,

Constantine, ever more convinced of the power of the Christian church, decreed that people condemned by the courts could appeal to Christian bishops to hear their cases. This means that even if Nicholas didn't literally snatch the sword out of the executioner's hand, as a bishop he could have heard the prisoners' appeal and declared them innocent.

This story circulated on its own centuries before any of the other stories: before the three girls and their bags of gold, before the demolition of Artemis's temple, and at least five hundred years before the three pickled boys. This is one of the earliest stories told about Nicholas.

Given that, it seems like it might be one of our only glimpses of the real person behind all these myths: fierce in protecting the innocent, wise, merciful, and just.

That would be a person worth remembering.

DEATH AND THE SACRED LIQUOR

More than fifty years had gone by since young Nicholas, wandering into a church one morning, was first made bishop of Myra. Now he was in his late seventies or eighties. Most religious paintings show him at this age, as if he was never young, never the boy who looked out over the harbor of Patara and snuck out at night to hurl bags of gold through windows. But in these paintings, despite his white beard, he does not look like our Saint Nick, clad in furry red, fat and jolly. He is balding, thin, and gaunt. He is dressed as a bishop. He scowls.

The day came when it was time for Nicholas to die, because death, we are told, is "the common law of nature." Everything must eventually die. Nicholas had been sick for a few days. He did not fear death. "While he desired to remain in the flesh, Nicholas equally desired to be unyoked from it." This was another one of the elements of Christianity that appealed to people: The body was merely a vehicle the soul rode in. Death was not the end.

And so Nicholas died. We are told that "at his passing, the heavenly choirs were heard."

His body was borne through the streets of Myra by priests and bishops carrying torches and candles. This was the city he had nurtured. The people followed along in slow procession.

They buried him in a crypt in the church at the south end of town. According to the story, his body would lie there under a marble slab for more than seven hundred years, until a crowd of thieves broke in to steal it and take it home with them.

He died on December 6, and this day is still celebrated by some Christians as Saint Nicholas's Day.

Immediately after his death, people began to notice something: "His body, buried in the church, straightaway gushed forth a sweet-smelling perfume, turning away all destructive powers, but providing a saving remedy that wards off evil." This liquid would later be described as an oil, a balm, an ointment, a potion, a sacred liquor, myrrh, or holy manna (named after the miraculous food that appeared to Moses and the Israelites wandering in the desert). The technical name is *myron*.

People began to drink this strange ooze or rub it on their bodies for its healing power. I am not sure who first had this idea. But soon, we are told, pilgrims were coming from all over the empire to buy the liquid that gathered around the bones of the dead Nicholas. "To the spot come multitudes of the weak, lame, blind, withered, deaf and dumb, and ones who are vexed by unclean spirits. When they are anointed with that holy liquor, they are restored to their original state of health."

A Greek hymn from a few hundred years after Nicholas's death sings the praises of this liquid.

It is sprinkled on those who approach
In order to drive out the ugly stench of the passions,
O Nicholas,
And to put to flight the host of demons.

This is the miraculous substance that would lead a gang of merchants, nobles, and nautical thieves to steal the body of Nicholas seven hundred years later.

And though Nicholas was dead, a little death didn't stop him from continuing to appear to people and working to help where he could.

ADVENTURES AFTER DEATH

Of course, a saint's adventures do not end when they die. In fact, for someone to be declared a saint officially by the Catholic Church, there needs to be credible evidence that after they died, they performed miracles.

There are many stories of Nicholas—transformed, after death, into *Saint* Nicholas—swooping in to save people despite being buried under a slab. Most of them are about rescues at sea: shipwrecks, lightning, huge waves, and suddenly, there Nicholas appears, glowing, in the sky, and quiets the rage of the storm. Even William the Conqueror, who famously invaded England in 1066 AD, claimed to have been saved once from drowning by Nicholas.

The stories shift and change through the centuries. One frequently repeated tale, for example, tells of a family who traveled to Saint Nicholas's tomb in Myra on a pilgrimage. On the way, they were attacked by pirates or slavers, and the son of the family was dragged off to a distant court. The boy served as a cupbearer for the cruel ruler there. A year later, on December 6, Saint Nicholas's Day, his parents were praying to the saint that their son would somehow find his way home, and Nicholas heard their plea. He appeared at the tyrant's court, at a feast where the boy was pouring wine. Saint Nicholas grabbed the boy by the hair, yanked him upward, and teleported him through the skies and over the ancient seas. The boy found himself back in his own country, in the courtyard of his own home, with a goblet in his hand and a napkin still spread on his wrist. His parents were astounded.

In different versions, the boy can be named Adeodatus or Dieudonné or Basil. Depending on when the story was written down and whom the writer was most afraid of, the country where the boy is imprisoned can be Babylon, North Africa, Sicily, or the island of Crete (which was a haven for Arab pirates in the ninth century). The "facts" changed for each generation.

Nicholas changed, too. Generally, the early *Lives* describe him as charitable and humble. Increasingly, though, storytellers picked up on that element of fury and rage he showed when he appeared to the emperor Constantine and Ablabius in the tale of the three generals. Starting around the year 1000, Saint Nicholas begins to appear regularly as a phantom punisher with a whip: kind to the innocent, terrifying to the guilty. He whips thieves until they return a cave full of treasure to the rightful owner. He whips a young poet-musician for creepily hitting on a pious widow, as singer-songwriters tend to do.

The idea of heroism changes over the centuries. In Nicholas's own time, during the Great Persecution, a new kind of heroism was introduced: not the military heroism of ancient epics, not the heroism of sword and shield and sandal, but instead the heroism of suffering or sacrifice, befitting a religion that worshipped a crucified

Son of God. The heroes from the Christian stories of that time are not heroes who spear their enemies, but martyrs, people who themselves are tortured and die, and in that death find victory. It is a radically different form of triumph. In the stories of Nicholas himself, we see the hero who converts people, which was the work the church wanted to accomplish in the centuries after the end of the Great Persecution, as the Roman Empire shifted from its ancient paganism to Christianity. It wasn't until much later that Nicholas was transformed into the kind of hero who dealt out justice with his whip—more active, more violent, less merciful. He was very testy in those years.

This starts to get at the answer to a question we asked a while back: *Why would historians bother with these stories when they're basically just made up, just folktales?* Because though they may not tell us much about the actual Nikolaos, fourth-century bishop of Myra, they tell us a lot about the people who made up the legends of his deeds. They tell us about how people conceived of ethics, morality, and heroism. They show us the different structures of belief through the centuries. That helps us understand the things we ourselves believe. We can start to ask: How do we build our heroes today? Who do we worship?

And these stories can still tell us a lot about the time when they were written, little details of daily routine or practical reality the authors took for granted. Sure, it is very unlikely that a demon goddess tried to detonate the church of Saint Nicholas with a jar of hellfire. But it's interesting that the author of that story described a substance that we know was a feared military secret at the time the story was written (mid–ninth century): a mysterious flammable liquid called

Greek fire, which literally could set the waves aflame, and that the Eastern Roman Empire used to defeat invading navies.

The story about the three grain ships that came sailing in to Myra sounds like a fable or a Christmas carol ("I saw three ships come sailing in, come sailing in . . .")—but it actually reflects a surprising social reality: The Roman government actually did requisition grain from all over the empire and transport it on huge grain ships across the Mediterranean so it could feed the poorer city dwellers at public expense. This was the Roman form of welfare. Everyone could have bread. The grain was shipped north from Alexandria. Reliable northwest winds blowing along the coast of Lycia made Myra a frequent stop for ships on these grain runs from Egypt; hence the huge granary that still stands, almost two thousand years old, in the ruins of Myra's port. Across the river stand the ruins of a water-powered gristmill that could grind that grain into flour. The old story has a lot of truth to it. There actually were grain ships traveling by order of the emperor from Alexandria to Constantinople, stopping off at Myra, and it's interesting to see Nicholas bartering for some of the surplus and the captains explaining how their cargo was measured out and accounted for at each end of the voyage. It tells us how that granary was used. The stories about Nicholas are filled with little details like this that show us the past and all the many fascinating ways humans have lived upon this earth.

So now we've told his stories. It's time cut away all these centuries of myth and legend and to ask: *Who actually was Saint Nicholas? What, truly, do we know about him?*

THE REAL SAINT NICHOLAS

W*hat, truly, do we know about him?* In a sense, almost nothing. There are no surviving mentions of Nicholas, Bishop of Myra, from his lifetime at all. He left no letters or memoirs. No inscriptions in stone. No paintings by anyone who saw him or met him.

So how do we decide what to believe about him? How do we know anything about what actually happened in the past?

Ironically, in our own great information age, it is hard to get good information. Knowledge rushes in great invisible streams all around us through the air, but many of those streams are contaminated with untruth. We have to be savvy. We have to be careful about which sources we trust. We have to know who says what and why they say it.

That's also true for the distant past, though usually the problem is there is too little information, rather than too much. Historians must work like detectives, asking, *Why would this author tell this story? Can I believe them? Are there things they might leave out?* It's useful when more than one surviving text tells the same story from a different point of view. Then the historian, working like a detective questioning several witnesses to a crime, can build a more accurate picture of what actually happened.

But remember that in the periods we're talking about—Nicholas's life, around the year 300, and the theft of his body, in the year 1087—those sources were scanty. There were no printing presses. All books had to be copied out individually by hand. We've lost many books we know existed. By bad fortune, no copies survived. We might know their names or a couple of quotes that appeared elsewhere, but some fantastic stories have been lost to the world forever through rot or fire. The Goths who burned the city of Ephesus, where Artemis had her great temple, destroyed one of the world's most famous libraries at the same time.

Here's an example of how historians consider the reliability of their sources when they're trying to reconstruct lives like Nicholas's.

The earliest mention of Nicholas to survive—possibly—is in a list of attendees at the great meeting of Christian bishops that the emperor Constantine called together at Nicaea. Constantine realized the Christian church could be used for political ends to hold the empire together, but he was worried by how many disagreements there were among bishops from different regions. As a result, in 325, he paid for bishops and archbishops from all over the empire to be brought together in the city of Nicaea to agree on a set of official doctrines to define Christianity. They arrived by boat and carriage and on horseback. Many of them had been tortured at the time of the Great Persecution, and now hobbled into the great meeting chamber missing eyes or legs or hands. Over the next several days, the bishops hashed out their differences. They argued about the details of Christian faith. They decided on how they should calculate the date of Easter. They made a list of their common beliefs. The resulting document is still said out loud, in unison, each week by Christians all over the world: the *Nicene Creed* (the statement of belief from Nicaea).

In a list of over three hundred bishops who attended the conference, we find, at number 151, *Nicholas of Myra in Lycia*. There he is!

The problem is, this list was first written down around 515 AD; and the one copy of this list that survives is actually from around the year 1200. It's a copy, or even a copy of a copy. That means there are at least seven hundred years in which someone could have stuck his name in. Several other versions of the guest list for the Council of Nicaea survive. The lists that contain around three hundred names (which is supposedly how many people actually attended) include Nicholas of Myra. The lists that contain two hundred names do not. It seems very possible that he attended but was simply not one of the more visible and important bishops at the time. No one knew he would become world-famous and would appear on pajamas and wrapping paper. But of course, we can't say for sure that he was there—or even that he existed at all. (We can probably discount entirely the later stories in which he won arguments at the council by ☞ **miraculously causing a brick to burst into flames in his hand** or by punching an arch-heretic in the face.)

If he was indeed there at Nicaea, it means—delightfully—that Santa Claus, the patron saint of Christmas, helped choose the date of Easter.

We know that starting around the year 400, the name Nikolaos, "Victory for the People," started to become popular in Lycia and spread outward from there across the Eastern Roman Empire. That makes it more likely that his cult began that early, shortly after his death. We know that in the mid-sixth century, the emperor Justinian built a beautiful church dedicated to Saint Nicholas in the reigning city of Constantinople, "driving back the waves of the sea," a sanctuary rising out of the billows on a rocky spit of land—the perfect location for a building dedicated to the patron saint of sailors. So by that time, even though we have almost no other surviving evidence, clearly the cult of Nicholas had reached the capital of the Eastern Roman Empire and had impressed the court with miraculous stories.

We know that in the century that followed that, churches devoted to Saint Nicholas sprang up all over the Mediterranean—wherever seafarers might stop and pray for a safe voyage. In Myra, after an earthquake, a new church was built to hold Nicholas's bones on the site of his own church. It was a fancier church, a *basilica*. Portions of it still stand to this day. It was this church, changed much over the centuries, that the thieves would eventually invade to steal his body. On the island of Rhodes, off the coast of Lycia, the giant shanks of the bronze Colossus were torn down and a church of Saint Nicholas was built in their place. We find ancient churches named after Nicholas all over the Mediterranean world: from grand cathedrals with gilded domes where kings and princes bowed down before his altars to tiny stone chapels on lonely isles.

The first surviving biographies of Saint Nicholas were written in the ninth and tenth centuries—five or six hundred years after his life—by scholars named, with appropriate fantasy-novel flair, things like Michael the Archimandrite, Symeon the Metaphrast, and John the Deacon. Almost all the stories I have told you are from these

Lives of the saint. I took their different versions and created versions that made sense to me. But of course, in doing that, I did exactly what they did, recombining and retelling with my own emphases, my own biases. This is the way stories change slowly and evolve.

John the Deacon, for example, wrote many lives of many different saints. Here is his description of how he filled in the gaps in their biographies:

> Where I could not uncover a story or determine what kind of life they led, either from the most aged people or from inscriptions or from any other source, to avoid a blank place in my list of holy pontiffs, I have with the assistance of God through your prayers invented a Life for them. And I believe that no deception is involved. . . .

That is terrible news for a modern historian. John is basically saying that in his saints' *Lives*, he's either finding previous sources and copying them out in Latin (which is what he did in the case of Nicholas)—or he simply made up some facts that seemed good and assumed that the Christian God approved. That is the kind of statement that makes historians gnash their teeth and tear at their tweed jackets.

It has led some to throw up their hands and declare that they don't know if there was a Nicholas of Myra at all. In 1940, some of the greatest scholars of the Catholic Church, the Bollandists, got together to examine the sources for the stories of Nicholas and, afterward, admitted they were completely frustrated. "We know nothing of the actions of the famous miracle-worker," they complained.

So what can we say? What do I believe? The question of belief always bedevils Santa Claus. Do I believe in Saint Nick?

In the end, all I can offer you are probabilities. It is very likely that there was a bishop of Myra named Nikolaos who lived from roughly 260 to 340 AD. It is likely he was thrown in prison during the Great Persecution. (That would not have been unusual for a bishop, in those troubled times.) It would not be surprising if he attended the Council of Nicaea in 325 AD. Following Constantine's announcement that bishops could hear appeals for condemned prisoners in 318, it is not impossible that somehow Nicholas intervened to save innocent men from execution in Myra, and perhaps even the three generals accused of treason by the unfortunately named Flavius Ablabius. (One of the earliest surviving documents about Nicholas tells this story alone.)

But, I guess, here's the most important thing of all: I don't think his name would have survived in folk legend if he had not truly been loved by his city. I think he fought for the people of Myra. I believe in his generosity. I believe that stories of his kindness (giving random gifts, arranging for grain to be delivered to his starving city)—these would not have clustered around him if he had not been the kind of person who devoted his life to making sure, in a brutal world, that people took care of each other.

This is what survives of him in the figure of Santa Claus, seventeen hundred years after his death.

One blustery, cold spring day when the wind blew in off the Adriatic Sea, I met the most famous of the monks who are responsible for protecting the body of Saint Nicholas: the Dominican Father Gerardo Cioffari, the world's foremost expert on the saint. He has devoted his life to studying the hard historical facts of the case. "When I speak of this," he told me, "I forget I'm a priest: I'm a scholar." He is a brilliant man. His office is ringed with bookshelves that are haphazardly stuffed with texts in Latin, Greek, Russian, German, French, English. He reads all of them. He has cautioned people against believing everything about Nicholas—and also against leaping the other way and dismissing the existence of Nicholas entirely, just because there are fanciful stories about him. That evening, we talked about all the theories and confusions, the bizarre tales, the historical realities of Constantine's reign.

Finally, I asked him frankly: *So do you believe in these miracle stories?* He is a Dominican monk, a man who has devoted his life to Saint Nicholas.

He gave a little smile and shrugged. "Several of the miracles," he said, "if you take away the miracles, might be real."

But now we move on—and the real life of this bishop in an obscure corner of the Roman Empire does not matter to us anymore. What matters are the stories I've told—because these are the stories that the saint hunters of Bari, the relic thieves, the League of Saint Nicholas, believed. This was who they thought they were snatching: a man who'd flown through the storm, a man who'd brought the dead back to life, a man whose body drooled holy healing oils.

So step back and let seven hundred years pass.

Things change. Christianity spreads across the empire. Constantine becomes a legend—the emperor who saw a cross blazing in the sky. Diocletian becomes a fairy-tale monster to frighten children. Nicholas's name spreads across the seas.

The old gods die hard. For hundreds of years, people still visit their ruined temples. It is difficult, after a thousand years of believing a place is filled with watchful spirits, to see it instead as empty. We have records from two hundred years after Nicholas's death of a monk named after him chopping down a cypress tree in the moun tains outside of Myra; **people were frightened it was inhabited by a demon**. This is almost certainly the memory of some previous sacred spot where a god of the forest was revered. It is difficult to unhaunt the world.

The Roman Empire falls apart, invaded from all sides. Rome itself is plundered, and with it, the Western Roman Empire topples. The Eastern Roman Empire continues, however, centered in the shining capital named after Constantine, Constantinople. Now stories are told about how, when the emperor laid out its walls, he was led by an angel. It is a Christian empire, and the average citizens can barely remember the names of the gods whose statues crumble in its squares.

Pilgrims come to Myra from all over the Mediterranean to see the tomb of Nicholas. They pay for bottles of the liquor that flows from his body. (Archaeologists have found the bottles at Myra's old port.)

Three hundred, five hundred, six hundred years go by. There is no flesh on that body.

The saint sleeps beneath a marble slab that is pierced with holes so the oil can be extracted. The church is burned and rebuilt. Wars are fought. Starting in the seventh century, a new religion arises and spreads quickly across the deserts and seas: Islam, the teachings of the Prophet Muhammad. This new faith spreads throughout Arabia, Syria, North Africa—as far west as Spain and far, far into the eastern steppe.

Ships still carry grain and lumber and spices from city to city—but the day of the giant Roman grain ships is over. Ships are smaller now and hug the coast. They don't dare go often into the deep waters of the Mediterranean. There are too many dangers. Every night they tie up at dock or anchor themselves in a harbor. They follow the shorelines.

And across the sea, from a city in southern Italy, the city of Bari, come three shiploads of thieves, racing the Republic of Venice to try to steal Saint Nicholas's body from its tomb in Myra.

Their story is about to begin.

Part
II

THE LEAGUE OF SAINT NICHOLAS

1087
AD

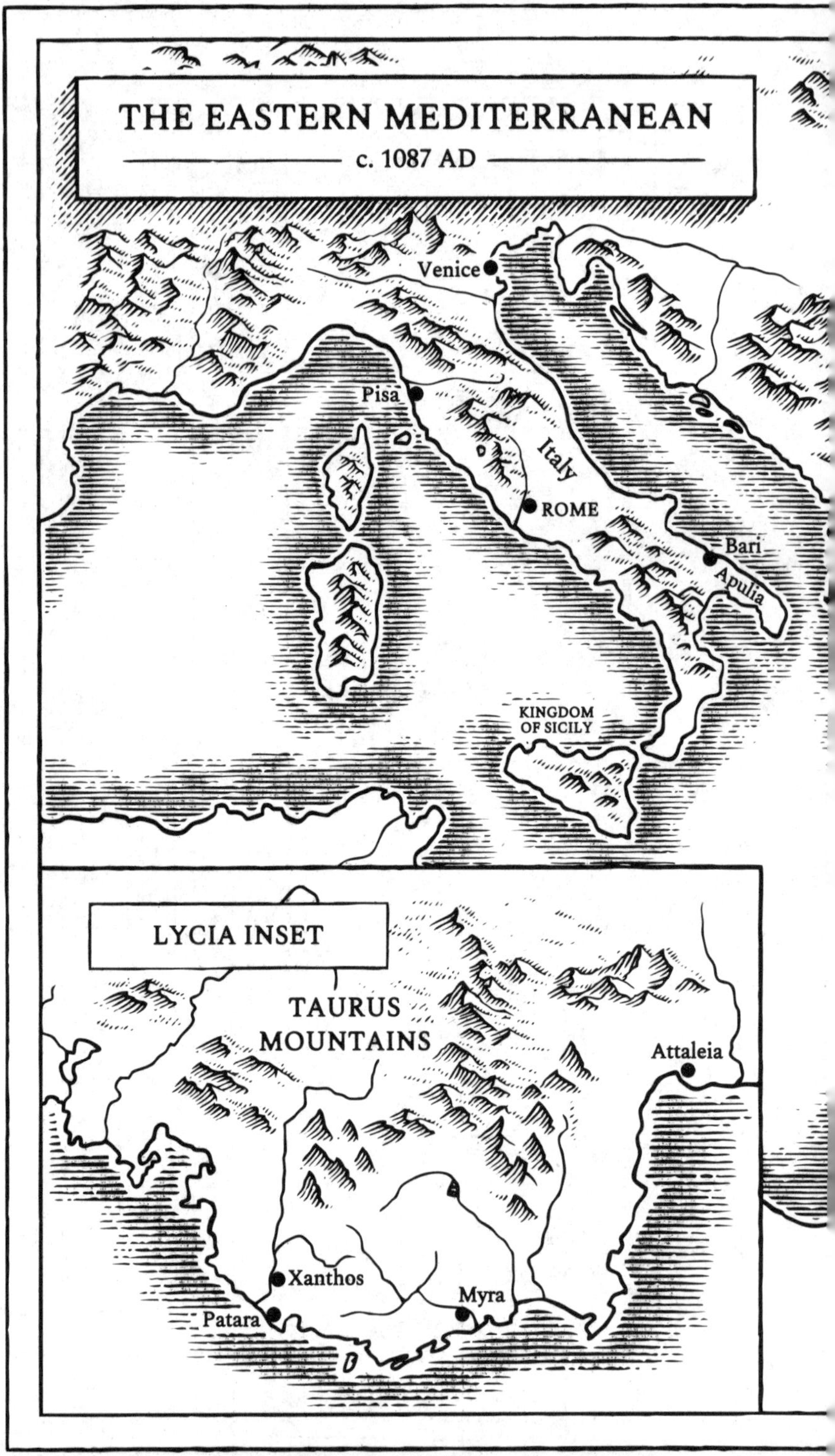
THE EASTERN MEDITERRANEAN
c. 1087 AD
Venice
Pisa
Italy
ROME
Bari
Apulia
KINGDOM OF SICILY
LYCIA INSET
TAURUS MOUNTAINS
Attaleia
Xanthos
Patara
Myra

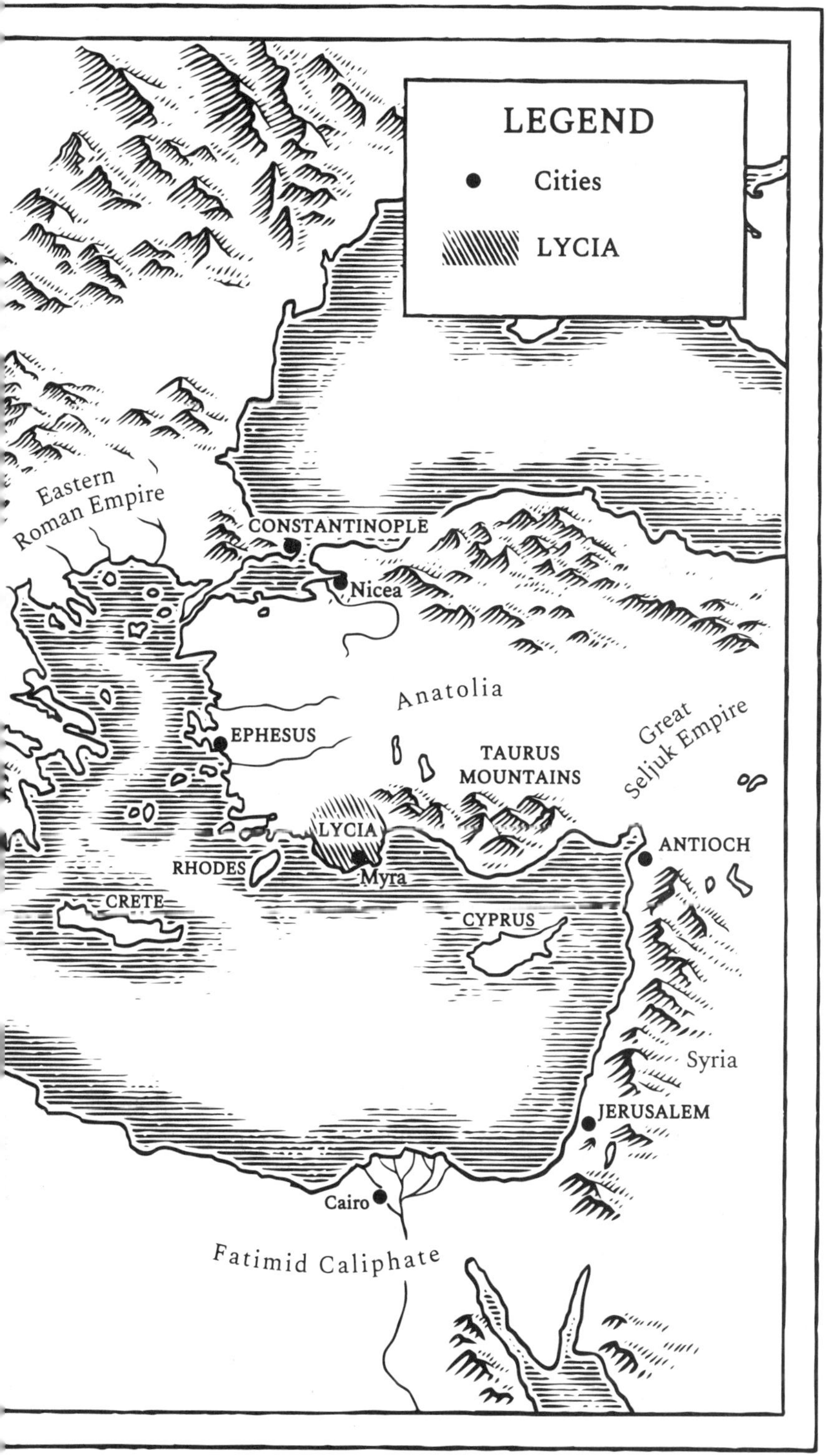
LEGEND
Cities
LYCIA
Eastern Roman Empire
CONSTANTINOPLE
Nicea
Anatolia
EPHESUS
TAURUS MOUNTAINS
Great Seljuk Empire
LYCIA
Myra
RHODES
ANTIOCH
CRETE
CYPRUS
Syria
JERUSALEM
Cairo
Fatimid Caliphate

THE BARI HEIST

One night, in the spring of the year 1087, three ships rested in a harbor—three grain ships, just as in the old legends of Saint Nicholas.

On one of the ships, sailors sat around on the deck, cross-legged, bored in the long evening, talking. Their conversation had turned to the city of Myra.

"There won't be anyone there," someone said. "We could just snatch the body and take it back with us."

They were speaking of the relics of the Blessed Nicholas, which had lain for seven hundred years in a tomb.

Some of the men were shocked. But the idea caught hold of several of them.

They were on a long voyage. It was going to last a couple of months, crawling along the coasts of the Adriatic and Aegean and Mediterranean Seas from southern Italy to Antioch, in distant Syria, to sell bushels of grain from their hometown, Bari.

Bored men. Men with too much time on their hands. Sailors, a few rich merchants, a few noblemen, a few priests. They would be sailing right past the port of Myra anyway. Why not steal the city's saint?

"The church will be abandoned. We can just walk right in."

We don't know who suggested first that they should steal the sacred body of Saint Nicholas, one of the most famous holy men in the world, and take it home with them to Bari. Some of them, we are told, immediately thought it was a fantastic idea, "and were claiming resolutely, as if they knew with a certainty, that this could be carried out with divine assistance."

Others said it couldn't be done. It had been tried before. No one had succeeded.

They knew the stories of failure.

Centuries before, when the word of the sacred healing ooze that came out of the body of Saint Nicholas had reached the ears of the Eastern Roman emperor, he decided the holy corpse should be moved to the capital, to Constantinople. He sent a representative to Myra to fetch the remains. But when his emissary got to the church where Nicholas was buried, the monks in charge of the body refused to give it to him.

The remains of Saint Nicholas were important to Myra. Travelers specifically came to the city to visit the tomb and buy the Nicholas liquid. In fact, by this point, people assumed that the name of the city, Myra, was taken from the word *myron* (the holy ooze, which was perfumed with an incense, *myrrh*, made from the sap of a local tree).

☞ **Ooze was big business.** Saint Nicholas was not the only saint whose body drooled it out. Saint Catherine, Saint John the

Apostle, and Saint Glyceria, for example, also produced it occasionally. There is a technical term for saints whose corpses sweat sacred oil: They are *myroblytes*.

There was no way Myra was going to willingly give up its myroblyte without a fight. The guardians of the tomb told the emperor's representative that they would not let the body leave their basilica under any circumstances.

The messenger did not want to go back to the emperor's court in Constantinople empty-handed. He prayed to the saint that he would be granted some lump or fragment of the body that he could take with him, something to give to his boss.

Then he went to the church of Saint Nicholas and asked for a bottle of the healing oil.

We have a description from a tenth-century song of how the system of extraction worked:

There are four guardians
Found in the atrium.
With a sponge they extract
The liquor, in fact.

It appears they must have lowered a sponge on **a long stem, or some other similar implement**, down into the sarcophagus of the saint. (The word I have translated as "sponge" here is very unclear. It could also be a brush or, more speculatively, some kind of thin tube.) They would draw out the liquid and pour it into a special souvenir jar so the pilgrim—or the emissary of the Eastern Roman emperor—could take it home with them.

The emissary watched as one of the guardians lowered the implement down into the sarcophagus and drew it out.

This time, however, the device, in swiping across the saint's face, had snagged on a tooth. The emissary had prayed for some fragment of the saint's body that he could take back to the imperial court—and here it was, a bicuspid or molar. Somehow, without the guardian seeing, the emissary grabbed the tooth and hid it in his hand. He'd have a relic after all. He'd smuggle it home to Constantinople.

When he was alone, he held the tooth in his cupped hands and kissed it. He found a golden box to put the tooth in. He must have been staying at a residence with its own chapel. He put the tooth in its box on the altar.

Shortly after, he walked by the room, poked his head in, and saw that there was a problem: The tooth hadn't stopped exuding the magical liquor. Oil was flowing down the sides of the box, pooling all around it.

He'd never be able to keep the stolen tooth hidden if this happened. He had to soak up the excess oil. He found some cloth and wrapped it around and around the tooth. "But in vain! For the more he bound the cloth around it, the more the liquid itself was flowing out, soaking the cloth. Therefore he began to despair since he could not keep it hidden as he had hoped, since the Lord was revealing all." His hands were goopy. The altar cloth was oil stained. His guilt could not be concealed.

That night, he had a dream. Saint Nicholas appeared to him. "Here I have satisfied your request, and given you part of me so you may see it—but you cannot take it with you, as you desired. I do not permit even the smallest part of my body to be separated from the whole."

When the emissary woke up in the morning, the tooth was gone.

We may picture him staring openmouthed at the box open there on the altar, the cloth unraveled, blotched and translucent from the oil.

With a saint's oil, even the stains make things clearer.

There was another story the sailors from Bari must have known.

In the year 808, the famous Caliph Haroun al-Rashid ordered one of his generals to lead a fleet to attack the island of Rhodes (where the Colossus had once stood). The assault on Rhodes failed, perhaps even at the walls of the Fortress of Saint Nicholas there. Irritable, the defeated general decided to destroy the famous tomb of Saint Nicholas in Myra instead. It was on his way home to Syria.

He arrived at Myra and sent men ashore. They smashed a tomb. But, according to a Christian chronicler, the saint misled them: It was the wrong tomb.

Saint Nicholas got his revenge. He caused a great storm to engulf the general's fleet. "Thereupon a great disturbance of sea waves, thunder, and lightning fell upon the fleet so that several ships were broken up." The general himself, who managed to live through the storm, grudgingly admitted that the saint had real power over the seas.

These were the kinds of tales people told about the kings and caliphs who'd tried to break open the saint's tomb.

The Barian men on the three grain ships told each other the stories of the previous attempts to steal the corpse. But they were sailing right past Myra. It was one of the ports on the way from Bari to Antioch. Why not just anchor there for the night and check out the tomb? Snoop around. What harm could that do?

The thing was, the city of Myra was very dangerous just then.

It had recently been invaded. A group of nomadic warriors under the command of the Seljuk Turks to the east had swept down out of the mountains and had taken the town just a few years earlier. Rumor said that these Turkish warriors still occupied the city. The Eastern Roman Empire was too weak to seize it back from them. The Seljuk Turks, galloping out of the vast grasslands of the east, were toppling nations one by one. Though at first they were considered nothing more than uncouth sheepherders and mercenaries, they quickly defeated many of the old kingdoms and thriving cities of the Middle East, capturing even fabled Baghdad. Christians and Muslims alike were astonished by their successes. Now bands of Turkish warriors were pushing their way further west, deep into the lands of the Eastern Roman Empire.

The men of Bari knew this. This is one of the reasons they thought it might be a good time to catch the citizens of Myra off guard and steal their saint. Everything was in turmoil in Lycia because of the recent invasion. The tomb would be abandoned, unguarded. The soldiers of the empire would be off fighting the Turks in the Anatolian highlands, unable to protect the church from looting. The men of Bari talked it over as they sailed closer to Saint Nicholas's city, edgy with excitement.

They passed through the islands off the Lycian coast, rocky isles bare but for low shrubs and tough grasses. The abandoned ruins of ancient Greek towns dribbled down the hillsides and vanished into the sea. They'd been destroyed centuries before in earthquakes. The foundations of houses and churches could still be seen carved into the stone where the waves lapped. The three ships would have sailed over sunken towns where pillars lay on the flagstones of village squares. The sea was an unearthly blue.

Nicholas had met those other three grain ships, centuries before, at Myra's ancient port. But it was in ruins, too. Over the centuries, the harbor had filled with silt. The quays where the huge imperial galleys had once docked were now swamps overgrown with rushes and reeds. The great steps where Roman emperors had processed up from their ships to the wide marketplace flanked by statues and tombs were now cracked, buckled, and uneven. The storehouses had fallen in. The walls of Nicholas's granary still stood, though there was no roof.

The three ships from Bari sailed into a little cove around a spit of land to the east and lowered their anchors. The three crews met with each other and talked about what to do next. Though they had heard that the city had been conquered by the Turks, they needed to find out more.

There was a pilgrim on board one of the ships—a man planning to visit the holy sites in the east.

Go ashore, they told him. *Go to the Basilica of Saint Nicholas, as if you just want to pray. Come back and tell us if it's safe.*

He agreed to act as a scout.

Alone, he disembarked. He headed toward the occupied city.

It must have been eerie for that lone pilgrim, walking through that desolate landscape. When the Turks had thundered down out of the Taurus Mountains and invaded, the people of Myra had abandoned their homes. Saint Nicholas's city was largely empty.

The pilgrim wandered past empty farms and villas that had been evacuated a few years before. Perhaps as he walked on the vacant road up from the harbor, once thronged with merchants trading lumber from the mountains and royal purple dye from the sea, he thought of the old lamentation from the Bible: "How solitary sits the city that was full of people . . ." The only sound would have been the razzing of the cicadas in the trees.

But there must have been a few lone figures lurking in those deserted houses, someone the pilgrim questioned—for he discovered that the city was not quite as abandoned as it appeared. Hundreds of Myrans were still huddled inside a fortress up on a hill just north of town. They had been hiding themselves there for at least two years and must have reached some kind of uneasy agreement with the invaders. They were probably paying the Turkish warrior-nomads tribute to avoid violence. Perhaps they ventured out during the day to tend their farms and their orchards and their olive groves. But it was not safe: They had not returned to their homes in the city below. They lived, packed together, in their hilltop castle.

The pilgrim could have seen their distant fortress, high on a cliff above the city, rising above the ancient, craggy tombs in the hills, bristling above the ruins of the pale limestone theater where the Romans once had watched plays filled with blood, and where later, during Nicholas's life, they had watched combats in which the blood was real. From the fortress, the people of Myra could have spied on the walled compound that held the basilica of the Blessed Nicholas, their city's saint.

Meanwhile, the hills and plains belonged to the nomad warriors.

The basilica of Nicholas itself was still staffed by four Christian guardians. But this was a terrible time to visit: The church's courtyard was completely occupied by the Turks right then. A local chieftain in charge of captured Myra had just died. Warriors from the whole region had gathered at the church for his funeral.

This is an intriguing historical detail. In the absence of a local mosque, the Muslim Turks apparently decided to use a Christian sacred site instead. There was considerable overlap between Christianity and Islam; the tomb of such a famous holy man, a "friend of God," was appropriate enough for a funeral, regardless of religion. Nicholas's bones were said to be miraculous and sacred; that was enough.

So the Turks had ridden in from the hills to pay tribute to their dead leader in the courtyard of Nicholas's church. The number of their horses alone, tied up in the basilica's courtyard, must have been staggering.

The pilgrim returned to the shore. The seventy-some men of Bari were waiting for him impatiently aboard their ships. They were ready for plunder.

Once aboard, the pilgrim reported that it would be suicide to attempt a heist at the moment. The church compound was bustling with armed warriors. It was just too dangerous.

So the Barians gave up their plan to steal the body of Nicholas. They pulled up their anchors and headed east. "With sails stretched wide they directed the prows of their ships towards Antioch," where they were bound to sell their shipment of grain.

It seemed like their theft of the saint was called off.

Then, when they reached Antioch, a chance encounter changed everything.

Antioch had also just been conquered by the Seljuk Turks a couple of years before. It still was a loud, crowded market city, though, one of those centers of trade where the camel caravans that had traveled all the way to the Far East, into the empire of the Song in China, met with ships which had sailed from the gray, steely waters of the North Atlantic.

There you could find fine cloth from Damascus and Baghdad and Dhaka, ebony from India, writing paper from Samarkand, fruits from Basra, and swords forged in the smithies of the barbarian Franks far to the west.

The men of Bari went about their business in Antioch. They visited the noisy marketplaces to sell their grain and buy whatever cargo they hoped to carry home to Italy.

Some of the sailors from Bari also ran into old friends. Venetians.

Venice was an Italian city far to the north of Bari, famous for its trade. Due to a special agreement, Venetian merchants could sell things throughout the Eastern Roman Empire without paying any tax. That agreement was making the Republic of Venice very rich. It was hard for anyone else to compete. The Venetians and the Barians respected each other, occasionally even helped each other—but they also were rivals.

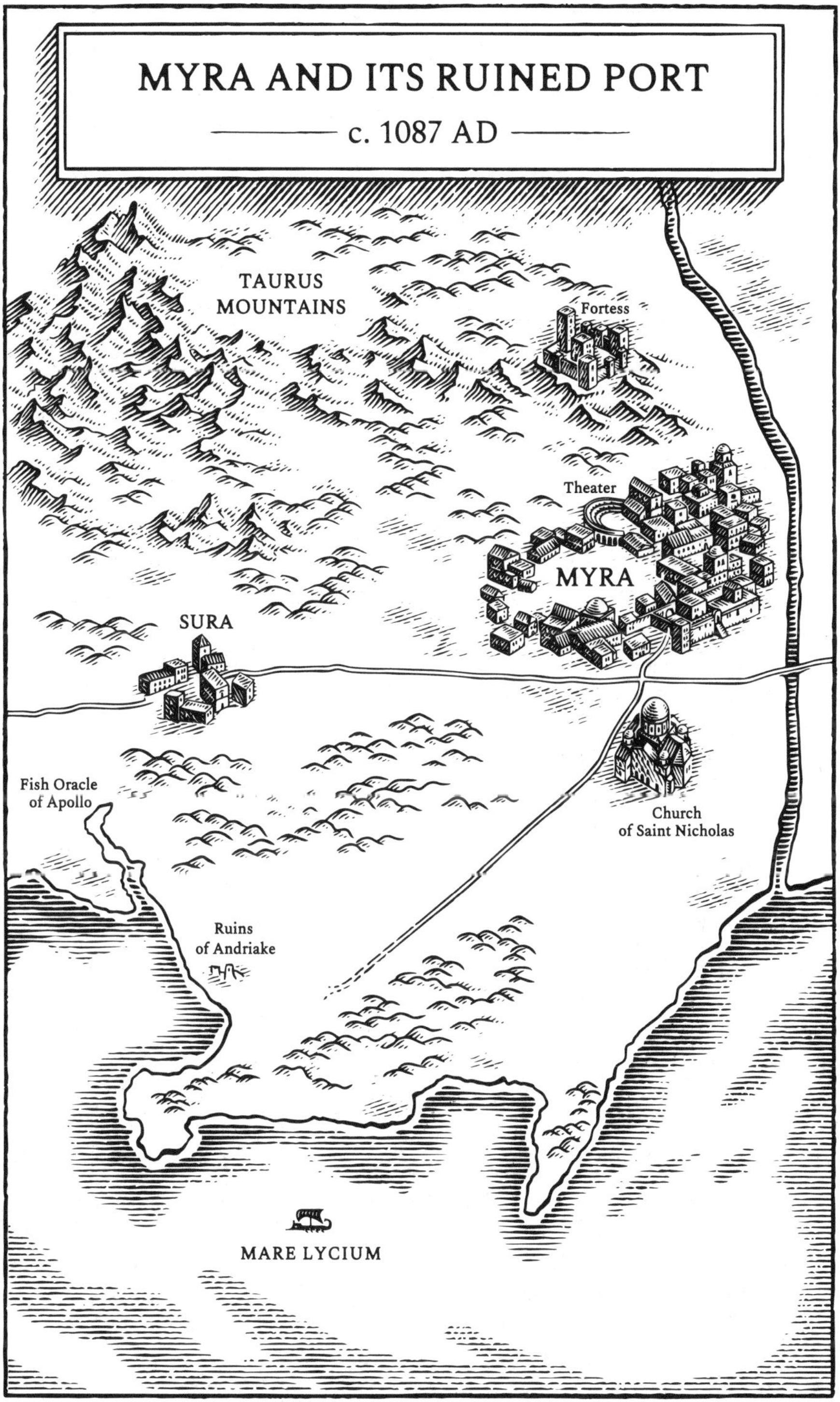
MYRA AND ITS RUINED PORT
c. 1087 AD
TAURUS MOUNTAINS
Fortess
Theater
MYRA
SURA
Fish Oracle of Apollo
Church of Saint Nicholas
Ruins of Andriake
MARE LYCIUM

In a spirit of both rivalry and friendship, the sailors from Bari went out with a few of the sailors from Venice for a drink at some local seaside tavern. They sprawled around a table, swapping stories. At some point, the Barians mentioned they'd paid a quick visit to Myra to see the body of Saint Nicholas. They must have bragged that they'd considered stealing it and taking it home with them. Impossible, though, they said: The place was crawling with Turkish warriors.

And this is when the Venetians, apparently pretty drunk on local wine, revealed their big plan: *They* were going to be the ones who stole the body of Saint Nicholas. They had everything they needed with them in the holds of their ships. They had mallets, pickaxes, metal spikes. They were going to smash the sarcophagus open, snatch the bones, and head back to Venice and glory.

The Barian sailors could not contain themselves. As quickly as possible, they got away and returned to their ships. They made an announcement to the rest of the crew: *The Venetians are going to grab the body if we don't.*

Rival cities. Rival merchants. "When our men of Bari heard this, they were inflamed with a greater desire for the undertaking and accomplishment of this task. And they began to think in a bolder and more ardent way about it, not so much on behalf of their own glory and honor or for the greatness of our whole homeland, but for the shame and reproach of fearing that the Venetians themselves might accomplish it before them."

Their competitive streak came out. They started to make plans.

We can understand how the Barians must have felt. Venice, with its special trade agreement, was absolutely taking business away from Bari.

Moreover, Venice was sucking up holy relics from all over the Christian world. Most famously, a few centuries before, they'd gone and stolen the bones of one of the most important saints of all, Saint Mark, the author of one of the four Gospels in the Bible. It was one of the most famous heists in history.

Saint Mark had been buried in Alexandria, in Egypt. The Venetians had gone shamelessly to his tomb and, in the dead of night, replaced his bones with the bones of another saint, Claudia. Then they'd stashed Saint Mark's bones in a cart of butchered pork. Why?

The city of Alexandria at that point was Muslim. The Muslim authorities wanted to make sure Saint Mark remained in their city—not only did it seem to be good luck, it was good business. The Venetians knew this, and they had a plan. The eating of pork is forbidden (*haram*) under Islamic law. So the Christians heaped pork on top of the bones of the saint. The customs inspectors looked at the load of butchered pig and turned away in disgust. They weren't going to paw through a slaughtered pile of unclean meat looking for contraband.

Thus Saint Mark's holy body made its way back to Venice under a pile of pig parts—or so the story goes. The Venetians built a new church for it, the Basilica San Marco. It is still one of the most famous religious sites in the world.

So Venice had the great Saint Mark. The Barian sailors, eager to win a victory for their own hometown, declared that they'd get Saint Nicholas for Bari. They'd show Venice. Saint Nicholas wasn't just any saint—he was the patron saint of sailors. Any port city that had the body of Saint Nicholas could count on constant traffic—shiploads of wealthy merchants coming and going across the Mediterranean. Anyone starting out on a voyage across the sea would want to leave from a city where they could pray to the bones of this wonder-worker who saved sailors and quieted storms. If the crew could steal the Blessed Nicholas, they would bring Bari not only the fame that came with a major saint, not only the added business from pilgrims and travelers—but also, they believed, the favor of God Himself. Once they had His holy man, things would start looking up for Bari.

They called themselves the League of Saint Nicholas.

The game was on.

The League of Saint Nicholas finished their business in Antioch as quickly as they could and set out on the return trip west to Myra.

Let's stop for a moment to look at who these men were.

There were more than seventy of them traveling on those three ships. Thirteen of them were noblemen; ten were merchants; five of them were priests (or other clergy); four were sons of the priests (at the time, Christian priests could marry); and four of them were ships' captains. Three of them were enslaved, perhaps prisoners of war: Peter, John, and Andrew. Two of them were pilgrims who got on board at Antioch. None were women.

As in all good heists, many of the gang had nicknames. One was called Elephant, and another one Topaz, after the precious gem. One was called Good Guy. There were priests named Father Bear and Father Wolf, though those names—Urso and Lupo—were not unusual in that era, when it made sense to declare yourself a predator. In the same vein, there were a few Leos ("Lion"). One man was just named High (Summus) and another was named Summissimus, Even Higher.

Summissimus was the captain of one of the three ships. The other two captains were named Giannoccarro and Albert.

Their ships were most likely quite small, broad in the belly for stability, whisked across the waves mainly by lateen sails, rather than the long ranks of rowers pulling on huge oars that had powered the old Roman ships, and which still provided the muscle for the empire's ships of war. These merchant ships had a few oars to paddle them into and out of harbors. There would not have been much space belowdecks, except for the grain they shipped out and whatever cargo they carried home. Instead, the crew and the passengers would have sat on the deck under canopies, playing dice and swapping tales of sacred teeth and, for the few who'd never been to sea before, vomiting over the gunwales. The spray from the bright Mediterranean dashed over the deck sometimes and drenched them. Each ship was steered by two men standing aft, at the back of the ship, carving a course toward Myra through the waves with huge, rudder-like oars as the sails billowed above.

The men on board those three ships were from cities all around Bari: from Monopoli, Trani, and Polignano a Mare, a town built on the white cliffs above the sea. Their whole region, Apulia, had been conquered a few years earlier by the Normans, a group of barbarians from what we now call France. The Normans were infamously brutal, harsh, and hungry. The lords and merchants and sailors of Bari had gone from being subjects of the Eastern Roman Empire, able to trade freely in any of the imperial ports, to being subjects of these northern invaders, squeezed hard by the chain-mail fist of their new overlords. The Norman dukes punished Bari severely for standing up against them. Business had been bad since these barbarians had swarmed the narrow streets and ejected the old Roman governor. The Barians were desperate for anything that would revive their city's fortunes. Especially in the face of their rivals in Venice.

So their ships sailed back toward Nicholas's city, hoping a saint's corpse would bring their God's favor and lots of tourist business to their town on the Adriatic Sea.

They only began to have doubts again as they approached Lycia.

After all, none of them were professional relic hunters. That was an actual job at the time: Specialists were hired by churches and monasteries to seek out and buy (or steal!) the sacred bones or beards or bloodstains of saints. It was a crooked business. Skeptical Christians pointed out that if all the relics of the saints were real, then there must have been "ten hands of St. Prokopios the martyr, fifteen jawbones of Theodore, up to eight feet from Nestor, on top of this, four heads of St. George, and five breasts from that victorious contender Barbara," which would almost put her in the running with many-breasted Artemis. There were heads of Saint John the Baptist all over Christendom. If these relic specialists couldn't find bones from the saint you asked for, no problem: They'd just paint a sheep's bone with saffron so it looked old and yellow and then sell it to you for a fortune so you could kneel in front of it and sing it hymns.

But these men aboard the three grain ships from Bari weren't trained in saint hunting. They were a boatload of amateurs. They were very aware of that fact.

So despite their enthusiasm, they might have sailed right past Myra again if the wind hadn't changed. A cold northern breeze stalled them as they were coming within sight of the Lycian coast. They had to stop there for the night anyway.

On April 20, 1087, they glided back into the harbor near Myra. They threw out their anchors.

This was it. Here they were. Time for the heist. They gathered to discuss strategy.

The first order of business was to scout out the church of Saint Nicholas again. A few weeks earlier when they'd passed through town, it had been crawling with Turkish warriors. Someone had to make sure the coast was clear. Before, they'd sent a pilgrim inland as a scout. This time, the crew chose two pilgrims who were paying for passage home to act as their surveillance team. The two men—one a Greek pilgrim, the other a Frenchman named Alexandre—would disembark and walk the two miles inland to the church.

In the language of heists, they'd case the joint.

Solemnly, the two men waded ashore.

They disappeared into the grassy hills. The rest of the crew waited. They made preparations for their assault on the church. They divided themselves into two teams. Forty-seven of them volunteered to head into the occupied city so they could loot the church and "liberate" the corpse of Saint Nicholas. The other twenty-five or so said they'd stay by the ships in case the Turkish occupiers attacked. The three captains—Giannoccarro, Summissimus, and Albert—declared they'd wait in the harbor with their ships. Their ships were, after all, the getaway vehicles.

Both groups armed themselves, preparing for the worst. The

raiding party had swords and knives, but also iron bars and a huge metal hammer to smash open walls and floors so they could get to the saint's sarcophagus.

It must have taken the pilgrims a couple of hours to hike to the basilica, look around its courtyards and domes, and then return to the shore.

Finally they reappeared. They signaled to the rest of the League: The coast was clear. The church was empty except for three or four priests. The Turks were nowhere to be seen. Neither were the Christian citizens of Myra. They were still locked up in their fortress on the hill.

It was time to move. Forty-seven men, armed and ready to kill, headed off to steal a saint.

They marched up from the harbor into town in battle formation, ready to repel attack. Peering left and right, they crossed the empty squares and filed down unpeopled streets, perhaps past the hulks of burned-out houses destroyed in the raid a couple years earlier.

It was a nerve-racking hike of more than two miles. They were terrified they might run into a patrol. The Turkish nomads were famed for their mounted archery. There was almost no way a company of mariners, on foot, armed primarily with swords, could withstand their attack. The Italians would fall, bristling with arrows, eyes wide and white, throats pierced with wooden shafts, before they even got within two thousand feet of the Turkish warriors.

Probably forty-five minutes or an hour later, they reached the courtyard of the church surrounded by its protective walls.

The Basilica of Saint Nicholas, hundreds of years old, rose before them, a series of domes and pillars that burned in the Mediterranean sun like an announcement of holy intention.

The team posted lookouts around the church and unstrapped their sword belts and bucklers and laid them down before continuing into the sanctuary. It was not unusual for men to carry swords in that age—but it would seem suspicious, even blasphemous, to carry them into a holy place.

They entered the church, passing from bright sunlight into the shadows and dark pomp of the sanctuary. As they went through the great ceremonial doors, they were immediately confronted with paintings, on the arches over their heads, of severe councils of holy men—perhaps gathered at Nicaea under Constantine to argue about the date of Easter. The men glared down in judgment, all bearded, watchful, even wrathful. They looked more like spectral guardians than living people. The thieves filed past beneath their gaze.

As the League of Saint Nicholas walked through the arches into the *naos*—the main hall of the church, the sanctuary, three stories tall, capped with a dome—they saw an altar raised upon a dais, and, behind it, the rising steps of an amphitheater where priests and monks and bishops would act out their holy rites in happier times. Over the altar was spread a cupola of stone or marble on four pillars, as if to protect the altar from unseen, radiant energies. An octagonal pulpit stood near the front of the church, where, in earlier days, the bishop would have trod up a flight of stairs to deliver sermons. (The marks of it remain on the kaleidoscopic stonework floors to this day.) The walls were doubtless covered in bright frescoes of saints and the threefold Christian God—with bands of bright color and dazzling designs, tricks played upon the eye, so beloved of the Eastern Romans.

The thieves were greeted by four custodians, four monks who had pledged to watch the church, their city's most holy place, despite the Turkish occupation. These men assumed the Italians were pilgrims who had come in peace to worship at the altar of Nicholas the Navigator, protector of sailors, the long-dead bishop of Myra.

Acting the part of good pilgrims, the mariners went one by one to kneel in front of the altar and pray to Nicholas and to their God. Some doubtless actually meant the words they said. Others glanced out of the corners of their eyes to take in the side galleries and try to figure out where the body was stashed.

To the northeast of the sanctuary was a spacious domed room where the ceiling was painted with Christ, standing beneath a domed cupola, giving bread and wine to His disciples. A caption hung near Christ's head: "Take, eat: This is my body." The heads of the disciples bobbed with haloes that almost crackled with yellow energy. This was probably the baptistry, where people were sprinkled with water by a priest to welcome them into the faith—but the thieves barely paused to notice the painting overhead. They had another body to find, and this chamber may also have been the entrance into a suite of rooms where the corpse of Nicholas lay.

To the south were several small chapels and galleries. In some of them were sarcophagi—the hulking tombs of long-dead Romans. (The word *sarcophagus* literally means "flesh-eater." The limestone that lined them was highly acidic, and therefore devoured the bodies that were laid within.) Several of the sarcophagi were from the age of Roman paganism, and on their lids and sides they had carvings of gods and beasts and tussling cupids. On one was carved a couple, husband and wife, lying together as if on a bed, holding hands even in death. The sarcophagi in the church had been reused more recently by wealthy Christians, just as the tombs outside town had sometimes been repurposed for new dead in a new age.

The thieves peered around, wondering where the wonderworker's body was hidden.

They could not wait any longer. "Brothers," one of them said to the monks who guarded the place, "show us where the physical body of the holy confessor lies."

The monks did not suspect any foul play yet. They led the thieves to **the spot where the sacred oil, the ichor, the myron, was extracted**. We don't know the details of this well-kept secret. We can imagine that behind an altar, there might have been some kind of **a plate in the floor** which, when lifted, revealed a narrow hole drilled into the marble flagstones. "Behold the place, as it has been passed down by our predecessors, where we believe without doubt Nicholas lies." The guardians showed the fake pilgrims how they used an implement to draw forth oil from the tomb and deposit it in beautiful little glass bottles, fine as perfume bottles, so the juice could be sold to visitors who wanted to taste the saint's miracles.

Several of the visitors said they wanted oil to take home. One of them, the priest named Lupo, filled his own small glass flask, squinting and peering at the golden-green oil, and set it down on a short pillar. There were so many people leaning in to see the extraction, however—so many sailors pushing and nudging for a better view—that the flask was knocked over in the excitement. It fell. It hit the marble floor.

Everyone swiveled their heads, aghast at the loud *crack* as the sacred fluid hit the flagstones.

But the bottle was intact. It hadn't shattered.

We are told by the chronicler Nicephorus that this was taken by the thieves to be a direct message of encouragement from none other than Saint Nicholas. "At that point they knew for a fact that the confessor of God himself had gotten their attention by that sound, and was saying, 'Why are you so slothful performing your duty? It is my will that I leave here with you. This is the spot in which I have rested through many cycles of years. Regard that as a miracle; but now leave, taking my body with you. For under my protection all Barians will prosper. You will lead happy lives under my rule.' "

That sure is a lot of meaning to extract from a bottle falling on the floor.

Remember, however, that the thieves were also believers: They somehow had to convince themselves that Saint Nicholas specifically wanted to go with them to Bari. You don't exactly *steal* relics—theft would mean they were nothing but an ordinary object. A saint's relics are not so much objects as people. The saint is still hovering by the bones, as the old gods hovered by their statues. If you take the bones and the saint doesn't want to leave with you, you're not just a thief. You're a kidnapper.

For this reason, the Barian sources would never call this a heist, or say that their sailors were *stealing* Saint Nicholas. They used a more polite word: They called it a *translation*. They schemed to *translate* the body of Saint Nicholas from Myra to Bari.

The League of Saint Nicholas had to convince themselves that the removal of the bones from their ancient crypt was the saint's own will. Otherwise, he would curse them. They would suffer bad luck. They could even be damned after death.

This put them in a difficult position as they clustered there in the side chapel, watching the monks sponge up ooze. The mariners were thieves, deceptive, prepared for violence—plotting, planning—and yet they also had to be innocent as children, welcoming this supernatural being, convincing him to follow them home.

But in order to steal the body, they had to get the guardians to reveal it. The thieves started asking lots of other questions about the body and where it lay beneath the floor. They were getting very specific.

At this, the guardians really looked at these pilgrims and started to catch on: This was no humble visit from sailors who wanted to pray for fair skies and southern winds. Something was wrong. The monks were suddenly very aware that they were alone—just four of them—surrounded by around forty men—and the rest of their townspeople were a mile away on a mountaintop, locked behind the walls of a fortress.

Suspicious, they demanded, "Why do you ask these questions? Can it be that you want to take the body? Don't you know that we cannot possibly agree to such a thing—in fact, we would rather die than permit him to be taken?"

It was time for the thieves to lay out the situation. "We wish to remove this sacred body and take it back to our homeland," one of the looters declared. "Indeed, for this reason we have come, carried by three ships." At this point, he popped in a little lie. "We have been sent by the Roman Pope." Not true, but maybe convincing. And if that wasn't convincing enough: "If you are willing to agree to this, we will give you one hundred gold coins from each ship."

Another looter added that the pope had been specifically visited by Nicholas in a dream and that Nicholas had requested, as a special favor, "to be transported to our land." Nonetheless, the sailor said, "We are prepared to pay you any price you name for this great treasure, in order that we may receive your blessing and leave here peacefully."

The monks were horrified. It was an outrage. "The saint won't allow this," roared one of the guardians. "He won't allow his body to be touched. Take our advice: Leave as quickly as you can, before the townspeople hear what's going on and put you to death."

That was it. The time for pleasantries was over. The mariners moved to grab the monks. The monks blanched—"The color left their faces, and blood drained from their veins." They realized things were about to get violent. One or more of them apparently made a run for it, trying to get out of the building to signal to the Myrans up on the hilltop.

The Barians seized the monks, threw them to the floor, and trussed them up. Most of the expedition filed out of the church to stand guard not only around the courtyard, but to keep watch on all the crossroads and plazas around the city. Things were getting serious.

A young man—a hothead—a sailor we know only as Matteo—was sick of all the waiting, all the pretending. He pulled out a sword and held it to the neck of one of the monks. He growled, "Either you tell me where the tomb of the saint is or I will kill you with this sword."

Another monk, a senior monk, "more prudent and saintly than the rest," tried to calm the sailor's rage. "Why are you roughing up a servant of God like that?" he demanded. With some sarcasm, he said, "Look there where the holy liquid comes out. Obviously the body of the saint must lie in that same place."

The company cast glances at the marble floor.

The saintly monk continued, gently: "We know for a fact from the tales of men of old that many emperors and other potentates have tried their best to carry out what you now plan—but they had no luck because the saint of God was unwilling."

Then, surprisingly, the monk expressed a doubt. He told the thieves standing around him that a year before, three Myrans had all had dreams in which Saint Nicholas scolded the people of the city for hiding in their fortress while his church and his holy relics went undefended. The saint told the people of Myra, supposedly, that if they didn't protect him, "he would migrate elsewhere."

Having admitted this vision, the old monk said sadly to the snarling Matteo, "Put up your sword, soften your threats, and rid yourself of those war-like looks." There was no reason for violence, the old monk said: If Saint Nicholas really wanted to leave Myra, then he would find a way to leave with the Barians. But if the saint did not want to go back with them to Italy, then he would somehow stop them.

The small group of thieves who remained inside the church looked at each other. The light outside was dying. It would be dark soon. This was the moment when everything would be decided. If the saint was going to curse them, it would happen when they started to burst into his tomb.

Two of the priests, Lupo and Grimoald, started to sing chants to Saint Nicholas, asking for his favor. Their voices echoed in the domes, drifting up past the scowls of painted councils and the dazed eyes of angels. But their voices petered out. "Having been seized by a fear of God and a trembling, as if driven mad, with tongues tied, they were not able to continue clearly chanting the prayer which they had begun."

Matteo, the hotheaded sailor, was tired of this bull crap. He threw down his sword, grabbed the iron mallet, and started to slam it savagely against the marble floor where the drain led down into the crypt.

It was a shocking sound: the sick thud of the hammer on stone in that sacred place. Chips of marble flew.

Now that the sacrilege had started, other men moved in to help. Fathers Lupo and Grimoald ordered them to pry up the stones.

Under the marble was a layer of concrete. The sailors fell on it with their iron bars. They reached in and pulled broken chunks out, tossing them over their shoulders. They used a small ax to hack at the grout, widening the pit.

And there, in a cavity under the floor, was an ancient sarcophagus with holes drilled in its lid to extract the oil. They had found the corpse's resting place.

The raiding party straightened up, peering down at the sarcophagus. "They were exceedingly fearful of striking it, dreading that something terrible might happen to them. But Matteo, who was more audacious than the others, could no longer restrain his hot intent; he scoffed at the notion that any evil would come to him."

As the captive monks wailed, Matteo took the hammer and smashed open the lid of Saint Nicholas's coffin.

Some archaeologists believe that we have found the sarcophagus that held Saint Nicholas, the same coffin Matteo attacked with his hammer nine hundred years ago. It still stands in the ruins of the church in Myra—now the town of Demre, Turkey.

The lid, which the looters would have seen first, is carved with fish scales; scallop shells run along its edge. It is a treasure box appropriate for a saint connected with the seas. Appropriate, but not made for him: It appears this sarcophagus was made in the first or second century AD, more than a hundred years before Nicholas was born. (It was not unusual to reuse expensive sarcophagi.) On the side of the coffin, which may not even have been revealed as Matteo smashed the concrete from above, there are deeply carved vines that grow out of a crude central cross. Though it's a box of death, the tendrils writhe with lush green growth, curling out of that cross, each capped with a blooming flower. Tiny animals play around them: roosters strolling in their shade, rams butting horns. The Christian burial service says, "In the midst of life, we are in death." But this carving seems to suggest the opposite. In the midst of death, there is still abundant life.

It was not originally a Christian message, however. The cross at the center is crudely carved—because it was originally a fertility goddess, standing with her arms outstretched. She has had her face and hands knocked away until she became the Christian symbol of resurrection. The coffin is a perfect resting place, in other words, for a saint who faced off against Artemis, fertility goddess, and took over many of her functions.

The really fascinating feature of this tendril sarcophagus, however, is its plumbing. There are two holes bored into the lid, both with sockets for some kind of metal neck or ring. The archaeologists who described it in the 1970s argued that these holes were the siphons into which holy oil was poured and drawn out of the coffin. We don't know if they were right, and if this was the actual sarcophagus in which Nicholas lay. But regardless, whatever vessel the saint was buried in must have had fixtures like this in the lid.

This is the kind of thing that Matteo must have seen as he, elated with victory, smashed the lid of the sarcophagus apart.

The lid cracked.

Matteo hurled the fragments aside. In the shadows, some of the sailors quietly picked them up and pocketed them. Even the lid of Saint Nicholas's coffin was holy. They'd be able to pray to the chunks—or auction them off—when they got back home.

If the tendril sarcophagus is indeed the one Matteo uncovered, it would make sense: half the fish-scale lid is shattered and survives only as crumbled pieces stored with the rest.

By the fading light of early evening and perhaps the oil lamps that often lit altars, the company could see a glimmer inside the black depths of the coffin: the holy liquor of Saint Nicholas. It filled half the box. It shook when they hammered like a bowlful of jelly.

We are told that the priests Lupo and Grimoald, "who had ordered the smashing, and some of the sailors and others of the company who had taken part in the action, were standing there. Immediately such a wave of delightful perfume arose that everyone thought himself to be standing in God's paradise." If we are to believe the sources, this smell wafted down through the abandoned streets to the harbor, where the sailors who'd been left to guard ships inhaled it and sighed in relief. "As they breathed it in, each was at once overwhelmed with joy, knowing that the holy confessor of Christ had consented to join their company."

Matteo got down on his knees—not to pray, but to fumble around for bones. To the horror of the guardians, he dunked both hands right into the sacred liquor and started pulling bones out of the soup. Father Lupo took off his outer tunic and laid it down on the floor, and Father Grimoald received each bone that Matteo fished out and placed them on the silk. The grease stained the fabric.

Was Matteo frightened of his sacrilege, grabbing at the limbs of a holy man protected for seven centuries by a curse? He later told the scholar John the Archdeacon that he had not been scared in the slightest: "For just as he himself recounted to us, he conveyed that he had never before stood so firm and undeterred. Hence who would doubt that in so great a deed, this youth was strengthened against fear by some angelic aid?" Whether angels or devils whispered him onward, he pulled up a little less than half the body. "Yet with the other limbs having been taken out of the sarcophagus in a disorderly and heedless way, the head was still missing." They needed the head. The head was the best part. "With the head still not found, they became somewhat saddened."

So once again, Matteo took a plunge. In this case, literally. Without even taking off his shoes, he clambered down into the saint's coffin, landing right in the middle of the skeleton, and began groping through the sludge for the skull.

This was horrifying: Moses had taken off his shoes when he had walked on sacred ground. Yet here was this upstart Italian kid sloshing around in the blessed ichor without any sign of reverence for the holy place or the man whose body he knelt in. It is probably at this point that the saint's delicate rib cage and pelvis snapped in pieces.

Watching this awful spectacle, the four guardian monks began to weep. They'd risked their lives protecting this tomb—and for what? The bones were being stacked up and stolen by a group of bumbling thugs. It looked like the Barians were going to get away with their heist—which meant Nicholas had decided to abandon his own city of Myra after seven hundred and fifty years as its guiding light and bishop. "Alas for sorrow," the monks muttered, "how great an evil has happened to our country." In their grief, they scolded Nicholas himself bitterly: "Holy father, why do you leave us as orphans? Here you are, faithful to strangers, unfaithful to your own children!" they accused him. "You don't care about all the ways we've served you, all the ways our forefathers served your glory. Is this how you repay your subjects for all we've done for you, all the hundreds of years we've served you?" They cried that they would rather die than allow their saint to be taken from them. Not just that: It seemed likely that when the townspeople discovered the saint was gone, the monks would be killed for their failure anyway. "How can we escape?" they hissed.

Too late. Matteo crowed and held up the skull. He'd found it. He rose from the pit, dripping. His clothes were soaked with holy oil. In his hand, browned, was the head of Saint Nicholas of Myra.

He pulled himself out of the hole. They laid all the relics on the tunic and wrapped it up into a bundle. It was time to go.

There was an ancient icon of Saint Nicholas on the wall. One of the sailors went to snatch it. Grimoald or Lupo stopped him: Let the Myrans keep something, they said. Let them have some memory of their saint.

The looting was done. The League of Saint Nicholas shouldered their tools and prepared to leave. They had a tough route back down to the ships, over two miles. They had to get away before darkness fell and they were discovered either by angry Myrans or the Turkish marauders.

Father Lupo slung the package of Nicholas over his shoulder, just as Santa Claus, centuries later, would carry his sack of gifts. Without any further ceremony, they fled the church. They gathered their watchmen from the squares and crossroads. They formed back up into their military line and marched down through the countryside, leaving devastated Myra behind them. They sang a ragged chant as they marched—the priests led them in a victory song. The bones of Nicholas clacked at each step against Father Lupo's shoulder. The oil drooled from the sockets and ran down his back, staining it.

Back in the basilica, the four guardians had somehow escaped from their bonds. Maybe they'd been released before the company left. Somehow, one of them scampered out and headed for the fortress on the top of the hill. Did he find a mounted rider who could carry a message more quickly? All we know is that swiftly, he got word to the people of his city that their saint was being hauled off by a gang of thieves from Italy.

And the people of Myra responded. They poured out of their fortress. Shouting in fury, they ran down from the hilltop toward the abandoned town. There were hundreds of them, supposedly. As the forty-seven looters returned to their ships, they may have heard the distant cries of anger far behind them. Evidently, they didn't worry about it too much. They were too busy singing their victory chant.

A mob surged toward them, hungry for blood.

The League of Saint Nicholas would have gotten away easily if they hadn't started arguing.

The crew members who had remained by the ships heard the hoarse singing of hymns as the looting party returned, and they realized it meant the expedition was successful. They rushed ashore to meet the thieves. They all congratulated each other and "praised Almighty God in unison for the great gift with which he had crowned the Barians. Certainly they shed many tears that day, knowing themselves to be unworthy of such goodness."

After this victory lap, however, they started to bicker. The question was: *Which ship should have the privilege of carrying the bones back to Bari?* The three captains—Giannoccaro, Summissimus, and Albert—all claimed the prize. They all wanted the credit. So the whole crew stood and debated this minor point while a tide of furious Myrans poured down toward them through the empty city.

Finally the League made its decision: The third ship, under Captain Giannoccarro, should transport the relics, because that was the ship that carried both Father Lupo (who had the bones in a sack slung over his shoulder) and Matteo (who had taken the lead in seizing the bones).

They took the body aboard. Though they wished they had a special casket of some kind to carry the bones, there was no golden box, no gilded reliquary with protecting angels on its lid. They had to store the remains in a wooden box usually used for their wine—a sort of cooler, or perhaps even a barrel. The crews of each ship assembled and prepared to cast off.

Too late, though. They had delayed too long, arguing. They looked up and, in the light of the setting sun, saw a surge of people sprinting down from the abandoned city. The whole Christian population of Myra had come to stop them from leaving. The mob poured out onto the beach.

There was a shouting match. The mob demanded to know who the thieves were. They screamed that Nicholas had been theirs for 775 years (close enough). They wailed that he was the only thing protecting their city. They yelled that the looters should return him—even a part of him—some bone to mark their special connection with the world-famous wonder-worker.

The thieves answered, almost taunting them: "You should know that we have come out of the territories of Apulia and have made our way here from the city of Bari because of a revelation that we should take the holy body to that place. Why do you so irrationally flay yourselves for this calamity? Just as you said—more than seven hundred years have passed since Nicholas died. It is enough that you have had his benefits all that time. Now he wants to leave your city and to shine his light on other parts of the world!" They argued that the Myrans could be comforted by the whole sarcophagus full of sacred ooze left behind and the miraculous icon of Nicholas that still hung above his ruptured tomb. But sorry, they said: He's coming with us to Bari.

While all this went on, the Myran crowd noticed one of the four monks who'd been assigned to guard the body had also come down to the shore. A cry went up: He must have accepted a bribe to betray them all and sell the saint to the looters. He protested he was innocent, but it was no good. The mob surrounded him and began to beat him mercilessly. He collapsed under the blows, pleading for mercy. It was a miracle that he lived. Nicholas, "the most blessed confessor of Christ, freed him from their pounding," we are told, and the crowd "stood dumbfounded, acknowledging that he was blameless."

The ships were starting to pull away from the shore, however. At this, the Myrans pushed and shoved forward, desperately plunging right into the sea, still in their clothes and their shoes. Wading through the waves, wailing like children being dragged from a beloved parent's arms, they grabbed at the ships' railings and at the oars. The crew strained to row. It was chaos.

The harbor was too deep. The Myrans began to topple away from the ships. The little fleet started to pick up speed.

The cause was lost. The Myrans stood in the lapping water, looking after the retreating ships and thinking of Nicholas's own life lived entirely in Lycia—his childhood in Patara, his strange early election as bishop of Myra, his suffering during the Great Persecution, his gifts to the city later. "You are taking our inspired Father, who has been with us since the time of the great Emperor Constantine! You leave us orphaned!" They were devastated that Nicholas would choose to leave.

"The mourners cried out these things and others, with sorrow, pain, and anger all intermixed, and the saddest of them, soaked by their own tears, began to return home. However, as they went they kept turning their heads to the shore and looking out at the ships.

Indeed both their own and their fatherland's glory was being borne away in those ships. Now and then, full of longing and as if driven mad they would stop and would roar like wild lionesses and tigresses in heat.

"The citizens left. In their grief, they trod with slow footsteps upon the sand. The sailors in turn swiftly abandoned the shore, filled with happiness and with rising spirits, and sitting on their benches they began to row briskly. I am not able to express in speech or in writing how much happiness there was in them, nor can I comprehend it in my mind without astonishment."

We are told that the citizens of Myra kept calling out for a long time, and that even when the sailors were a mile or two away, they could hear the wailing of the desolate townspeople on the evening air. "Indeed there were very few among them who could even with great effort keep themselves from tears, as they sympathized with such wretchedness."

As the sun set over the Mediterranean, it turned the blue seas red, as if all the ocean were itself a miraculous ichor, as if water were turned to wine or blood.

How do we know all this? How do we know these details? From two accounts written shortly after the theft, one by a monk named Nicephorus, who describes himself as "the lowliest clerk in Bari," and one by a much more powerful man of the church in that city, John the Archdeacon. They agree pretty closely about events, although occasionally they put them in a different order.

But here's the question: Given that they're both celebrating the "miraculous" delivery of these relics to Bari, their own city, why do they include so many details about the brutality of the looting and the deep sorrow of the locals? Why record all the things that make the League of Saint Nicholas look like a band of pirates? Nicephorus and John the Archdeacon don't just report the complaints and lamentations of the Myrans; they occasionally even write those complaints as poems. Why would they take so much trouble to record the League's lies, strife, coercion, and even violence?

An anonymous Russian account of the theft, written about seven years after it happened, brushes over all the unpleasantness. It presents a version of the story that is gilded and pretty, with no harsh edges at all. In that version, there is no argument between the Barians and the guardians of Saint Nicholas. No one gets tied up. No one is threatened with a sword. Two of the monks even agree to come along on the voyage home, presumably to keep up their work as guardians in the new city. It's all very friendly. Here's the whole section of the account having to do with the theft itself:

> Having taken council they armed themselves and entered the church of St. Nicholas, where they met four monks, whom they asked where St. Nicholas was. The monks showed them the tomb where St. Nicholas was resting.
>
> Then they smashed the floor of the church and found the stone coffin full of sacred liquor. They poured the sacred liquor in some vessels and took his relics as well as pieces of the stone coffin where the relics had been, and took them to the ships.
>
> They set sail again, leaving two monks in Myra, while the other two accompanied the relics of St. Nicholas. And they got under way toward the city of Bari, on the other side of the sea.

If that was the only account that survived, we wouldn't know anything about all the anger, all the sorrow. It would be erased from history.

So why didn't Nicephorus and John the Archdeacon clean up the story like this before they told it? Why tell us that the thieves themselves actually shed tears because the Myrans' grief and desolation were so moving? Why make it so clear that this was a true looting, a brutal assault on a holy place?

Well, for one thing, it is clear that both Nicephorus and John the Archdeacon are enthusiastic storytellers, and they enjoy the little details. Perhaps they even felt some kind of duty to record the truth. (Though if they left out some really disturbing detail—that a citizen of Myra was beaten with an oar and killed, say, or drowned in the waves—we will never know it.) But that's not all.

No, there's a deeper motive here: *In order to prove that the bones were real, they had to prove that the loss of the bones was a calamity.*

It's 1087. There are no photographs. There's no way to circulate snaps of the thug Matteo grinning in the pit, holding up the skull of the saint, dripping with ichor. There was only word of mouth and word of honor.

So this is a heist that can't operate under cover of darkness. It would be a disaster if there was an oath of secrecy and all the thieves kept mum. They don't want to slip in and out unseen. Because if they just show up in Bari with half a skeleton and say it's a saint, they can't prove it. It could just as easily be sheep's bones painted with saffron to look aged, or a random skull they found in a graveyard.

They have to be as loud about the heist as possible. The more the people of Myra tried to stop them and the greater a disaster for Lycia that the theft appeared, the more the people of the world would believe that these truly were bones worth protecting. The story mattered. The story was of central importance. All the threats and the lamentations and the desperate citizens plowing through the waves and grabbing at the oars authenticated this fragile body in a wooden lunch box as the true and precious relics of Saint Nicholas.

That night, they moored at the nearby island of Kekova. They had not made it far—just three miles or so from Myra. That's understandable: It was getting dark, and the straits off the coast were perilous with half-submerged lumps and pillars of rock. Worse, the wind was against them and they couldn't use their sails. They had to row. It was hard work.

The three ships paused there and waited for first light. The island was fringed with ruined towns and tombs now girdled by the waves.

We can follow their progress away from Myra on a map. John the Archdeacon and Nicephorus list each of their stops. We can see that their progress for the first few days is slow—just a few miles a day. They were exhausted from the rowing. A wind from the north had picked up and made the seas choppy and shoved them back where they were coming from. They gritted their teeth and rowed onward, straining at their oars for hours at a time, battered by spray.

It only got worse. On the fourth day they had only made it as far as Nicholas's birthplace, Patara, about forty or fifty miles away, and they were being blown off course. These ships were not good in a storm. They must have been flung about on the waves, thrown by swells. It was dangerous to stray too far from shore into open water—but the shores were lined with treacherous, tiny islands and deadly rocks that could easily smash a hull to smithereens.

The sailors were beginning to mutter. If they had the real body of Saint Nicholas the Navigator on board, why did the seas try to push them back to his home? Maybe he didn't want to leave. Maybe it was not God's will that they "translate" him to Bari after all. Nature itself seemed to resist them.

And in the depths of the night, as the anchored ships heaved uneasily, a sailor named Eustasius woke from an awful nightmare: A flock of swallows was crowding his open mouth, pecking at his tongue, and he was gagging on his own blood.

I find that image horrifying—the beating, suffocating wings, the avid little eyes, the beaks piercing the tongue's flesh as he tries to scream. Some versions of the text say it was not swallows, but leeches that ate at his tongue, squirming in his mouth. (In Latin, *hirudines*—leeches—instead of *hirundines*—swallows—which sound like each other.) Take your pick.

Either way, he woke up screaming and told everyone his vision. There was no question in their minds that Nicholas was angry. Something had gone wrong with the heist.

The sailors tried to force their way north from Patara. It would probably not be a good idea to anchor in the harbor town Nicholas was from. Never mind supernatural intervention: If people discovered they'd stolen the relics, the crew would be assaulted by another angry mob. So they tried to continue on their route along the coast.

"After expending every bit of energy that they had, yet not being able to proceed beyond, possibly, twenty-four miles, they unwillingly altered their course to a place called Perdikca, with all their strength gone." They moored the ships and disembarked.

Now that they were no longer trying to sail away, the seas dropped and were still. There was an ominous silence.

Then, accusations started. Why had the winds shifted against them? They called each other out and said that someone—one of them—had stolen part of the body. Someone had tried to keep some fragments back for himself. That must be problem: not that the theft of the body itself was against the Blessed Nicholas's will.

They pointed fingers. They got into a screaming match there on the shore. Then someone spoke up and prophesied. The contrary winds would not stop blowing until whatever parts of the body had been stolen were returned to the wine cask, to the bundle of the saint's bones. "For in truth, certain among us have secretly taken pieces of the sacred remains and have hidden them. But if we all desire to return happily home, whatever each person has hidden should be given back to the sacred body."

One of the priests brought out a Bible. He ordered everyone to swear on it that they hadn't stolen anything—and if they had stolen something, this was the time to confess. Otherwise, God's wrath would fall on all of them.

At this, a man named Romuald stepped forward and opened his hand. He had two teeth in it and a few chips of bone. Another man pulled out a leather pouch, which was soaked with holy ichor. There were five men in all who'd stolen body parts: Romuald, Byzantius Saragolla, Sire Azzo Cavallo, Nicholas of Monopoli—and Eustasius, the same man who'd dreamed of leeches or swallows mobbing his tongue. Perhaps his dream had been more about his own guilt than the rest of the crew's.

They were filled with shame. They handed back their knucklebones and teeth. They swore an oath they had no more body parts that were not their own.

Once again, we might ask why Nicephorus and John the Archdeacon report this story, which doesn't reflect well on the Bari mariners. The answer is simple: Both writers were trying to establish the fact that all of the bones of Nicholas belonged to Bari. None, supposedly, were missing.

We know that is not true. When the remains were examined in the 1950s, the doctor presiding over the forensic study discovered that only about half the body was there beneath the altar in the crypt of the Basilica of Saint Nicholas in Bari. The relics had been seized in a rush job. Not only that, Matteo had literally been standing on bones as he groped around to find the skull. He'd crushed bones under his shoes, fragmented them. Something had seriously damaged much of the skeleton, probably either Matteo's fumbling in the bath of oil or the retreat down to the shore, when the bones were slapping against Father Lupo's shoulder in a sack.

The sailors did not have anatomical knowledge. They apparently didn't pay a lot of attention to what bones were there and which ones were missing. The reality of the corpse didn't matter. The important thing was to establish an international reputation for having all the bones in one place. Pilgrims had to come to Bari to see Nicholas. It was an exclusive deal. That was what the world had to believe.

That's why it made sense for Nicephorus and John the Archdeacon to tell this story of petty theft. It underscored the wholeness of the saint's pilfered body.

Once the body was made whole and wrapped up again, the wind shifted, and they realized they could sail on.

"After celebrating mass, with quieted winds and becalmed sea-swell, they left the shore under swollen sails with joy among them all."

We can follow their route across the Aegean Sea, around the Peloponnese, working their way up toward the Adriatic and their home. They stopped almost every night at a port to replenish their water and avoid rough weather in the deepest parts of the sea. At this time navigation was difficult without a landmass in sight. The magnetic compass hadn't been discovered yet in the West and wouldn't be discovered by Europeans for another hundred years. If they couldn't see the stars, ships had to follow coastlines to be sure of where they were in the great expanses of blue sea.

But the days were apparently fair and bright for the League of Saint Nicholas. One night, a sailor named Disigius dreamed that an old man approached him and said, "Do not be afraid, but be bold, for I am with you."

Disigius asked, "Who are you?"

The old man answered, "I am Nicholas, who now travels with you. As proof that I speak the truth, you will arrive at the port of Bari on the twentieth day after you took away my body."

With that he disappeared.

"Therefore," we are told, "with a prosperous wind blowing and with their ships cutting through the calm sea, praising the greatness of the Lord, happily they were carried along on a swift voyage."

As they crossed the Aegean, a lone bird, a lark, flew down out of the clouds and settled on the box of bones. She sang and then leaped to land on a sailor's outstretched hand. She flew in circles around the ships, chirping welcome.

And so, on the eighth of May, 1087, the three ships came to the shores of Apulia, in Italy—to the port of San Giorgio, just a few miles south of Bari. And there they stopped to announce their victory before sailing triumphantly into their home port.

Unfortunately, their arrival turned out to be more complicated than they had anticipated. So far, no one had gotten killed in the course of the expedition. Oddly, it was only when they got home that the heist became lethal.

At the port of San Giorgio, the League of Saint Nicholas prepared for their triumphal return home. They sent messengers ashore to ride up to Bari and announce that they were on their way and would arrive the next day.

The crowds were already gathered on the docks of Bari when, on May 9, 1087, the ships finally arrived at the port. The shore was crowded with gawkers. The sailors' relatives rowed out in their boats to meet the returning ships, waving their arms. People darted through the narrow streets of town, shouting the news. Quickly, the Christian clergy of the city threw on their holiest vestments and raced out to meet the ships.

Already, there were grumblings in the crowd about what was

going to be done with the bones. Who would own them? You can't really own a saint. But where would the relics be held? Who would profit from them?

These questions would become important. The sailors had talked amongst themselves and had already decided what they wanted to happen: A new church should be built for the relics of Saint Nicholas, a special church devoted entirely to the saint.

The first important clergyman to arrive at the docks was Elias, abbot of the Monastery of Saint Benedict, surrounded by a flotilla of monks. Blessing and praising, he boarded Captain Giannocarro's ship. There, he delighted in the delivery of the bones of Saint Nicholas from far across the sea. In delicate language, he suggested that the sailors should hand the bones over to him for safekeeping—just until arrangements could be made to keep the sacred relics in a suitable church.

The sailors weren't stupid. They knew that as soon as the bones were out of their hands, they'd have no bargaining power. They demanded control over what happened to the body and, equally important, a cut of the profits the Church would make from the visiting pilgrims who would come from all over Europe to pray before the relics. What followed, as the crowds waited restlessly on the shore, was a secret series of sharp negotiations.

Elias had no choice but to agree to their terms. They had the body. He did not.

While the narratives of the delivery fill this scene with generous speeches and prayers, we have documents that show that in fact, a tough, legally binding agreement was struck that day between Elias and the mariners.

Here is what the sailors demanded:

1. The relics of Saint Nicholas would be housed in a new church built on the site of the old Roman governor's palace.
2. Each and every one of the sailors would have the right to be buried by the walls of that shrine, a huge honor and a boost for those trying to scrabble their way into Heaven.
3. During services in the church, they would all be granted chairs for themselves and their spouses.
4. If any of them ever hit really hard times and lost everything, the Church would support them.
5. And finally, most importantly, each one of them would get a percentage of the income that the Church made from pilgrims who would come to be blessed with the saint's holy liquid. They would get a cut of those profits—and so would their descendants in years to come, after their deaths.

They drove a hard bargain. But Dom Elias, abbot of Saint Benedict's, agreed to it. **His verbal oath was later written down by lawyers.** We even have financial records showing that, a century later, the Church was still paying out those profits to the descendants of the sailors.

With this decided, Dom Elias returned to shore to prepare for a triumphal entry of the relics into their new home city.

Meanwhile, the Archbishop of Bari—arguably the most powerful Christian clergyman in the city—was nowhere to be found. He was thirty miles away, in the port of Trani, preparing to get on a ship to sail to Jerusalem on a pilgrimage. The writer of one of our narratives, John the Archdeacon, was with him, acting as his secretary. A messenger arrived and told them the unexpected news: One of the most famous saints in Christendom had just drifted to shore in Bari.

The archbishop abandoned his trip to Jerusalem. He needed to get back to Bari as quickly as possible. He needed to take control of the Nicholas situation. He rode off along the shore. "His horse did not gallop as fast as his burning desire made him pant to get back."

Back in Bari, the monks of Saint Benedict had thrown together a hasty welcome ceremony, a triumphal celebration for the arrival of the bones in their new home.

> So the sailors and the Abbot Elias disembarked with the saint, and the people and the clergy fell to their knees before his relics with joy and reverence, raising their voices in praise of the greatness of God, who alone is the author of miracles; and joyful tears flowed from many eyes. Therefore, in this way, with the monks supporting Nicholas in their arms with deep love, he was brought down from the ship, while clouds of incense floated above him; before him filed ranks of psalm-singers in white robes and embroidered capes; he was both preceded and followed by an innumerable crowd of men and women who praised God and said: 'Blessed is he who comes in the name of the Lord; peace on earth and glory in Heaven'; therefore St. Nicholas, whose name means 'Victory to the People,' made his entry into the city of Bari, while flocks of bells rang out all around him.

They processed through the streets to the monastery of Saint Benedict, where Abbot Elias had agreed to hold the saint's bones until another resting place was prepared. Singing hymns, they laid the bones on the altar and fell to the floor on their faces in front of the sacred bundle.

But the sailors were still wary. "Those who had taken him away from the city of Myra surrounded him, armed, ready to die rather than to allow any violence from the great and powerful people of Bari," who were apparently already asking questions about why this rabble of sailors was determining the fate of a saint.

When Archbishop Urso arrived in the city, he rushed to the monastery to see the relics. He prayed before them and then explained that he was going to take them to his cathedral.

At this point, there was a violent disagreement in the mob that had gathered around the remains. On the surface, it was about who would control these bones and where they would rest; but clearly it was about something more, since the people of Bari actually started to riot in the streets. Historians have wondered whether it was an ethnic clash or a political clash—the archbishop, after all, owed his position to the new Norman overlords of the city, who ruled it with an iron fist. He was a close advisor of the Norman duke. Did people resent his interference? It is unclear.

In any case, rightly or wrongly, there were rumors that the archbishop was "plotting to carry away the body by force or guile." When the archbishop sent some guards to pick up the relics of Saint Nicholas, the watchful crowds drew their weapons and moved in for a fight.

The stone streets of Bari are narrow and deep as chasms. We can only imagine them echoing with the shouts of rioters, people hurling stones, people beating each other with sticks.

There was blood. Screaming. Bodies fell. When the encounter was over, two teen boys—one from each side—were dead.

At that, it appears shock filled the crowd. A day of celebration had turned into a day of mourning. The archbishop must have been horrified. The whole thing had spun out of control. Archbishop Urso renounced his claim to the bones.

This episode is a good illustration of the kind of detective work historians have to do. Our two written accounts—by Nicephorus and John the Archdeacon—tell very different stories about the Bari riots. Though they were both written around the same time—1087 or 1088—one of them covers up the violence of the disagreement.

Nicephorus is the one who tells us about the two young men who were killed. That detail is not in John the Archdeacon's account. In fact, John's account smooths over the Bari riot and makes it sound like a debate that was settled by the time the archbishop arrived panting on his horse from Trani. John the Archdeacon, as I've said, was the archbishop's man. It was the archbishop himself who asked him to write his account of the Translation of Nicholas. It is even possible that he wrote his version to counter Nicephorus's, in which the archbishop comes off looking dictatorial, even obnoxious, riding in late and making demands about the bones. John's plan worked to a great extent: His version of events was more widely circulated.

In a case like this, historians have to squint past the stories that are told by the witnesses to try to recognize the truth that lies behind them. They have to ask themselves: Why does this witness want to tell me this story? What are they trying to convince me of?

Without this kind of detective work, victims of history like the two boys killed over an argument about where to stick some bones simply disappear as if they never lived, never breathed, and never died.

Both accounts agree on one thing about the arrival of Nicholas's relics in Bari: The miracles started immediately. Even when the box of bones was sitting in the monastery of Saint Benedict, lines were forming of people from all over the region, coming to file past and pray for healing.

According to Nicephorus and John, the prayers worked. The blind could see again. The mute could speak. The paralyzed could move. The sick were well. Demons fled. The two authors provide running tallies for how many people were healed each day. As the years went by and their stories circulated all over Europe, new copies included more and more miracles from far-flung countries.

What was the experience of being healed like? Three days after the relics arrived in Bari, Nicephorus interviewed one woman to find out. She told him that as she lay by the relics, close to death, she had seen a great hawk fly over her and land on her chest, and he had spread his wings to cover her. As he flew away, a sweet scent had filled the air, "so sweet that she thought she was in the garden of paradise." When she arose, she was better.

How any of this healing actually happened is up for you to decide. The important point for historians is to notice how Nicephorus and John were trying to sell their saint to western Europe. These rosters of miracles were an advertisement, an invitation for pilgrims to come from far away to visit the holy relics newly fetched from the

East. They were not merely selling Saint Nick: They were selling the port of Bari.

There's one interesting detail about these lists of afflictions and cures: Not one of the miracles involves the famous myron, the holy liquor of Nicholas. These pilgrims we hear of in John and Nicephorus kneel in front of the box and pray. No oil is extracted. The flow is not mentioned. One woman with leprosy arrives late to discover that the church is closing for the evening. A custodian is washing the floor, which is covered in mud from the huge crowds of visitors who arrived during the heat of the day. The woman throws herself down in the mud and covers herself with it, streaking her face and limbs—and it cures her. Even the mud near Nicholas is pure and miraculous. But no myron.

It's time to ask what the Nicholas liquid was, and why it may have stopped flowing at first when the saint arrived in Bari.

When describing the sarcophagus that may have contained Nicholas's bones in Myra—the tendril sarcophagus—I mentioned that there were two holes drilled in the fish-scale lid, and that they could have been used to draw liquid out, but also to funnel liquid in. Whether this particular lid was Nicholas's or not, this seems like the system the guardians in Myra probably used.

By 1087, the bones of Nicholas were roughly 745 years old. There was no meat on that carcass. There was no juice. What seems most likely is that Nicholas's caretakers in Myra were pouring in a mixture of holy oil, perhaps some holy water, and myrrh, a scented perfume.

Let's break this recipe down. Holy water is simply water that has been blessed. Holy oil would have been olive oil that was blessed. It would have been produced locally, as Myra was surrounded by olive groves. Myrrh was also produced locally. We are told that the Myrans made an incense from the sap of a local tree, the *zygia*, boiled with the wood of another local tree, the *stourika*, which had been gnawed "by a fat worm." This incense accounts for the tales of miraculous sweet scents that waft from the corpse. There is also a symbolic power in myrrh for Christians: One of the Three Kings, the Magi, supposedly brought myrrh as a gift to the infant Christ child.

These three ingredients would have been mixed together and then drained into the casket for contact with the bones. Archaeologists may even have found a manufactory for the sacred liquid in the church compound in Myra, several rooms where the oil was pressed and blessed. The ruins appear to include the remains of some terracotta plumbing—a pipeline for the oil—and a basin where the olives could be ground up before the oil was stored in stone jars. The floors there are still laced with chemical traces of olive oil and myrrh, the two major ingredients of the Nick liquor. Throughout the complex, archaeologists have found bowls used for crushing and grinding olives to produce oil. They have also found the small, delicate glass bottles, which the guardians of the monastery filled with the oil and sold to pilgrims in exchange for donations to the shrine.

The fact that the monks and priests of Myra may have been producing the saint's oil themselves does not make it a scam, however. Relics supposedly radiated holiness. They infected whatever touched them, whatever was near them, with their sacred power. This is why the Barian mariners were grabbing chips of marble from the tomb.

Simply by being near Nicholas's body for so many centuries, those chips, in the eyes of those men, would have been steeped in divine energies. And any oil that cascaded through those ribs and touched that grinning skull would have been irradiated with blessings. This was considered a perfectly legitimate way to replicate a saint's power, even if the body didn't exude the stuff itself. Just because a miracle is mass-produced doesn't mean it isn't real.

And in Bari, they quickly went to work to put an assembly line for the mass production of salvation into place. They apparently did not realize that they could not draw sacred oil *out* of saint's tomb unless they poured sacred oil *into* the saint's tomb. But that didn't stop them from trying to make the saint's miracles available to pilgrims.

Work started immediately on the new church of Saint Nicholas. While armed guards stood around his bones, a crypt was dug and workmen started to disassemble the old Eastern Roman governor's palace to use its pieces as the building blocks of a new sanctuary.

They designed it for heavy tourist traffic. The white stone steps that descend to the crypt were fifteen pilgrims wide. One grand staircase leads down into the crypt and another, on the far side, leads back up to the sanctuary, to cycle people efficiently past the holy relics.

By 1089 the crypt was complete, though there was no church on top of it. The Barians wanted to welcome pilgrims to visit the bones of Nicholas the Navigator as quickly as possible, so they opened the tomb to the public, though the sanctuary above it was only half constructed.

The crypt where Abbot Elias laid Saint Nicholas to rest still stands today beneath the basilica in Bari. Tens of thousands visit it each year. The crypt itself, sunk below the church, is a forest of pillars of marble and oolite, striped and spotted and scarred with patterns like frost or ferns. Each has a carved base with different beasts and birds and flowers. These were taken from the palace of the Roman governor.

And at the center of the crypt is an altar surrounded by oil lamps, protected with iron bars. And under that altar is a metal plate which shields the bones of Saint Nicholas, laid to rest there for the first time in a ceremony conducted by Pope Urban II on October 1, 1089.

It took many more years for Bari to complete its new church, the Basilica of Saint Nicholas (Basilica di San Nicola). It stands to this day, a stark, gorgeous monument to this strange story of deep faith and cynical theft.

It looks as heavy as a fortress, with small windows that seem almost designed to repel attack, like arrow loops, and yet it is also miraculously light, built of shining white stone, scribed with blind arches that seem to bear the weight upward toward Heaven. It is a church of chaste simplicity. Yes, it captures the military might of the Norman dukes who ruled Apulia—but it also, I like to think, recalls the faith of that long-dead Nicholas, Bishop of Myra, who found holiness in what was plain and simple. If there is a majesty to the building, it is accomplished through a lack of ornament, an austere humility.

So let us leave the Barians with their sacred relics and their mighty church by the city's seawall, looking out across the gray Adriatic.

Because the story isn't over. Have you forgotten the Venetians? What happened to them? They were beaten by the Barians in 1087—they must have arrived in Myra a few days later and heard about the theft—but they were still hungry for those relics. They wanted Saint Nicholas for their city and would do anything to get their hands on him. It wasn't long before they decided to do something about it.

Today, Bari claims to have the bones of Santa Claus—but so does Venice. How did this happen?

For the story of this second heist, the next chapter in this strange story, we need to move a few years forward, into the 1090s, and a war that would scar the world forever.

THE VENETIAN HEIST

We have dealt with small events: one man, a bishop of a provincial city by the sea; seventy men deciding to steal his bones. Though the lives of individuals (even our own lives) seem to be made up of small things, behind them lie the sweeping actions of great nations and powers. The vast gears of history turn, dwarfing us all.

To understand the Venetian heist, we need to step back and look at history from a distance for a moment.

As we've seen, the Turks had spread across quite a lot of the Eastern Roman Empire, from the blue waters of Lycia, where Myra lay, to the high grasslands of central Anatolia, to the underground beehive cities of Cappadocia, to the deserts of Syria in the east. This invasion had taken several decades. The Eastern Roman emperor wanted all that land back. He couldn't force the Turks out of that vast territory by himself, though—he'd need a lot of military assistance. He made the mistake of turning to the Christians of western Europe—from the regions now called France, Belgium, and

Italy—and asking them for help against the Muslim invaders. Suddenly, a territorial war became a holy war.

The emperor himself did not find it particularly important that the Turks were Muslim. Constantinople had formed alliances and agreements with members of the Turkish Seljuk clan over the years. The emperor's own armies had thousands of Muslim troops on their payroll. The emperor wanted to expel the Turks from Anatolia not for any religious reason, but because they were a rival nation that was occupying land that the emperor considered his own.

But to draw the western Europeans in, he had to sell the conflict as a war against the infidel, the unbeliever. In the West, the pope, Urban II, embraced the cause because it served his own purposes. He began to preach about the need for kings and knights to travel on violent pilgrimage to the Holy Land and purge the old sacred cities (Nicaea, Antioch, Bethlehem, Jerusalem) of the infidel. Crowds eager for glory, loot, blood, and salvation took up the cause and screamed back at him, *"Deus vult!"—God wills it!*

Starting in 1096, waves of Christian barbarians from the West poured into the Middle East, seeking to "free" Jerusalem, the Holy City—and to grab as much other territory as they could in the process. We now call this assault the First Crusade, the first War of the Cross. Princes and soldiers sewed red crosses to their surcoats and even branded the sign of the cross onto their own skin with hot irons. They headed east by land and sea.

Many of them set out on ships for the Holy Land from the port of Bari. For as it turned out, Bari's bid for prosperity and recognition through Nicholas's relics had worked—his shrine was incredibly popular. The city was bustling with business as troop transports and ships of provisions for the Crusaders were stocked on its docks. Nicholas had truly and miraculously transformed the city's economy. Bari, blessed by the patron saint of sailors, was the perfect setting-out point for a sanctified expedition. Crews preparing for departure across the sea first prayed for safe passage at the half-built new Basilica of Saint Nicholas, bowing before the bones in the crypt. Crusading princes and sailors all knelt in the darkness of that cool, subterranean grove of marble, asking for calm seas and victory.

Almost immediately, the Eastern Roman emperor regretted his decision to invite these brash Westerners with their upstart princes, their armies of hungry vagabonds, and their homicidal zealotry. The emperor got much of his territory back, but at great cost. The Crusaders ravaged and despoiled whatever land they passed through, often including the emperor's own territory. They weren't interested in his directions or in his careful alliances with certain local Muslim rulers. They did not seem deterred by their strategic disasters.

The Muslims of Anatolia and the Middle East looked on in some bewilderment as these European barbarians hurled themselves into battle. For the Great Seljuk Sultanate and other Muslim powers, there were more important rivalries to worry about than any war with far-off Christian Europe: there were rival princes, rival caliphates, rival sects of Islam. But the Crusaders saw all Muslims as one undifferentiated mass of unbelievers. They were simply pagans to the Western barbarians, who referred to all Muslim enemies, regardless of nation, as "Saracens," ignorant of the divisions between them. The Muslims, surprised and divided, could not mount a unified defense. City after city fell to the Crusaders.

Finally, after many sieges and battles, the Crusaders reached their goal, the prize they sought, the city of Jerusalem. Christ had entered its gates a thousand years earlier, riding humbly on a donkey. The Crusaders had more spectacular plans. For weeks, they surrounded the city, besieging it. On June 13, 1099, parched with thirst, they marched barefoot around the walls, singing hymns. Early the next morning, they attacked from several sides at once. They mounted the walls with siege engines and poured into the Holy City.

The slaughter was overwhelming. No one was spared: man, woman, or child, Muslim or Jew. "Now that our men had possession of the walls and towers, wonderful sights were to be seen," crowed one triumphant Christian chronicler. "Piles of heads, hands, and feet were to be seen in the streets of the city. It was necessary to pick one's way over the bodies of men and horses. . . . In the Temple and porch of Solomon, men rode in blood up to their knees and bridle reins. Indeed, it was a just and splendid judgment of God that this place should be filled with the blood of unbelievers, since it had suffered so long from their blasphemies. The city was filled with corpses and blood." When Jews (who had aided in the defense of the city) tried to seek sanctuary in their synagogue, praying for mercy, the Christians barred the doors, set the building on fire, and murdered anyone who tried to flee the flames.

The Crusader princes "ordered all the Saracen [Muslim] dead to be cast outside because of the great stench, since the whole city was filled with their corpses; and so the living Saracens dragged the dead before the exits of the gates and arranged them in heaps, as if they were houses. No one ever saw or heard of such slaughter of pagan people, for funeral pyres were formed from them like pyramids, and no one knows their number except God alone." Many thousands died in the massacre.

In this way, the Christian invaders announced to the broader world the good news of salvation, and their work in Christ, the infant of Bethlehem, the Prince of Peace.

The Venetians did not want to join the First Crusade. They had too much to lose. They had made their fortune by trading both with Christian kingdoms like the Eastern Roman Empire and with Muslim nations like the Great Seljuk Sultanate and the Fatimid Caliphate. They had strong economic ties all over the Mediterranean. If the Venetians joined the Christian cause, their trade routes to Muslim ports in Egypt and the Holy Land would immediately dry up. Their Islamic trading partners would become enemies. Simply put, it just did not pay to join a holy war.

So what they did was wait until it was absolutely clear that the Christians were going to win. Once Jerusalem had fallen, the Venetians loudly declared that of course they had been on the side of Christianity all along—and though the war had already been won, they were on their way to help.

One of the only ways we know about this Venetian expedition during the First Crusade is through the document that retells the story of their supposed theft of Saint Nicholas's bones. We don't know much about the author of this story. He was an anonymous monk from the monastery of Saint Nicholas where the sailors were all blessed before the voyage. He is a cheerleader for Venice, a city he clearly loves deeply.

As we hear this medieval monk's account of theft and violence, keep in mind his motivations for telling us his story, just as you would if you were watching a police interrogation: He is trying to make Venice's contribution to the Crusade, which was in fact somewhat late and feckless, sound impressive. The triumphant return to Venice with Nicholas's bones—or what they said were Nicholas's bones—would really be one of the only victories they could claim.

And yes, the Venetians had decided to send out their own expedition to Myra to steal Nicholas's relics—despite the fact that the Barians announced they'd stolen them back in 1087. Clearly, for twelve years, the Venetians had been fuming about the success of the Barian heist. So in the middle of the Venetian voyage to blood-soaked Jerusalem, they stopped to seize these bones.

This is how it happened.

Once the Venetians had heard that Jerusalem was sacked, the ruler of Venice, the Doge, appointed his own son to lead an expedition to the Holy Land, accompanied by a powerful cleric, Enrico, Bishop of Castello, so that Venice could protect its commercial interests in the Middle East. They assembled a crew of soldiers from many nations: Greek, French, English, Italian, Hungarian, and German sailors and mercenaries who were ready and willing to head off to Jerusalem under the banner of Venice. Before they set out from Venetian territory, they all sailed to the local monastery dedicated to Saint Nicholas the Navigator, begging the saint to bless their voyage. Then "the ships were dispatched from the port. The sails began to swell as they entered the wide sea."

Whereas the Barians had seized the bones with a little merchant fleet of just three ships, the Venetians launched thirty warships and tenders manned with hundreds of sailors and marines. Their flagship was a powerful trireme, a Roman-style galley bristling with three ranks of oars. For long voyages, it used sails—but in battle, it lanced through the waves propelled by three hundred oarsmen grunting and rowing in deadly unison.

These military ships were highly maneuverable when confronted with enemies, but sea crossings were slow. Given their dart-like slenderness, they were even more unstable in rough waters than Bari's merchant ships. They had to be careful of storms and deep water. That slowed them down. More than that, three hundred rowers drink a lot of water. It was vital that these ships pull into port almost every night to "refuel"—to get fresh water, wine, and food. (In fact, the First Crusade would see the replacement of these old Roman-style galleys by new warships that were powered solely by wind.)

This is all to say that after the brave start with prayers and good winds and full sails, the Venetians made incredibly slow progress toward Jerusalem. They bumped and dithered down the coast of Dalmatia and agonizingly crossed the Aegean and had only made it as far as the isle of Rhodes when they decided they'd better stop for the winter. Their triremes weren't ready to take on the Mediterranean chop in the cold season. They'd gotten started on their voyage pretty late in the year. (Jerusalem, remember, was taken in the middle of the summer, so it was probably not until September or October that the Venetians set out.) They unloaded all their provisions from their ships and settled down for a few months in Rhodes, where once the colossal statue of Apollo had welcomed travelers to the harbor.

That winter, the Eastern Roman emperor, hearing they were

anchored at Rhodes, wrote to them and told them to pack up and go home. He had lost all interest in the Crusade. The Crusaders filled him with fury and horror. He begged the Venetians to turn around.

The Venetians, however, were not going home. Bishop Enrico might have been reluctant to set out on the voyage, but once they were underway, he was committed. He gave the fleet a pep talk. Neither God nor men liked quitters, he said. They had to finish what they'd started.

Nonetheless, the only thing they achieved that winter was attacking another Christian fleet, a fleet sailing out of the Italian city of Pisa. Though the Pisans had more ships (fifty to Venice's thirty), the Venetians really were masters of the waves.

They met in battle off the shores of Rhodes. The Venetian galleys with their ranks of oarsmen were fast and powerful in battle. With their prows, they smashed in the sides of other ships. Archers released flocks of arrows and quarrels strong enough to pierce armor and pass right through the body of a soldier. Men poured off the galleys' high decks onto enemy ships, engaging them in bloody hand-to-hand combat.

The Venetians quickly captured thirty-eight enemy vessels and forced the surrender of the entire Pisan fleet. They took a lot of prisoners.

Why would a Christian fleet attack another Christian fleet in the middle of this holy war? Who knows? The brief description of the battle we have is primarily an excuse for the author of the narrative to boast about his hometown team.

In the spring of 1100, the Venetian fleet left Rhodes, and Bishop Enrico ordered them to sail for Myra. It was time for them to lay their hands on the bones of the Blessed Nicholas for the glory of Venice. Now that they had defeated the Pisan navy, it was time for them to even the score with Bari.

As the Venetians row across the strait between Rhodes and the mainland, with their Pisan prisoners aboard and their marines giddy at the prospect of action, let me pause to say this: There is a lot about the Anonymous Monk of Lido's account that is suspect. Clearly, he has read the reports of Bari's earlier theft written by Nicephorus and John the Archdeacon. He wants to outdo them. He goes to great lengths, therefore, to tell a story in which *the men from Bari did not get the right bones at all*. But he tells the story using exactly the same structure and details as the Barian reports. A modern historian has created a chart lining up all the similarities between the Venetian story and the Bari stories. There are many of them. The Anonymous Monk of Lido seems to be saying: *We did everything the mariners of Bari did. But more, and better.*

So it is hard to trust him. But let's tell the story as he did first, before we ask questions.

Here, then, is what he said happened.

The Venetian fleet anchored about five miles away from Myra. Like the Barian League of Saint Nicholas, they sent scouts ashore, since "it was reported to them that more than five hundred Turks closing in on that area were not far off."

When the scouts reached the church, they discovered it was full of Christian clerics. Apparently someone had seen the thirty ships anchoring nearby and assumed that it was Crusaders who might want to stop in to pray at Saint Nicholas's own church. They were hoping for rich offerings.

The people of Myra were still living in the fortress up on the hill, leaving their city abandoned below. The priests came down to perform their rituals for Saint Nicholas four times a week. Having received this intelligence, the scouts excused themselves from the church and said they'd be back soon with the army. They did not reveal what the army was expecting to do.

When the scouts got back to shore and reported all this to the Venetians, the soldiers onboard the ships "eagerly took up arms and rushed to the city in swarms," not even waiting for Bishop Enrico or Commander Giovanni Michiel to give the order.

Without fanfare or the announcement of a herald, they pushed their way into the church.

There was no pretense that the army was just there to pray. Their prayer at the altar was loud and clear: "Blessed Father Nicholas! Visit our country, which has always been devoted to you! Venice, your daughter, invites you. It has prepared a place where it would receive you. And if you go there, Venice will enhance that church further and improve it so it is fitting to house a patron as powerful as you. We know we are unworthy to look upon you with our lustful eyes and hold your bones in our soiled hands." But God's will and their faith, they announced, would make everything come out right for Venice. It was time for another translation of relics.

The priests of Myra, astonished, realized that this was a theft. Most of them fled. They must have run up to the fortress on the hill. The army held four of them back to answer questions. The

Venetians posted guards all the way along the old city walls, armed and ready for combat.

The soldiers interrogated the four guardians who remained. They asked where the bones of Saint Nicholas lay. The guardians were confused—we might assume, because the bones had already been stolen thirteen years earlier. The soldiers offered them bribes to give answers. *Show us where the bones are.*

Bewildered, the guardians pointed to the sarcophagus, with its broken lid, which was now resting against one of the sanctuary walls. "This is the coffer from which the Barians took some of the relics and left others behind. If you want them, take them and let us go."

Matteo, of course, had left behind lots of fragments of the skeleton. He had probably shattered the pelvis and ribs when he crawled around in the coffin, groping for the skull. It makes sense that there would have been plenty of shards left behind: More than half the skeleton didn't make it into the bundle that Father Lupo carried on his back.

If you ask someone in Venice today where their fragments of Saint Nicholas came from, this is what they'll tell you: *These are the parts the Barians left behind in the casket. These are from the same body.*

The thing is, that is not what their own account says.

Grabbing the leftovers from the carcass that Bari had picked clean was not good enough for the Venetians. To outdo Bari, they had to deny that the bones the Barians had stolen were from the real skeleton at all. The Venetians demanded new bones, bones that hadn't been touched in the previous raid. They threatened the guardians with violence if they couldn't point to another set of Nicholas relics entirely. "So far we have used soft words and flattery with you.

But unless you tell us what we asked, we will punish you quite severely with beatings and torments." Where, in other words, was the *real* body of Saint Nicholas?

The guardians, understandably, were totally at a loss. If the body the Barians had taken wasn't the real one, they had no idea where another body of Nicholas might be hidden. "Even if you burn us with flames or threaten our heads, how can you possibly get the truth out of us, when no one knows it?"

The soldiers dragged the lid off the sarcophagus that Matteo had breached and predictably found it filled with water and oil—the myron. That wasn't what they were looking for. If there were bone fragments lying deep in the murk, they ignored them. This is important. They refused to believe that any bones the Barians had discovered could be the real thing. So someone was holding out on them. The real skeleton was still to be found.

Furious, they took out their rage on the church itself. They smashed altars and battered the walls until the plaster and stone collapsed and the rubble used to fill the walls was revealed. Darkness didn't stop them. Throughout the night, they continued their vandalism by the light of torches and oil lamps. During the long years of the Turkish occupation, more than a decade, the Turks had never done the kind of damage the Venetians did to the church in that one night. The Muslim invaders had shown more reverence than these Christian men with their mallets, their iron bars, and their impossible demands.

They threatened to torture the guardians if something didn't turn up soon. That's when one of the guardians broke. He whimpered a promise: If they would go back to their ships and bring their spiritual leader, Bishop Enrico, the guardians would tell him everything they knew, the whole truth.

The soldiers agreed. They rushed to the shore and told the bishop that there were secrets waiting for him at the church, if he'd only come ashore.

Surrounded by troops of soldiers, the bishop and Commander Giovanni marched to confront the weeping guardians.

Giovanni led the procession through the abandoned city, surrounded by a phalanx of soldiers in full armor. Enrico and his attendant clerics followed, singing psalms, walking in bare feet.

When they got to the church, the elderly bishop hobbled through the scene of chaos the soldiers had left—piles of rubble and dirt—and he painfully lowered himself and lay face-down on the floor, arms spread wide in front of the altar to show his humility before his God and the saint. He prayed for Nicholas to reveal himself to the Venetians and asked for permission to remove the bones.

If his prayers didn't work, surely the platoon of soldiers in chain mail standing around the sanctuary would help.

The bishop rose awkwardly to his feet and made his way over to the four church wardens who sat miserably under guard. "Blessed son," he said to the one who'd promised to reveal all, "when I received your message, although I'm slowed by painful infirmity, I came here at once, lifted up by hope. For I know that you did not send for me without good reason. If you have some bit of truth, do not conceal it from me."

The guardian answered truthfully, but it was not the answer

the bishop wanted to hear. "Holy Father, with God as my witness, I know not a single trace of proof of what you're looking for. I sent for you only wanting to avoid impending punishment and to be freed by you."

The bishop, saddened, said nothing but walked away to some dark chapel where he could be alone and think.

This left the four guardians unprotected—it exposed them to the rage of the soldiers who'd been tricked. Immediately after the bishop wandered off, the soldiers began to torture the lying monk "with exceptional punishments."

Beaten and pierced, he eventually could not take it anymore: He screamed for help.

The bishop heard the echoing cry. He limped over as quickly as he could. He scolded the soldiers for torturing the man—and in a church, too. He pulled the guardian away from them.

Panting as he recovered his breath, the guardian complained about the torture—but in thanks for being saved, said he could show the bishop where there were some other relics—not of Nicholas himself, but of two other saints.

Reading this story, I wonder whether the bishop didn't know about the torture all along. I wonder if the Venetians weren't playing a pitiless game here, a version of good cop/bad cop. The bishop walked away, letting the soldiers assault the guardian. Then he could come back and win the man's trust by saving him. Was the bishop truly horrified at the torture—or was his disgust at the violence just another interrogation technique?

If so, the trick worked. The guardian revealed that inside the main altar of the sanctuary were the relics of two saints associated with Myra: Saint Theodore and Saint Nicholas the Uncle. Saint Nicholas the Uncle was not the right Nicholas—he was the uncle of a saint (also named Nicholas) from the sixth century—but he was, after all, one Nicholas more than the Venetians had discovered so far.

Quickly, the Venetians surrounded the holy altar where the bishop had just been praying face-down on the floor. It might have been holy, but that didn't stop them from smashing it open. They found two sweet-scented boxes of cypress wood, and inside them, the bones of the two saints. Each was conveniently labeled.

This was a victory. They carried them out of the church, raising them on high in their arms, singing hymns of glory while the army's heralds blew trumpets and waved banners.

The church was quiet again. Most of the army had left.

But a few remained amidst the rubble. A few skeptics. They put together some clues. They saw the icon of Saint Nicholas that the Barians had left behind. They supposedly smelled the sweet, tart aroma of myrrh right beneath it. They recalled that the priest had celebrated a ritual on that spot, even though there wasn't an altar there. He had set up a tripod on the flagstones right there under that sacred image.

That, they decided, must be where the *real bones* of Nicholas must be buried.

They ran after the army, which was well on its way back to the fleet. They told the bishop that they'd been thinking, and it seemed like the priests paid a lot of attention to this particular spot. Surely—surely—that was where the real relics were hidden.

The evidence seemed scanty, but somehow it convinced the army. They all turned around and marched back to the church. The four exhausted guardians watched the Venetian invaders return to their work of destruction.

Who knew what they would find?

Inspired by the idea there might still be more secrets to reveal, the soldiers "took up once again tools of every kind and applied themselves once more to blessed labor. First the previous pile of rocks and soil, which they had thrown this way and that in their previous efforts, was removed. Then they excavated all the way to the pavement, which they also broke and pulled aside. After a huge weight of rock was lifted away, they discovered a glassy mass which was hard to break and difficult to penetrate."

They chipped away at the glassy mass. Some of the men held chisels while others, standing over them, walloped the chisels with mallets. When their arms got tired, other soldiers moved in to take their place. The mass was so hard the tools broke and they had to find new ones.

Then under the glassy mass was a layer of hard, congealed charcoal.

Never mind that they didn't even know exactly what they were searching for. They started to chip away at the charcoal. It was even more dense than the glass.

And yet there, in that mass of charcoal, they found a chunk that contained bones and copper. This, they decided—this was Nicholas himself.

We are told that at this discovery, the scent of myrrh unfurled and angels were all around them. A palm tree grew up right in the spot. They discovered a placard in Greek that confirmed that this truly was the body of Saint Nicholas, Bishop of Myra. That chunk of bone and charcoal was a miracle.

This, at any rate, is what the Anonymous Monk of Lido tells us. Santa Claus was entombed in coal, ironically, like a gift for naughty children.

Bishop Enrico took the bones, many of them still fused together in the blackened lump, and wrapped them in his cloak, weeping in gratitude.

Now, finally, the Venetian army truly did leave the church. They marched back down to the shore, singing hymns et cetera—the usual. You know the drill at this point.

As a sign of thanksgiving and celebration, they released their Pisan captives, all the mariners they'd taken prisoner when they had defeated the Pisan fleet that winter. They gave them a ship and a map and sent them home.

Meanwhile, the people of Myra had ventured out of their fortress and were standing in their church, looking at all the rubble and ruin. It was ghastly. The sanctuary had been torn apart. The archbishop of Myra wept. He pleaded with his city's saint, "Holiest father, Nicholas! Why do you abandon your homeland? Why do you let yourself be carried violently away by those men?"

He sent a delegation down to the shore to beg the Venetians to leave something for Myra. He couldn't bear to go himself. He didn't even want to look upon the vile men who'd done this to his church.

Powerless, he cursed the looters. "O cruel Venetians! Why have you done this to us? Why did you destroy our church, break apart our altars, and snatch our church's patrons and relics? Although the

Turks destroyed this city, they left us with a great hope for well-being until now. But you, who are Christians, have reduced us to nothing."

The Myran delegates went down to the beach where the fleet lay at anchor, and they begged for the return of what had been stolen. Though the Venetians would not give back the saints themselves—Saint Theodore or Saint Nicholas the Uncle or the blob of coal that they said was Nicholas himself—they did give back a precious box that had been hidden inside the broken altar, and they donated one hundred gold coins for the restoration of the church's interior. They said the place was going to need a lot of work.

Once again, the citizens of Myra came down to the shore to see off their saints. This time, however, there was no hysteria. No one plunged into the waves and grabbed at the oars. Instead of three small merchant ships, this was a fleet of thirty warships manned with armed marines. There was no hysteria because there was no hope. Once again, Myra had been plundered.

"Eaten up by sadness, they returned to their homes, their eyes flooding with tears."

The Venetians, on the other hand, were ecstatic. They sent word back to Venice that they had secured the bones of three saints, including, they claimed, Saint Nicholas the Navigator, bishop of Myra. They built an onboard shrine for the relics they'd found. They surrounded the relics with curtains and cushions and the sailors all tossed coins at the saints, as if the remains were a wishing well. They kept candles and oil lamps burning around the bodies, and the clerics sang hymns and nocturns day and night.

Sure, we are told, a few of the men occasionally tried to steal a joint or a bone chip, but "These men were either afflicted by disease, struck down with harsh beatings, or disturbed by terrors in the night."

So with their sacred cargo, the Venetian fleet set off again—finally—for their original destination, the Holy City of Jerusalem.

Do I think the blob of coal was really the body of Santa Claus?

No. I don't.

If I had to guess, I'd say that what they found beneath the floor was an old portion of the church that had been burned to the ground in one of the Arab raids of the eighth or ninth centuries—or even the charred remains of an older church destroyed in an earthquake in the sixth century. The bituminous mass, even the glass (which is superheated sand) suggest the remains of a building after a huge fire. At other archaeological sites, clay bricks that were subjected to great heat fused into a glassy mass of slag. I suspect that the people of Myra just constructed a new wing of the church over the ruins of the previous one. There is plenty of archaeological evidence that the church was rebuilt and renovated many times over the thousand years or so that it was in use—and there's evidence of fire damage elsewhere in the ruins.

It is entirely possible that Venetians did find the remains of a body that had been entombed at some point with a copper box beneath a floor in the old church, and which had been engulfed in slag during a disastrous conflagration. On the other hand, I find it extremely unlikely that they found a perfectly preserved placard announcing that these fragments were Nicholas. That sounds like a stretching of the truth or even a complete fabrication.

The eleventh-century tradition clearly stated that in Myra, Nicholas's body had been placed in a location where it could be doused in the sacred oil and the oil could be drawn up and squeezed into bottles for pilgrims. That was a tradition that stretched back several hundred years. The small collection of bone fragments the Venetians were now celebrating was in no position to yield up holy oil: For centuries it had been encased in glass and coal so thick it required teams of men with chisels and hammers to get through to it.

Given that, these small pieces are no more likely to be Nicholas of Myra than they are to be anyone else who lived in the region and was buried in that church. Many important Lycians must have been entombed there at some point.

I wonder what that nameless person would think if they knew their bones still lie, more than a millennium later, in a church in Venice, with believers whispering secret demands and requests before them on their knees.

The Venetians continued on to Jerusalem. The other Crusading armies apparently were not very impressed with their timing when they arrived. Jerusalem had fallen to the Crusaders a whole year earlier. Bishop Enrico gave a sermon in which he defended the idea of people arriving late to a war. "Those who fight bravely in a later battle are just as victorious as those who wrought slaughter in the first battle." It sounds like he's trying to convince himself.

The Venetian Crusading record in the Middle East is not particularly impressive, though the Anonymous Monk of Lido really tries to sell it as a portrait of Christian heroism. The Venetians seem to have accomplished two things: They set up a profitable trading partnership with the Christian occupiers of the Holy Land, agreeing to provide provisions and other needed goods. And they assisted in besieging Haifa, a completely neutral city that happened to be populated almost entirely by Muslims and Jews.

Bishop Enrico offered to let the people of Haifa go if they would convert to Christianity and pay a huge annual tribute. They refused. Eventually the Venetian army built a mammoth siege tower out of planks from their ships and rolled it up to Haifa's battlements. As in Jerusalem, what followed the breaching of the walls was a pitiless massacre of everyone in the city.

The Anonymous Monk of Lido boasts that the terrified civilians fled to Bishop Enrico to beg for mercy, "But the Christians, who were stationed behind them, struck with their swords, without regard to age or sex. They spared no one within the city. The virtue of Christ and the ingenuity of His men had conquered at last, and when the anti-Christian city lay open to the Christians, no one could take a step on any street or square of the city without touching the blood or remains of a pagan." This was a new kind of heroism: killing unarmed women and children in an attack from behind.

In this way, the bishop, the anonymous monk, and the Crusaders themselves showed the quality of their Christianity.

Why study the First Crusade, something that happened a thousand years ago in the middle of the Middle Ages? That was a long time ago. Things change.

But some things are broken forever, and that's why the study of history is important.

The clash of sword on shield from the First Crusade still echoes today in the rhetoric of religious extremists, both anti-Western jihadists and Islamophobic terrorists. American white supremacists, for example, still take inspiration from the Crusades. They march wearing Crusader crosses on their T-shirts. Their websites include the phrase "Deus vult"—*God wills it,*—first spoken by Pope Urban II as he stirred up the fury of medieval mobs—and they're proud to post pictures and memes of noble Knights Templar, pale as cream cheese, taking the knee with their swords in hand as beams of heavenly light pour down on their raised faces from above. In 2016, for example, a group of white American Christian nationalists planned a massacre of Muslims using car bombs and arrows dipped in pigs' blood; they called themselves "The Crusaders." Thankfully, the FBI intercepted their plans and foiled them.

Associating yourself with the medieval Crusading movement is an odd choice for people who value brute victory so highly: The 1099 Fall of Jerusalem was basically the high point of the Crusades. What followed was two centuries of incompetence and failure as the Europeans floundered in the Middle East and lost every bit of territory they had gained in that first surprise campaign. None of the later Crusades were successful. Again and again, waves of Christian invaders were soundly defeated by superior and committed Muslim adversaries. By the Fourth Crusade (1204), the Christians didn't even bother to get as far as the Holy Land: They realized it was more profitable to just attack Constantinople, the capital of the Eastern Roman Empire. They spent the next few years besieging and sacking other Christians. Praise the noble knights of the Cross as you will, but the Crusades were basically a two-hundred-year pageant of stupidity, greed, delusion, retreat, and military ineptitude.

The only good things that came out of the European occupation of the Middle East were the elements of cultural exchange, which profoundly affected both the European West and the Middle East. The famous Knights Templar, for example, living in the Holy Land over decades, started to develop alliances and even friendships with local Muslim rulers and warriors, as well as political rivalries. Trade goods and ideas flowed east and west through the Crusader states, for the brief time they held on, before the amateur war making of Western kings prompted the whole edifice to topple and the Christians were expelled.

It is important to know this history, though it happened so long ago, because it's important to understand the roots of modern conflict. When a contemporary US politician refers to a war in the Middle East as a "Crusade," he sets off a series of echoes he may not intend. That kind of gaffe makes it almost impossible to win hearts and minds in the Middle East. It stirs up extremists to violence and prolongs conflict. If a leading politician with access to the country's military proudly shows off his Crusader tats—a Jerusalem cross, the phrase *Deus vult*, or *Infidel* written in Arabic—it puts Muslim allies on edge, understandably, and suggests an ignorant, blundering approach to Middle East strategy and diplomacy. Profound missteps like these connect modern political situations with a now legendary history of cultural clash that may or may not be relevant or strategically useful. They encourage mistrust, destroy useful alliances, and provoke opposition. Intentionally or not, they advertise an allegiance to the worst in human nature.

The First Crusade in particular is invoked by modern extremists because it was a moment where blunt religious hatred between Christians and Muslims really solidified. There is no real reason these religions necessarily should have been at each other's throats: They share a great deal of belief in their prophets and their God. Yes, before the First Crusade, rulers of one religion or the other would occasionally invoke holy war for political reasons. The Seljuk Sultan Alp Arslan, for example, cast his brutal attack on the Christian city of Ani as a blow for Islam; but at other times he acted with a notable generosity to Christian prisoners, making nothing in particular of their religious differences. The Eastern Roman Empire was a Christian nation, but they had allies among the Seljuk Turks as well as Christian enemies. Similarly, the League of Saint Nicholas, stealing the relics of the saint from Lycia, were frankly just as worried about the Christian townspeople of Myra as they were about the Muslim invaders—and they were arguably *more* worried about the rival Venetians. Religion did not need to be a defining characteristic in conflict. The mere fact of whether someone was a follower of Christ or Muhammad did not automatically make them an enemy.

This changed after the First Crusade and the bloodletting at Jerusalem. Increasingly, throughout the Middle Ages, Muslims and Christians understood themselves as part of a cosmic war, pitted against each other. That didn't mean that leaders didn't occasionally act with courtly gentility toward each other—but the poison had been injected. Believers of each religion increasingly found it convenient to define themselves by vilifying the other. In a French play about Saint Nicholas from the year 1200, for example, the roaring king of the Muslims stomping around onstage describes himself as a "pagan" who worships three idols: Apollyon (the demonic form of the god Apollo), Tervagan (a random demon), and a horned god called Mahom (Muhammad). There could not be a more glaring and willful misunderstanding of Islam. Islam was, of course, no more polytheistic than Christianity. Moreover, depictions of Muhammad were absolutely forbidden in Islam—if anything, Christians were the ones who bowed regularly before statues as if their company of saints was a pantheon of gods. The author of the play, preparing his Saint Nicholas's Eve entertainment, wildly distorted the rival faith to create a convenient Saracen fall guy. By 1200, when this play was written, French pilgrims had been traveling freely to the Holy Land for a century, if not longer. They had seen mosques. They knew mosques contained no idols. But truth was less important than the opportunity to fabricate grotesque differences. It's easier to think yourself holy when you can paint your enemy as outrageously satanic. This, to some extent, was the work accomplished by the First Crusade.

It is astonishing that white supremacists are proud of this shameful moment in history and rally around it: It's a history of ignorance, cruelty, wasted effort, and, after the first few successes, utter incompetence. But this is a good example of why it's vitally important to understand the complexities of the past instead of devouring the cheap and easy legends we tell ourselves.

The Venetians returned home after two years overseas. You can imagine the parades and the processions. The people of the city vowed to make a new church at the Monastery of Saint Nicholas on the Lido, one of the long barrier islands that protects Venice from the open sea. It was a place where fleets gathered before setting out on expeditions, a perfect home for the patron saint of sailors.

Boasting about Venice's two great saints—Nicholas the Navigator and the evangelist Saint Mark (the saint who had been smuggled into the city in a shipment of pork, and whose symbol was a lion)—the Anonymous Monk of Lido wrote, "O Venice, truly blessed, twice-blessed Venice! You shine today, relying upon twin pillars. Indeed, you have the lion, which makes you victorious in battle, and you have the holy admiral, who never fears a storm at sea. You seized the lion from Alexandria through ingenious deception and secured the holy admiral from Lycia with manifest strength. But does that mean you acted criminally in the theft of the one and plunder of the other? God forbid! For you did these things not for the sake of desecrating some place, nor for the sake of malice, but you acted with zealous devotion and piety."

The Venetians spread the story that the Barians didn't have the relics of Saint Nicholas at all; they'd been deceived. The real relics were in Venice, on the Lido, in the Monastery of Saint Nicholas, where the anonymous monk wrote his account.

Their set of the bones of Saint Nicholas of Myra was placed in a casket on an altar beside those of Saint Theodore and Saint Nicholas the Uncle. Conveniently, Nicholas himself appeared in a dream to a local priest shortly after to confirm that these were really his bones.

And so they sat for centuries.

But it is now the twenty-first century. Let's open up the caskets and see what's really there.

AN AUTOPSY FOR SANTA CLAUS

It's time to look again at all these sets of bones, as a detective might pace between the remains of victims in the morgue, trying to make connections and reconstruct how a crime really happened.

By the 1950s, the Basilica of Saint Nicholas in Bari was in need of repairs. It had been centuries since it was built by Abbot Elias, and time grinds down all things. To work on the foundation of the building, the sacred bones of Saint Nicholas had to be temporarily removed from the crypt where they had sat for 864 years, since they had been placed there with great ceremony by Pope Urban II.

On May 5, 1953, at 11:30 p.m., in the dark of night, the three giant slabs that lay across Saint Nicholas's tomb were lifted. Dr. Luigi Martino, a professor of anatomy at the University of Bari, was present to examine the remains. He writes of the sense of wonder in that moment when the final slab was lifted. "A shiver of emotion passed through the bodies of all present, a recognition that we were the first after eight centuries to see the corporeal remains of a man and a saint."

What they found was a somewhat haphazard arrangement: The

skull had been carefully placed on the northern end of the sarcophagus. The rest of the bones were largely fragmentary, with the largest bones placed closest to the skull. Martino and his assistant spent the next couple of hours sorting the fragments and picking out stone pieces left over from the rubble of the sarcophagus young Matteo had smashed all those centuries before. "In those two and a half hours all we could do was to catalogue most of the larger pieces, and we couldn't give consideration to the overwhelming number of bone shards." They sorted them into two silver cups: slightly larger fragments and smaller fragments. "There was a great deal of wasted time because of the necessity of cleaning and drying each fragment with gauze and cotton."

Drying: because of course the tomb was puddled with the sacred myron.

Yes, the myron eventually flowed again from the bones in Bari, supposedly. It took a long time after the bones were buried in their new home, but we do eventually find mentions of people scooping up liquid from the tomb through a hole in the floor. About eighty years after the Translation of Nicholas to Bari, his healing fluid was being offered to kings. By the seventeenth century, it was being extracted daily from the tomb, using a sponge tied to a sinker of pure silver. By the twentieth century, it had become an annual ritual, which continues to this day.

The body, today, lies under the altar in the crypt, guarded by ceremonial gates. Kneeling, you can peer through a decorative grating to see inside the altar, where there is an inscribed metal plate that covers a hole leading down into the burial chamber. On May 9 each year—the day the League of Saint Nicholas returned, triumphant, from their expedition—a priest will crawl halfway under the altar, lift off the metal plate above the body, and lower a crystal flask down into the burial chamber. Each year, when the priest withdraws the flask from the tomb there is liquid in it, a few ounces' worth. The priest holds it up the before the congregation in triumph. It will be dispersed in many, many bottles of holy water for believers and pilgrims to take home with them.

It is no longer oil, myrrh, and water, however—which required custodians to actually pour liquid *into* the tomb. Testing was carried out on Bari's version of the sacred liquid in 1925 by the city's Institute of General Chemistry and Hygiene. They found that the fluid was **water—unusually pure water**, free of bacterial contamination. "The manna of Saint Nicholas is an almost pure water, which has no connection with the waters that infiltrate from the external environment of the saint's sarcophagus." They are at pains to talk about its unusual purity, which they call "Alpine," as if the water appeared from the mountains.

Martino speculates that this water may actually have helped Nicholas's relics survive: "To me it appears that through the centuries this liquid permitted a better conservation of the bones, resisting the small pulverizations that through time microscopically damage bone. The purity liberated the bones from micro-crystallization of calcium phosphates."

Believers in past centuries were somewhat confused by the fact that after the Translation of the body from Myra to Bari, the liquid had changed from an oil to water. They made up a legend in which there were two streams of liquid coming out of the saint: oil pouring from his head, which people rubbed on themselves for healing, and sweet water from his feet, which they gave to the sick to drink. It appears, however, that after the bones were moved to Bari, the only substance drawn out of the tomb was water.

Where does this water come from? The most likely scientific answer is that it is condensation. The crypt is extremely cool, below sea level, and there are channels that convey air into the burial cavity. As in the eleventh century, however, the science of the answer doesn't really matter. Technically, for believers, however this liquid manifests, the fact that it touches the bones themselves irradiates the water with sanctity.

Martino and his assistant dried the bones and sorted them until 2:30 in the morning. Then the clergy placed all of the relics in a crystal urn, a reliquary, and they were installed in a side chapel of the church so that worshippers could see them while the repairs to the foundation were going on.

For the next four years, they remained on display. Martino was apparently not permitted to take another close forensic look at them during this time.

In 1957, the repairs were done, and it was time to place Nicholas back under his altar. On the night of May 6, 1957, Martino and two assistants were granted another chance to catalogue the bones more systematically before they disappeared forever into their tomb. It was brief and hurried, a strange scene: that ancient church at night, dark except for the glaring lights brought in for forensic examination and photography. The professor was prepared this time with anthropometric measuring instruments and radiographic equipment.

The examination revealed the details we've already gone over: The relics were the skeleton of a male, over seventy years of age, about five feet, six inches (1.67 m) tall, who'd probably suffered from back pain and headaches. His nose had been broken. In life, his lower jaw probably jutted out a bit. Significant portions of the body were missing.

In 1957, it would have been possible to determine the age of the skeleton through radiocarbon dating. (Living things, during their lives, absorb the isotope carbon 14. After their death, carbon 14 atoms slowly transform into other atoms. By counting the remaining carbon 14 atoms in a piece of organic material, scientists can determine how long ago something lived and died, up to about sixty thousand years.) This would have been extremely useful. It at least might have confirmed that the man whose skeleton is buried in Saint Nicholas's tomb in Bari lived seventeen hundred years ago, when Diocletian and Constantine were upon the throne.

Unfortunately, that also would have meant removing a chunk of the bone and treating it with various chemical emulsions, and apparently that was not permitted. Martino was given only one precious night to photograph all of the bones and to create a chart showing what was present and what was missing. Most of the pelvis and the rib cage were gone. He worked frantically through the night, frustrated at how little time he was allowed.

At dawn on May 7, 1957, the professor's time was up. That day, the bones were put in their reliquary and paraded through the streets of Bari. Then, in time for the May 9 anniversary of the Translation, they were buried again beneath the altar in the crypt, where, Martino notes, "they will stay for centuries to come."

I wish I could be there, perhaps another thousand years from now, when that tomb is next opened by whatever incomprehensible thing we have become. What will our descendants, human or virtual, think of who we are in this millennium, our attachment to bodies, our fascination with the scaffolding that our flesh and fat hang on?

The ancient man beneath the slab in Bari slumbers on.

So much for the Bari haul. What about Venice?

The Venetians had popped the top to check on their relics six times between 1100 and the twentieth century: in 1134, 1282, 1347, 1399, 1449, and 1634. During the 1449 checkup, they discovered that there was a skull in the midst of Saint Nicholas of Myra's bones that hadn't been there before. That was a little confusing. But in any case, they were not particularly eager to investigate further. Each time they opened his reliquary, whoever was abbot of the Monastery of Saint Nicholas would die. It appeared to be a curse.

In 1991, the Patriarch of Venice decided it was time to undertake a scientific study of the bones at the monastery. On September 17, 1992, experts opened the reliquaries again. (This time, the abbot of the monastery lived.) Here is what they found:

Saint Theodore's box contained a few nondescript pieces of bone. The reliquary marked as Saint Nicholas the Uncle's contained a virtually whole male skeleton, reasonably intact.

The reliquary that supposedly belonged to Saint Nicholas the Great, Bishop of Myra, Wonder-Worker and Navigator, contained pieces of several skeletons, one male, one female, with a five-year-old boy's jaw. They were surrounded by a litter of bleached white bone fragments.

The Venetians were not happy with this outcome. They were going to have to declare their relics null and void.

Desperate, they called in an expert: Dr. Luigi Martino, who had done the autopsy in Bari almost four decades earlier.

On November 11 and 12, 1992, Dr. Martino carried out an examination of the remains under the close watch of a Catholic cardinal, an abbot, and a priest.

Martino confirmed the likely sex and general age of the owners of the bigger bones in the Nicholas box. (Sex is typically determined from the pelvis or, failing that, muscle attachment points on the skull—but those decisions are not absolutely accurate, given the wide range of human body types.) This wasn't looking good for the Venetians.

But then he drew their attention to the smaller bone fragments. They were unusual: The other bones in the casket were brown with age. These were a peculiar white.

At this point, Martino, who seems to have been looking for a positive outcome for the Venetians, reread the two translation accounts of Nicephorus and John the Archdeacon. This gave him the answers he needed. Of course the bones of Nicholas wouldn't be whole! Young Matteo had stomped all over them in his haste! "The bones of the saint, preserved in Venice Lido, could only be in the form of a large mass of shapeless fragments! And not otherwise!" he exclaimed. It was hardly an impartial and dispassionate scientific inquiry.

He was assuming that the Venetians had carried off whatever the Barians had left behind. He therefore decided that the white bone chips were absolutely the missing pieces of Nicholas. He speculated that perhaps they had been hidden in a chest with another family to conceal them. "The Myran monks were smart to hide the crushed Holy Relics inside an anonymous chest." He wrote a report, dated May 6, 1993, and recommended that these white fragments be removed and given their own casket.

Here's the problem: Martino is not acknowledging the Venetians' own account of their theft. He says that the Venetians, engaged in "the same commando operation as the people of Bari," had discovered the rest of the remains "in a sealed wooden chest placed behind the high altar."

That would make sense. That would be very convenient. But that is nothing like what the Anonymous Monk of Lido actually says. The monk writes that the Venetians saw the broken sarcophagus behind the altar left over from the Bari expedition—and then ignored it, because they didn't want Bari's leftovers. Drawn on by intuition and a miraculous scent, they delved under the floor and hacked their way through glass and tar and coal to find a set of bones fused into a lump.

I would argue that if we are to believe the Anonymous Monk of Lido at all, it makes it incredibly unlikely that the bones from Bari and the bones from Venice are from the same body. On the other hand, the bone fragments that remain in Venice fit perfectly with the anonymous monk's account of them.

Dr. Martino speculated that the whited bones in Venice were bleached by some "special uniform treatment, unknown to us, that the pious guardian monks, after having patiently collected all the fragments, had subjected them to for a decade or more."

I would argue that those bones were bleached by some caustic substance the people of Venice rubbed on them to try to scrape off the coal and tar that bound the bones together. The Anonymous Monk of Lido specifies that the bones the Venetian army took back to their ships were "still stuck together with scraps of bitumen." They would not have left them in that state when they got home. It would have seemed neglectful, inhospitable, even blasphemous, to their beloved patron saint. They would have tried to clean them. And that, I'd argue, is when they were bleached.

I asked a forensic anthropologist, Dr. Angelique Corthals, if this seemed credible. It is her job to study ancient remains. She was working only from Martino's descriptions of the state of the bones, but she pointed out that the most likely cleaning agent monks would use on bones in the period was lye—and this would have bleached the bones bright white. While all this is speculative, it does suggest that the whited bone fragments could have been chipped out of a bituminous mass.

I believe that the two churches in the two rival cities, therefore, have two separate bodies on their hands: The Barians have a body from a sarcophagus, a body that the monks of Myra had believed was Nicholas and had bathed in oils for centuries; the Venetians have a body that was buried with a copper box at some point before a fire leveled part of the church, perhaps in one of the coastal raids of the eighth and ninth centuries that we know severely damaged the building.

Which of these was, in fact, the person of Nicholas, Bishop of Myra, in the fourth century? I'm pretty inclined to believe that Santa Claus now rests in the church in Bari. It seems likely that after his death, there was an unbroken tradition in Myra regarding the location of his body, because almost immediately, he was a distinguished person, a person people remembered. In the years after his death, people all over the region started to name their children after him. His church was celebrated as his burial place. His tomb would be remembered.

In situations like this, it's hard to establish truth, so I can't claim my solution is definitely right. For example, we might doubt the Anonymous Monk of Lido's account of how the Venetian bones were found. He gets a lot of details right about the First Crusade (at least, so far as we can corroborate them). But his account of the theft is clearly supposed to echo and outdo the earlier accounts of Bari's heist. He steals a lot of details directly from the earlier accounts. How much of it is just made up to discredit the people of Bari and boast about the triumphs of Venice? And what does this mean for the bone fragments, which, I suspect, have nothing to do with the saint on their label?

Some of this may be cleared up in the next few years by Turkish archaeological digs at the Basilica of Saint Nicholas in Myra (now Demre). Some of it may be cleared up by a more thorough examination of the bones.

In these cases, historians may have their beliefs about what happened—but it makes sense to hover above alternative worlds, alternative truths, looking down upon both of them equally, allowing both to run their course, waiting for evidence to confirm or deny one—at which point, one world fuses with ours, becomes real, and expels the other into uncreated night.

GIFT GIVER AND WONDER-WORKER

Venice did not manage to spread the story of their bones as efficiently as Nicephorus or John the Archdeacon sold the story of Bari's heist. John the Archdeacon's account survives in at least twenty manuscripts, spread across Europe; Nicephorus's survives in several different versions and was translated into Greek. The Anonymous Monk of Lido's work survives in only one manuscript, and that's still in Venice. It did not get much international attention. The Barians had set in stone the story that the world believed.

As the rollicking tale of Bari's sacred theft spread across western Europe, the fame of Nicholas increased. Many expeditions and pilgrimages to the Holy Land were launched from Bari's docks as a result; in fact, writers of the period often simply called Bari "the Port of Saint Nicholas."

As the League of Saint Nicholas grew older, Abbot Elias—who had become archbishop by this time—honored his legal promises to the sailors. Every year, thousands of pilgrims came to worship, especially on May 9, the Feast of the Translation of Saint Nicholas, and every year, the church paid out a percentage of its income from those visitors to all the mariners who had taken part in the theft back in 1087. Incredibly, we have an expense report from 1175—ninety years after the voyage—that shows the church was still paying out those annual dues to the descendants of many of the sailors as promised.

As the years passed, the mariners of the League of Saint Nicholas died one by one, and the church, true to its word, buried them against its walls. It was a great honor. Their names are still inscribed above their bodies. You can walk around the church, in the shadows of its imposing gallery, and find memorials to the sailors chiseled nine hundred years ago. Captain Giannocarro is buried right next to the grand main entrance to the church. A bit off to the left is Summissimus, the Highest—even in death, he goes only by this name. Disigius, who dreamed that Nicholas appeared to him and told him the voyage home would be swift, is buried nearby, and so is Byzantius Saragolla, who had stolen bits of the saint and had been foiled by the storm. There is a sweet forgiveness in giving Byzantius Saragolla his privileged burial, despite the fact that he was a thief among thieves. I feel this is what the original Nicholas, famed for his mercy to prisoners, would have done.

Back in Lycia, in Nicholas's homeland, the forces of the Eastern Roman emperor Alexios Komnenos reclaimed the city of Myra from its Turkish occupiers following the First Crusade. The Christians of Myra ventured back out of their hilltop fortress and down into the abandoned town. They reclaimed the city in the plain. It was around this time that the emperor paid for repairs to many buildings in the area, including the basilica, which, if we are to believe our chroniclers, had been damaged far more by Italians than it ever had been by Turks. There is archaeological evidence of these repairs, especially a set of lovely frescos painted in a corridor leading to the chapel where relics of Nicholas had probably once lain. They depict stories of his life: the rescues at sea, a demon thrown out of a boy, the three Roman generals saved from execution by a dream.

Though Nicholas's body was gone, pilgrims still stopped off mid-voyage and prayed, partially because Myra was a convenient harbor between West and Middle East. His icon, after all, was still in the church, and so was a tubful of his sacred liquor. On Nicholas's feast day, local fishermen supposedly tossed boiled wheat into the sea to ask for calm waters, just as their ancient ancestors, at the beginning of winter, had thrown sacrifices into the deep to gain the favor of Poseidon, god of the seas.

Now we need to step back and let the world spin faster. We have heard the stories of who Nicholas supposedly really was; we have watched the thefts that spirited his relics from East to West. Now it is time for us briefly to watch his transformation into the figure we know as Santa Claus. For that, we need to move forward another seven hundred years.

Saint Nicholas's churches continued to spread across Europe as his fame spread. So did his body parts, real or faked. Bones began to show up in France, Germany, Russia, Bulgaria, Poland—wherever he was popular. The stories of his life and miracles spread at the same time: painted on walls; fused into sparkling images in glass; read out to monks during their meals, chapter by chapter; and acted out in chilly chapels on the anniversary of his death, December 6.

In parts of England and France, cities recalled Nicholas's surprising youthful elevation as bishop of Myra by appointing boy bishops in loud, hilarious ceremonies. It was part of a whole series of chaotic midwinter rituals that turned medieval society upside down, treating donkeys as priests and parading them through cathedrals, making fun of the Latin used in churches by having boys hoot out nonsense words like sacred chant.

In these passing centuries, Nicholas was also remembered as gift giver—he who had tossed gold through the windows of virgins. By the twelfth century, we find nuns in rural France spreading out through their villages on the night of Saint Nicholas's Eve, December 5, and leaving bundles of foods—fruits and nuts—at the houses of poor families in their neighborhood. A few centuries later, reports begin to come in from all over Europe of parents delivering gifts of clothing or sweets to their kids on Saint Nicholas's Eve and claiming that it was the work of the saint and his servants sneaking through locked windows on a mission of mercy.

Over the years, more and more professions chose Nicholas as their beloved patron saint. Just as the Roman pagans had chosen gods based on their specialties, so did Christians choose saints. Each profession chose a saint who would represent them best, based on the saint's most famous miracles. Nicholas, obviously, attracted the interest of sailors, but also everyone who worked in jobs connected with the sea: fishermen, ferrymen, dockworkers, shipwrights, captains, navigators, stevedores, and, eventually, merchants themselves. Merchants needed to pray that their cargoes would make it safe and sound to distant lands. Even if they were sending goods overland, they began to pray to Nicholas for a successful shipment.

The story of the three grain ships meant that Nicholas was also patron of grain dealers, beer brewers (because beer is made from grain), millers, and seed merchants. The story of Artemis and the firebomb meant that he was a favorite of chemists and firefighters. Nicholas's reputation for exuding sweet-smelling myron made him patron saint of perfumers, apothecaries, and the embalmers who prepared the bodies of the dead. His severe sense of justice and fairness, performing miracles to make sure that the innocent weren't punished, made him a popular saint for lawyers and judges. His fame spread across Christendom.

And yet the world that Nicholas knew was falling away, ever more a dim memory.

The city of Myra, once his pride, disappeared. Sometime around the year 1300, there was a massive flood, and it inundated the church. Water rose up above its altars. Silt filled its chapels and covered its hypnotic mosaic floors. The church and the city around it were abandoned, filled with alluvial debris. No one bothered to reclaim the city this time or to rebuild the church. It lay, half sunk in earth, for six hundred years. Gray calcite deposits blanked out the scenes of Nicholas's life painted on the walls, as if the building itself, ancient and slope-shouldered, suffered amnesia and lost its memory.

In 1453, Constantinople fell to the Ottoman Turks—distant relatives of the Seljuks—and finally, after more than a thousand years, the Eastern Roman Empire died.

In 1492, on Saint Nicholas's Eve, explorer and infamously incompetent navigator Christopher Columbus landed in Haiti at the place now called Môle Saint-Nicolas, bringing to the people of the New World three gifts from the Old World: massacre, slavery, and syphilis. This was the first spot in the Americas to be named for the saint; it would not be the last.

At about the same time that Constantinople fell, in Germany, a monk named Martin Luther started a movement to rid Christianity of many things he considered to be abuses and superstitions. Among them, the saints. He and his followers preached a Christianity in which God communicated directly with His believers and did not need supernatural messengers or heavenly patrons. The old saints found themselves without employment, halos discarded like lanyards and security badges from jobs they'd lost.

Wars raged across Europe about which version of Christianity to follow: Catholicism, which believed in the authority of the pope and the saints; or Protestantism, which did not.

Saint Nicholas was one of the casualties of these wars. Ironically, one of the ways we know how far his story had seeped into the folklife of ordinary people is through laws passed by Protestants forbidding anyone to celebrate his December 6 Feast Day.

German Protestants, irritated that Saint Nicholas, a superstitious figment of the old religion, was getting more press than Jesus Christ, tried to suppress him in favor of focusing on the little Christ child—*Christkindlein*, or *Christkindl*—as a gift giver. This ended up backfiring a few centuries later, when Santa Claus had swept the field of midwinter revelry, and people began to assume that *Christkindl*—Anglicized as Chris Kringle—was actually just Santa Claus's civilian name. He's still occasionally called that in animated Christmas specials.

In the Netherlands in the mid-seventeenth century, laws were passed that outlawed baking cakes or cookies or gingerbread in the shape of Saint Nicholas or selling dolls that looked like him; these things were declared idolatrous (like the worship of pagan idols). There were even marzipan figures made into the likeness of the saint's miracles: sailing on ships or raising the three boys from their pickling tub. The city of Amsterdam passed laws against holiday markets that sold Nicholas merch: "On Saint Nicholas Eve various persons have been standing on the dam and in other places in town with candy, eatables, and other merchandise, so that a large crowd from all over town gathered." The city magistrates wanted "to prevent all such disorders and to take the superstition and fables of the Catholic papacy out of the youths' heads," so they outlawed those vendors and stalls. By this point, Dutch children were putting out their shoes to be filled with cakes or even small toys on Saint Nicholas's Eve.

We can see some of these rituals in a painting by Dutch artist Jan Steen, from around 1665, called *The Feast of Nicholas*, painted for a Catholic patron. It is an intimate scene of a family on the night of December 5, when Saint Nicholas was supposed to visit. The family has baked or bought dozens of goodies: breads and waffles and little glazed cakes. The saint has apparently already decided who's been bad and who's been good. (This is the residue from the later stories about Saint Nicholas being a stern judge with a whip who punishes sin as well as rewards virtue.) It looks like the big brother in the family has been naughty in the Year of Our Lord 1664. He's sobbing while his younger brother points delightedly at his older brother's shoe, which is filled with a bundle of twigs, a switch to spank him with. The rest of the family seems entertained by his sniveling. It may be that the grandmother in the background has something for him anyway.

She is drawing aside a curtain and beckoning with her finger. Meanwhile, the younger sister apparently found some toys and fruits and a sugar-rooster lollipop in her shoe. The shoe now lies discarded on the floor with a stitched ball like a hacky-sack nearby. She's holding a doll—though because it's a Catholic household, the doll is not a baby or a plush animal but an action figure of Saint John the Baptist. Her mother might be trying to coax it from her, afraid she'll play too hard and break it. It might be more an ornament than a toy.

In the background, a little sister cradles one of the forbidden Saint Nicholas gingerbread men, shaped like a bishop with a Catholic bishop's hat, a miter. A young uncle or an eldest brother holds her up and points up the chimney, explaining how Saint Nicholas got in, while another brother's mouth gawps open with wonder. This is early evidence of the idea that Saint Nicholas uses the chimney to break in to houses; usually, as in the story of the three sisters, he used the windows.

In the background, the father sits hunched in a chair and watches all the commotion. Is he amused or just kind of exhausted?

Who can tell?

This is not a noble scene or a scene of miracles or swashbuckling larceny. But it is a vital scene, nonetheless. Across the void of three and a half centuries, we see a human family. We see petty jealousies and small pleasures and private jokes and perhaps even love. These things are precious. In the face of all the history that rushes by—the rise and fall of nations, the invading armies, the homicidal tantrums of rulers and crusaders—let there be many inconsequential evenings where you are surrounded by the faces of people you love and those who love you, whether family or friends.

So Saint Nicholas's Eve was celebrated in some places, though the old rituals devoted to him were dying out. But as the years went by, he was only one of a number of supernatural beings credited with appearing in midwinter all over the face of Europe: There were witches, demons, imps, and Father Christmas himself, garlanded in druidic holly leaves. The Dutch and some German Catholics favored Saint Nick, but otherwise, he no longer had much of a profile in Europe. Even the Russians, who revered Saint Nicholas deeply and named several of their tsars after him, relied on a witch named Babushka ("the Grandmother") to deliver their midwinter goodies. In the year 1800, Saint Nicholas, humble and severe, was just one contender among a whole frosty night sky filled with magical beings ready to bribe children with sugarplums.

It was not until the nineteenth century that the metamorphosis occurred, and Saint Nicholas—gaunt, dressed as a bishop from the Turkish coast—became Santa Claus—chubby, jolly, dressed in red furs, summering at the North Pole. The story is a surprising one. It involves a writer playing a prank on all of New York.

Let's close our midwinter's tale there.

Part III

"A JOLLY OLD ELF"

1800 AD

On October 26, 1809, a mysterious ad appeared in a New York City newspaper. A local innkeeper complained that one of his guests had disappeared. It was an old Dutch man, Diedrich Knickerbocker, and he had left behind a pile of papers—but no sign of where he had gone.

Over the next several weeks, more updates appeared in the same paper, the New York *Evening Post*. Knickerbocker had not been found. The innkeeper was getting angry: He wanted someone to pay for the room. He announced that if no one came forward to pay Knickerbocker's bill, he was going to publish the stack of papers the old man had left in the empty room. Meanwhile, other New Yorkers were worried. They offered a reward for information that would lead to the vanished man's return.

The thing was, there was actually no man named Diedrich Knickerbocker.

It was all a stunt, a prank, carried out by author Washington Irving. On December 6, 1809—Saint Nicholas's Day—he published what pretended to be the great work that Diedrich Knickerbocker had left behind in his hotel room, *A History of New York: From the*

Beginning of the World to the End of the Dutch Dynasty. He had made up Diedrich Knickerbocker, and the innkeeper, and, frankly, most of the history of New York that he described in his book. Blurring the line between truth and fiction, Washington Irving poked fun at many of the city's loudmouths and blowhards.

Irving is best known today for creating another one of our favorite holiday-themed night riders, the Headless Horseman of Sleepy Hollow. But at the time, it was Knickerbocker's parodic *History of New York* that made him famous—and it was central in the creation of Santa Claus as a modern myth.

The book pretends to be a description of the Dutch settlement of Manhattan. In fact, much of it was made up as a gag, filled with quaint humor about New York's forgotten early history. Irving later described his purpose in writing the book: Few New Yorkers, he claimed, knew the history of their city, or knew that "New York had ever been called New Amsterdam or had heard of the names of its early Dutch governors or cared a straw about their ancient Dutch progenitors. . . . The main object of my work . . . was to embody the traditions of our city in an amusing form, to illustrate its local humors, customs, and particularities . . ."

In this made-up history, Saint Nicholas played a major role in the founding of New York. According to Washington Irving, when the Dutch first arrived on the shores of the New World in the seventeenth century, Saint Nicholas was carved on the prow of their ship; he led them safely across the sea, and once they arrived, Nicholas inspired them, through a series of dreams, to build a new city on the island of Manhattan.

The story he tells is that when a party of Dutch invaders went out to find someplace suitable for their city, they camped one night in the spot now called Bowling Green. That night, a man named Oloffe had a dream: "Lo! The good Saint Nicholas came riding over the tops of the trees, in that self-same wagon wherein he brings his yearly presents to children." He drifted down to the campfire where Oloffe lay, surrounded by sleeping soldiers. "And he lit his pipe by the fire, and sat himself down and smoked; and as he smoked, the smoke from his pipe ascended into the air, and spread like a cloud overhead." The smoke from Nicholas's clay pipe drifted over the forest, and to Oloffe's amazement, formed itself into "palaces and domes and lofty spires," a phantom city of the future; then the smoke drifted off, and left nothing behind. "And when Saint Nicholas had smoked his pipe he twisted it in his hatband, and laying his finger beside his nose, gave the astonished Oloffe a very significant look, then mounting his wagon, he returned over the treetops and disappeared."

Immediately, Oloffe woke up, shook the other Dutchmen who slept around him awake, and announced that "it was the will of Saint Nicholas that they should settle down and build the city here; and that the smoke of the pipe was a type of how vast would be the extent of the city, inasmuch as the volumes of its smoke would spread over a wide extent of country." This was a joke on Irving's part: In his lifetime, the many, many fires lit in fireplaces, kilns, and smithies all over the city already made New York a smoky, smoggy place.

Saint Nicholas, therefore, is a founder of Manhattan in Irving's fantasy. The Dutch, according to Irving's *History*, built their fortress right where Oloffe had his dream, and built a church dedicated to Saint Nicholas nearby, hanging the wooden Saint Nicholas from their ship above its door.

The Saint Nicholas that Washington Irving drew was not, however, dressed as a medieval bishop. He was dressed like a seventeenth-century Dutchman, "equipped with a low, broad-brimmed hat, a huge pair of Flemish trunk-hose, and a pipe."

That fortress and that church would eventually become the city of New Amsterdam, which would eventually be renamed New York when the English took it over, and so, Irving claimed, Saint Nicholas was and would always be the patron saint of the city.

But here's the thing: None of this is true.

The seventeenth-century Dutchmen who first settled on the shores of the Lenape island of Manhattan were deeply Protestant and would never have sailed with a statue of a Catholic saint on their prow. And anyway, as we've seen, when Dutch Catholics thought about Saint Nicholas, he wasn't dressed like a merchant in a wide hat and big pants—he was dressed like a bishop. The settlers didn't build a church to him (which, as Protestants, they would have thought of as blasphemous).

In the New York of Irving's day, where saints were not generally in vogue, certain saints had become connected with certain ethnicities, even among Protestants: The English had Saint George; the Irish had Saint Patrick; the Scots had Saint Andrew; the Welsh had Saint David; the French had Saint Denis; and the Dutch, with their tradition of Saint Nicholas's Eve, had Saint Nicholas. Asserting the importance of Saint Nicholas to the city of New York was part of Irving's attempt to emphasize the city's old Dutch roots.

He referred, later in the *History*, to the old Dutch traditions, the ceremony "still religiously observed in all our ancient families of the right breed, of hanging up a stocking in the chimney on St. Nicholas Eve; which stocking is always found in the morning miraculously filled; for the good St. Nicholas has ever been a great giver of gifts, particularly to children." Irving describes him "riding jollily among the treetops, or over the roofs of houses, now and then drawing forth magnificent presents from his breeches pockets, and dropping them down the chimneys of his favorites."

This tradition was only practiced in a few old Dutch families at that point. Descendants of the English in New York tended to give presents on New Year's Eve, without any mythical being to assist.

But as Washington Irving's fantasy history of the city caught on and became wildly popular, a bestseller, people started to pay more attention to the old Saint Nicholas customs he described. It didn't hurt that many of Irving's literary friends also started to write fantasies about this half-forgotten saint in imitation, creating a whole sack full of fake myths and traditions. Parents thought the idea of giving presents on behalf of Saint Nick was cute. Toy stores started to market Saint Nicholas Day presents.

Irving's brother-in-law James Paulding wrote a *Book of Saint Nicholas* that was in many ways a rip-off of Irving's *History*, a mixture of fake facts, New York humor, holiday cheer, droll stories, ghost yarns, a nonexistent Dutch author, and, like Irving's book, attempts to make the displacement of the Lenape Indians by the Dutch settlers into something quaint and cute. In Paulding's book, Saint Nicholas is the spirit of a Dutch baker addicted to greasy, deep-fried New Year's Eve cookies. (He's born on New Year's Day.) He accidentally becomes involved in the battle between Catholics and Protestants.

Somehow this leads to his spirit wandering the streets of New York three hundred years later in a one-horse wagon, scuttling up the sides of houses and down the chimneys to deliver gifts.

Paulding's book, successful at the time, was forgotten, as were hundreds of little drawings and articles that followed Irving's book with images of a transformed Saint Nick. The one snippet from this fad that endured was a poem called "A Visit from St. Nicholas," published anonymously in the newspaper, but almost certainly written by a professor of Greek and Latin, Clement Clarke Moore. It is that poem, beginning, "'Twas the night before Christmas, when all through the house, / Not a creature was stirring, not even a mouse . . ." that fixed in people's minds the idea of flying reindeer and that gave them names, two in Dutch ("Dunder and Blixem," in the original—from a Dutch exclamation, "Thunder and lightning!"). It depicted Saint Nicholas as an "elf" with a tiny sleigh. And it was clearly based on Irving's book, since both Moore and Irving have the saint knowingly laying his finger aside of his nose before he disappears. But Paulding and Moore were just two of the host of writers and illustrators who took up the Nicholas fan-fiction fad.

Some of these writers called the saint *Sinterklaas*—a slurring together of the Dutch words *Sint Nicolaas*. In the next few decades, as people wrote more tales and drew more pictures of the saint who flew over the rooftops of New York, they spelled this name in different ways and eventually settled on *Santa Claus*.

At the time when Washington Irving wrote his *History of New York*, the United States was a very young country, barely thirty years old. It looked back across the Atlantic at the ancient nations of Europe, which could tell heroic stories of their founding that reached back a thousand or two thousand years. Part of the appeal of Irving's book and its faked histories was that it gave America a past; it gave Americans a mythology. It gave them rituals—like hanging stockings by the chimney. Quickly, New Yorkers embraced these stories as if they were true.

Santa Claus became more and more popular each year. More stories were told about him. Each story added new details. Now, in the twenty-first century, we have a very complete mythology of Santa: He dresses in red. He comes down the chimney. He rides in a sleigh pulled by eight reindeer. We even know the names of the reindeer. He's from the North Pole, where he has a workshop. None of these elements were taken from the traditional stories of the saint—they were all concocted in New York's Santa Claus craze of the nineteenth century.

At the time, polar exploration was all the rage. The North Pole was the great region of the unknown. At the end of Mary Shelley's *Frankenstein*, the monster slips away into the snows of the Arctic; Gothic horror writer Edgar Allan Poe described cosmic mysteries in the impenetrable regions of the pole. Eerie paintings of ships trapped by icebergs made New York socialites shiver. Meanwhile, real expeditions set out to chart the far north. So, in the midst of the Arctic exploration craze of the 1850s, Santa Claus's magical home migrated up from sunny Myra, up past all known latitude lines, to the North Pole, an image of cozy fires and frosty windowpanes set against the vicious winds and snows of eternal winter.

Each of these elements—the red suit, the reindeer, the paunch, the pole—came from a different source. As different writers repeated them, they became part of the lore. But the details that stuck and became canon were kind of an accident. Other stories made up about him from the same period didn't last, but could have: He could have ridden a cart instead of a sleigh, pulled through the sky (or through the streets) by a horse. He could have worn a tricornered hat, like a Revolutionary War hero. He could have worn a blue jacket. He could have worn green, like the English spirit Father Christmas. He could have worn ice skates. He could have been tiny, like an elf. He could have carried a bundle of sticks to spank bad kids. He could have appeared on New Year's Eve. He should have appeared on Saint Nicholas's Eve. Instead, Christmas gradually won out as his busy night for gift-giving. He could have been from Amsterdam. He could have been from Finland. He could have been from downtown Manhattan. These were all stories that were told about him. The shape he took was based on the accidents of who read what and what story sold best.

So as Saint Nicholas stumbled out of the nineteenth century, he found himself unfrocked from the bishops' robes that he'd worn for sixteen hundred years, stuffed in red furs, and now with a new addiction to cookies. He had been transformed in the course of a few decades. No one remembered the stories of grain ships, pickled boys, the emperor Constantine, or angry demon goddesses with bombs.

At about the same time that Irving was scribbling his fantasies of Saint Nicholas in New York, a young English architect, Charles Cockerell, decided to poke around the ruins of the saint's church in Myra. He happened to be passing by in a ship and had pulled into a cove where he had cooled off in the evening with a swim in the turquoise waters of the Lycian coast.

The place was no longer called Myra. That name had sunk in the floodwaters and mud of the fourteenth century when the river had torn through the old city. The plain that had once held one of the busiest ports in Lycia now was busy only with the metallic rasp of cicadas. It was a landscape given over to spiky bushes burning beneath the sun; lazy cows wandering through grasslands, looking for shade trees; some shepherds' huts; and a few scattered ruins, a wall or a pile of stones, recalling nothing. That was all that was left of Nicholas's city.

Apparently, the Greek crew who piloted Cockerell's ship had heard of the ancient church, and so, that evening, as the heat lifted from the hills, they all put on their Sunday best and headed inland to find the Basilica of Saint Nicholas. They had to ford a river at one point; their Sunday best got wet.

The church was only a few half-fallen domes. The rest was now beneath the earth, buried in silt. Cockerell and his crew entered through what was once an upper window—and even that window was so low they had to crawl in on their hands and knees. The Greek captain had brought an offering of holy oil, as if he was returning to the saint what once had been taken from him. When they were inside the church, where they believed the tomb to lie, the Greeks lit candles around the chamber and then knelt down and bowed their foreheads to the earth, crossing themselves. They gathered dirt from the floor to take with them as a relic of the saint's tomb.

They discovered an old Greek priest there who had declared himself the tomb's custodian. When he was young, he had almost died of some disease, and in prayer, he had promised that he would devote his life to Saint Nicholas if he was just allowed to recover. He was healed. He now squatted by the sunken church and lived, he admitted, a somewhat miserable life. In the summer, he was basically the only inhabitant of the plain. The local Turkish village, a little collection of huts, emptied out each May when it got too hot. The farmers and shepherds made their way up into the mountains, not just because of the broiling heat, but because of the swarms of gnats and mosquitoes and vicious blackflies. The old priest stayed down near his saint, alone, in the hot fields and the buzzing swamps, praying and swatting.

Young Cockerell wanted to check out the ruins of the ancient theater and the necropolis, the city of tombs. His Greek sailors deserted him. There was a lot of friction between the Greeks and the Turks—a troubled history going back to the time of the Seljuks and the Eastern Roman Empire. They didn't want to run into any Turkish villagers. They headed back to the boat.

Cockerell reached the ancient amphitheater and was struck by its beauty, even in its fallen state. In Nicholas's day, it probably held ten thousand people. Now grasses grew over its steps.

The Englishman was admiring the carvings on the old stones, the faces of gods and monsters, sorceresses and violent lovers, when a group of Turks wandered by and started to mutter about him. He overheard one growl that if the foreigners were all attracted "by these blasphemous figures, the temptation shall soon cease, for when that dog is gone I will destroy the carvings." Shortly afterward, a larger group of villagers showed up and demanded that Cockerell and his friends come with them to the court of a local magistrate to answer some questions. It would be a march on foot of six hours. Things looked bad. Luckily, when the Turks found out that Cockerell was an Englishman, their attitude changed completely. They let him go with apologies. They had assumed he was a Russian, and they were very suspicious of Russians, who they said were "plotting to take possession of the place."

This seems like paranoia, but it turns out the Turks knew exactly what they were talking about.

Cockerell slept that night near the sagging domes of the basilica. The next morning, he swam out to his boat, troubled only by a five-foot-long snake, which swam along with him. He sailed off to other distant climes and ruins.

But as western European visitors began to trickle in over the next few decades to visit the ruins of Myra, they increasingly encountered the same rumors of Russian interference.

When a Frenchman visited in the middle of the nineteenth century, he discovered a small clutch of poverty-stricken Christians living in the ruins of the monastery next to the church. They were suffering from smallpox. One of them had died of it that morning. The dead man's aunt was standing in a doorway, wailing and tearing her hair out. The Frenchman asked them about the tomb of Nicholas. They claimed at first that his body was still buried somewhere in the silt and rubbish of the church. After the Frenchman told them the old legends of the heist and the Barian pirates, they changed their story, and said that the bones had indeed been stolen—but by the Russians.

This sounds like a conspiracy theory on the part of both Turks and Greek Christians—but oddly enough, there must have been something behind it. Because in the 1850s, the Russians actually did try to buy up the church and the surrounding land with the idea of founding a Russian colony on the Mediterranean.

The Russians had felt a particular connection to Saint Nicholas since sometime around the year 1000: Their ancestors, the Rus', had converted to Christianity at a time when Nicholas's popularity as a saint in the Eastern Roman Empire was at its greatest. When the League of Saint Nicholas stole his remains in 1087, an anonymous Russian in the capital of Kyiv had been one of the first people to write down the story of the theft. (As we discussed earlier, it is not a particularly accurate account, but it is extremely enthusiastic.) It is no surprise, therefore, that they took a particular interest in Nicholas's first resting place.

In the 1850s, during the reign of Tsar Nicholas I (named after the saint), Russians quietly started to buy a lot of the land around the church and the town of Demre (formerly Myra), just as the Turkish villagers had feared decades earlier. The land was discreetly purchased under the name of a Russian countess, Anna Galicia, with the help of the Russian Consul in Rhodes. The idea was to make a Russian settlement near this holy site and on the shores of the blue Mediterranean. The details are a little unclear, because the box that contained all the documents about the purchases mysteriously disappeared while en route to the Turkish capital. We do know that a European architect, Auguste Salzmann, was hired to restore the church. Renovations were started in 1862. The church was dug out of the plain. Domes were reconstructed in dark, heavy stone. But at that point, the government of the Turkish Ottoman Empire started to take notice. They didn't want a Russian colony on their coast.

They seized the land back from the Russians and expelled Salzmann. To discourage Russian settlers, they made it illegal to repair or renovate any buildings in Demre, including the church. If there was further meddling, the Ottoman government threatened to seize all the property in Demre by eminent domain and turn the whole valley into an imperial stud farm.

So the Russian project was halted.

When a German archaeologist, Hans Rott, visited in 1903, he found that due to the restrictions on repairing buildings in Demre, half the apartments in town had collapsed, and the whole place looked pathetic. Carved marble cladding that Salzmann was going to use in the renovation was just sitting around in piles near the church. It had been sitting there for fifty years at that point.

The vaults and domes the Russians had installed were starting to collapse. Water was raining down through the roof. As Hans Rott explored the building, he had to carry an umbrella inside and wear trout-fishing waders. He sloshed around the ruins for four days, making sketches and taking photographs. He and two assistants—also in thigh-high fishing boots—held up candles on long poles to see the faint remains of paintings on the walls and domes.

There, in the flickering candlelight, they saw the fading finery of the ancient court at Constantinople, armor worn by angels, unnamed conferences of men with smoldering eyes. Glimpses of a vanished world.

What had the world learned in a millennium and a half? As we have seen, the story of just one man, Nicholas, and the fate of his dead body cannot be told without telling the stories of whole nations, emperors, wars, the rise and fall of religions, monks and newspapermen, many-breasted goddesses, men being torn apart by animals in the arena, and children whispering prayers for gingerbread at bedtime. The wars of imperial Rome might seem vain and futile. But humankind had apparently learned little since then. As Hans Rott stood there in that dripping gallery, peering up through the gloom at the paintings of Jesus Christ serving bread and wine to his Disciples, Europe was readying itself for its first World War; the empire of the Turks would soon be convulsed with horrific massacres on an unprecedented scale.

When Hans Rott was done with his work in the church, he went out with his assistants to sit on the steps of the ancient theater of Myra.

"To the north of the church," he wrote, "the old burial temples look proudly down from the rock walls into the wistful loneliness of decay, where the Lycians rest in their stone cabins in view of the roaring sea. We shake our heads in amazement at the strength of a vanished people as we sit on the highest steps of the theater, a towering mass of stone, contemplating ourselves and, like the green lizard next to us, surrendering to the radiance of the eternal sunlight."

In each part of the story of Saint Nicholas I have told, he presides over a major religious shift: the shift from Roman paganism to Christianity during his life in the fourth century, and the shift in his homeland from Christianity to Islam in the eleventh century. In this third and final part of the story, his transformation from Saint Nicholas to Santa Claus, there is one last religious shift, from Christianity to secular American consumerism.

In 1931, the Coca-Cola Company confronted a big problem:

People did not want to drink a Coke in the middle of the winter. How could a company popularize the image of an ice-cold soft drink in the frosty holiday season?

Enter advertising artist Haddon Sundblom. He painted a series of iconic ads with Santa Claus winking and sipping a Coke before work. The red and white of the suit matched the red and white of the logo. The pictures caught on. They're still occasionally recycled today, almost a hundred years later.

But businesses all over were recognizing the boon and boom of Christmas sales—an unexpected outcome for young Nicholas's act of gift-giving seventeen centuries earlier. Department stores on major city streets created festive windows that perpetuated the new Christmas mythology and drew shoppers into their doors: little scenes in which mechanical elves made mechanical toys and little mechanical children swung in circles around toy beds, preparing themselves for the coming of Claus. The Macy's Thanksgiving Day Parade was overseen by Santa Claus, resembling the religious processions in Europe where saints were carried through narrow, winding streets by believers. The parade announced the opening of an annual season of buying. Over the course of the twentieth century, retail businesses enshrined the winter holidays as one of the most important periods for sales and income, key in determining annual profits. If consumerism is a religion, then these are its high holy days: the period from Black Friday (the frenzy of sales on the day after American Thanksgiving) up until the New Year. The whole rhythm of the year for retailers is shaped by these patterns of sale and inventory, in the way that ancient Romans celebrated Saturnalia and the sequence of the seasons; the way that medieval Christians celebrated Advent and

Christmas, Lent and Easter; the way that Muslims celebrate Ramadan and Eid al-Fitr.

In 1939, an ad writer at the Montgomery Ward department store came up with a poem for a coloring book about one of Santa's misfit reindeer, Rudolph, an addition to the original eight. The store gave the coloring book away free to shoppers to get them in the doors. A few years later, the adman's brother-in-law, a songwriter, had an idea—like a light bulb—and set the rhyme to music. It became the song we all know and love, "Rudolph, the Red-Nosed Reindeer." We've forgotten it began as an ad for a department store. It seems like it has been around forever. A folk song. An ancient tradition, lost in the mists of time.

It is strange that Saint Nicholas is used to promote material consumerism in the frenzy of the holiday season. With his three sacks of gold, he was a symbol of generosity, not greed. But the season of giving is also the season of buying. It's the season of spending, of sales.

This puts the mythical Claus—or Nicholas, Nikolaos, "Victory for the People"—in an uncomfortable position. The story goes that he rewards good children with toys and bad children with coal. As we said earlier: "He knows if you've been bad or good," runs the song, "so be good, for goodness' sake." He is given the power of omniscience, like the Christian God, all knowing, with the power to judge right and wrong.

But functionally, of course, Santa's generosity is based less on your behavior than on the income of the adults around you. Some very wonderful children get very little. In this sense, Santa Claus's gifts recall the gifts of the old pagan gods: You ask them for specific things you want—a list—and the gods grant them or don't, based on your material circumstances, not on any moral reality. As a result, the wealthy are invited to see themselves as righteous and favored by the gods precisely because they are wealthy.

Saint Nicholas's generosity truly does leave a mark on the season, too, though. As it happens, the American tax year ends on December 31. This means that people who want to make charitable donations—tax-free gifts to charities—have a deadline right after Christmas. If you want a tax break, you must donate by the end of the year. This works well with the messages of goodwill and gift-giving that circulate at that time of year in carols, songs, and shows. Every year, millions and millions of dollars are given to charities in December, and so the federal tax code participates in the glory of the season every bit as much as "O Little Town of Bethlehem" or "'Twas the night before Christmas" or the ghosts scaring rich Scrooge into charity in Charles Dickens's *A Christmas Carol*.

Santa Claus's economic entanglements have made this Christian saint unpopular among some Christians, just as Protestants turned against him hundreds of years ago when they split from the Catholic Church. Every year, there are campaigns to remind people that "Jesus is the reason for the season." One Baptist pamphlet, for example, compares Santa to Jesus Christ. (Santa is omniscient; so is Christ. Santa rewards and punishes; so does Christ. Santa wears a red suit; Christ was clothed "with a vesture dipped in blood"; etc.) The pamphlet suggests Santa is trying to take Christ's place. It points out that Santa is an anagram for Satan. And it warns believers: "Friend, don't glorify Satan by giving the glory and attributes of Jesus Christ to Santa Claus! Santa is a COUNTERFEIT GOD!"

So Saint Nicholas comes full circle. He began, in the fourth century, preaching Christianity in Myra by replacing the pagan gods, replicating their functions, calling them counterfeit. Now, in the twenty-first century, he is accused of being a vain idol who replaces the Christian God, point for point.

But as the patron saint of consumerism, he is not going away. The stories tell us that he circles the whole world in his sleigh. In a sense, that is true: Wherever the spirit of consumerism spreads, Santa Claus appears nowadays, even in countries with little history of Christianity. Decals of him stand next to mall Christmas trees in China and Japan; plastic inflatables bake in the desert sun. He invites the world to spend.

But I don't want to end this story with Santa Claus. In some ways, Santa Claus has stolen away Saint Nicholas in his sack and sleigh even more deviously than the Barians or the Venetians ever did.

Every year, thousands of people make a pilgrimage to Lycia, where the historical Saint Nicholas lived. They drive down along the coast, through the forests of the Taurus Mountains. The sunlight slants through passes. Down in the foothills and the fertile lowlands, there are orchards, olive groves, gardens.

Myra disappeared long ago beneath the apartment blocks of Demre. The Church of Saint Nicholas has been dug out of its silt—though it still stands a couple of stories below the level of the street. A statue of Nicholas, severe and clothed in his bishop's robes, has been replaced by one of a cheerier, secular Santa Claus, or as he is called in Turkish, Noël Baba.

The church compound itself is still being excavated. Its story is not yet fully told.

Inside the church, you can still see the remains of frescos on the wall, painted long ago, in the time of the Eastern Roman Empire. The church is more bare than it would have looked when the Barian pirates burst in. Much of it is simple stone and plaster, the dark domes restored by the Russians and by recent structural work. But still, there are saints on some walls, their eyes blank now as the paint has faded and the plaster has fallen off.

Russians brought in on buses wander through the arches. They gather to pray by one of the shattered sarcophagi. It is not, as it happens, one that anyone really believes could have been Nicholas's: It has a Roman couple on its lid, lying side by side. But it has been marked as holy by tourists, and so it is protected by plexiglass.

The pilgrims gather around it, reaching out to touch the plastic. Clothed in shorts and Crocs and holding up iPhones, they sing chants in an ancient language—*O Nikolai!*—resonant voices swelling in the empty stone chambers where dogs sleep to keep out of the sun. They press close to the tomb, believing they touch the majesty of the supernatural. Mothers push their children's faces up against the plexiglass for blessings.

What is important is not what they touch, but the power of human desire. The cry for safety, for prosperity, for love.

And across the Aegean and Mediterranean and Adriatic, there stands the Basilica of Saint Nicholas in Bari, where the bones were taken. Every year on the anniversary of the arrival of the League of Saint Nicholas in the city, May 9, the Feast of the Translation, there are great ceremonies that take place all over the city. A boat brings a statue of Saint Nicholas, bobbing, up from San Giorgio. He is carried through the streets while crowds of thousands follow him.

Down in the crypt beneath the church, hundreds gather in the grove of pillars to watch a priest kneel before the altar, open the grating on the front, and crawl in, his robed legs hanging out behind him. He slides the metal plate aside from Saint Nicholas's resting place. It is a strangely awkward act, this reverence of mortal for the immortal. He lowers down a crystal flask, an ampulla, and draws up the holy manna, about three and a half tablespoons' worth of pure and sparkling water. As he holds it up for the congregation, everyone applauds, and bells ring out above the city's square; believers line up to kiss the bottle.

I asked Father Cioffari, the historian who is a monk in the Dominican order that was assigned in the 1950s to protect the relics of Nicholas, "Why don't you have the bones on display in the altar?" Usually, bones are visible in a reliquary.

He gave a sly little smile. "Do I want another theft?" he asked.

When it is not a festival day, the crypt is quiet. Each morning, townspeople from Bari still come on the way to work to pray to their town's saint, the saint their city stole. Visitors come from all over the world. Some of them just take photos. Some of them kneel in front of his tomb, weeping silently in private prayer.

We are earthbound creatures who want so much of Heaven.

In the course of this story, we have followed this saint backward through time. We have sorted his fragments as carefully as a forensic biologist in a darkened church at midnight with only a few hours to work. Laying out these broken pieces, we have tried to make the outline of a human we might know, though so much is missing, stolen, or turned to dust. History, remember, is not the events that have happened in the past, but the investigation into those events.

So what can we learn by looking at this bizarre life, the life of Saint Nicholas of Myra—a life that extends seventeen hundred years beyond his death?

He was remembered because he was generous and just; he gave himself to a city, and they gave back, telling impossible stories about him, granting him the power to fly through the air and calm the waves. His name survived because he was part of a community he loved.

How will we be remembered in a hundred, in two hundred years? How will those who knew us—or who knew those who knew us—fit together the pieces and make a story about who we were? What will your children and grandchildren say about you? After our deaths, how will any of us be known? What will remain?

Saint Nicholas may not have performed the miracles ascribed to him—but he transformed every place he inhabited, alive or dead. He made Myra a place of prayer and reverence for a thousand years. He gave Bari hope in a time of oppression, when they were strangled by their Norman overlords. He gave New York new rituals, new reasons for families to perform strange rites together (hanging socks near a heat source; hiding fruit in socks; leaving out baked goods as an offering for an invisible visitor). His odd stories gave people reasons to celebrate and to consider kindness when, generation after generation, the poison of our worst nature led us to conquer, to kill, to end the stories of others forever. He encouraged us to give, but also to see wonders around us in the air.

One of the great joys of human life is these stories we tell about each other and the places we live. If we will listen to each other, we will discover we already live in a land of wonders, as fabulous as Lycia with its gods and goddesses, its peasants transformed into frogs, its fire-breathing chimera. In the small American town in the hills where I live, there is a church where a whole congregation decided that time was going to end on a particular night in the 1840s, and they gathered with a grandfather clock to watch the final minutes tick down. (It was awkward when the world went on.) There is a house supposedly haunted by a ghost with a rubber nose, as his real nose was eaten by a horse. Do I believe these things? It doesn't really matter: Telling these stories between neighbors makes us all feel like we live together and our place is interesting and is someplace we want to be—a community. There is nothing special about this town, and yet, asking questions, we discover surprises everywhere.

Look at the place you live. What are its stories of miracles? What are its strange tales? What do they really tell you about the people who once lived there? What are its histories? What are its hidden stories of cruelty that must be told if old wrongs are to be righted? What are its hidden stories of triumph? What are the things that give you hope for that place in the future? What do you wish it could become?

If we would all listen to the stories of others, there would be fewer senseless massacres, fewer bloody and incompetent Crusades, fewer tyrants who could hold power through lies and fear. Perhaps, in that sense, the miraculous can save us after all, appearing like the saint in the storm-tossed boat, raising his arms, and causing the waves, just for a while, to cease before we capsize.

Seventeen hundred years ago, there was a boy named Nikolaos, "Victory for the People," and he stood upon the shore in Patara, and he looked out to sea. He vowed to be useful and good.

His city was devoted to prophecies of the future through the dreams of Apollo; but how could the boy have foretold in any dream that his name would spread beyond those seas and around the world? How could he have dreamed that his body would be stolen? How could he have dreamed of all that would follow for him: the gifts, the songs, the reindeer, the hat, the rise of nations, new religions, the fall of old gods, impossible technologies that speak through the air, his face on plastic and tin? How could he understand the ebb and flow of future economies, a world inhabited by many billions, and that he would be asked to fly around it in one night in a sleigh, tossing incomprehensible gifts down to people with the powers of flight and of healing, people with the powers of gods?

Think of him there, standing on that shore, and then think of yourself, and what unimaginable destiny awaits you.

Will you rise to greet it?

APPENDIX: THE EVIDENCE OF THE CRIME SCENE IN MYRA

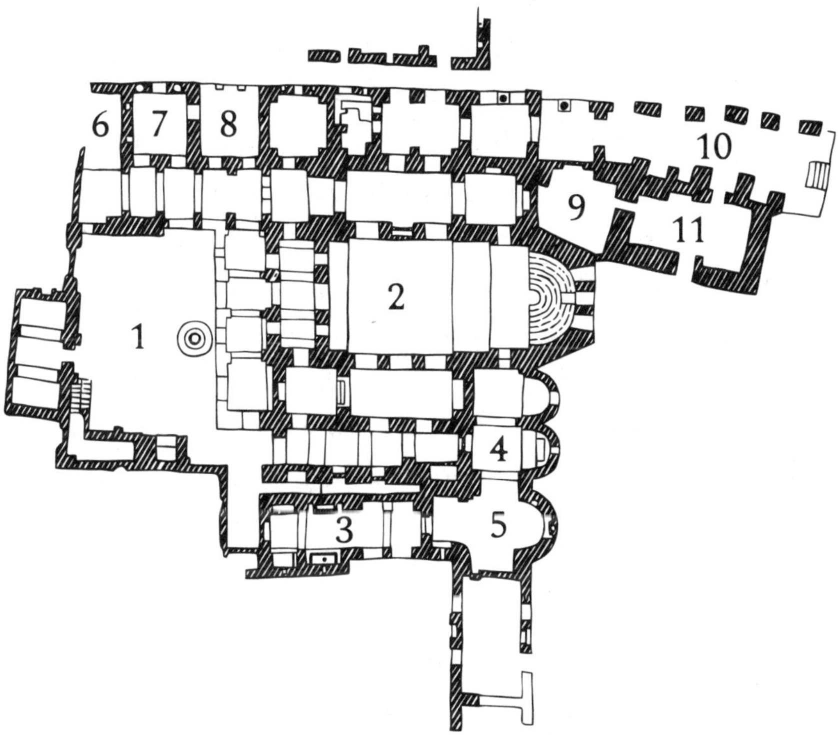

The scene of the crime: a map of the Basilica of Saint Nicholas in Myra, as the ruins stand today. Where in this ancient church was Saint Nicholas's body hidden? Archaeologists have discovered many clues, and there are several theories.

First, let's stroll around the church. You would probably come in through the courtyard (1). By the time of the heists, the whole church complex was surrounded by a protective wall. Inside the wall were a mansion for the bishop, a monastery connected with the church, and various other practical outbuildings. You would walk across the courtyard past a fountain, where you could pause to wash yourself off and where baptisms may have taken place to welcome new believers into the church. Then you would pass in through the main doors of the church and through an entrance hall into the naos, or sanctuary (2), which would have been beautifully decorated with wall-paintings and mosaics, glittering with oil lamps hung from chains. The only thing that remains of this rich ornamentation are some of the floors, which combine different shades of stone and marble to create kaleidoscopic designs. At the far end of the sanctuary you would have seen a series of amphitheater steps where the priests would have stood while performing their rituals. In front of those steps would have been an altar. This church, like many Christian churches, is oriented toward the east, where Paradise was supposed to lie—where the sun rose, resurrected, every morning. Though the sanctuary is barren now, it would have been full of vivid color in 1087.

So where would you have gone to look for Saint Nicholas's body?

Modern German archaeologists have concentrated their search for his tomb in the southern passages and side chapels (3, 4, 5). There's good reason to believe he was connected with that part of the church at some point. For one thing, in a funeral corridor with several sarcophagi (3), there are murals showing scenes of his life and miracles. It would make sense that pilgrims might have circulated through this passage on the way to pray in the saint's chapel. The delicate inlaid floor of one of those chapels has been savagely attacked and clumsily repaired with big slabs of stone. Maybe this was a place where the Barians or the Venetians broke through the floor in their search for the sarcophagus. One of the other clues that this might have been the spot is its similarity to the design of other churches around the Mediterranean. One German archaeologist has pointed out that in other churches in Lycia, there was often a burial chapel to the south of the sanctuary, just like these side chapels, where a martyr's body could be worshipped. Could the layout of the Nicholas basilica actually have been the model for these other, smaller, local churches?

A lot of recent work by a Turkish archaeological team, however, has concentrated on a different area of the basilica, a complex of rooms to the north of the sanctuary. Several of those rooms (6, 7, 8) may be the assembly line where the myron, the miraculous oil, was manufactured and ritually blessed—they include not only chemical traces of oil and myrrh in their soil, but also fragments of plumbing and a basin possibly used for pressing olives.

It is likely that at least for a time, Nicholas was buried in the rooms to the east of the sacred oil factory. The chamber labeled 9 is the prime location. It is domed, which suggests a special use, and it has a special cross above the door, one that seems to mark that you're about to enter a sacred space. Its floor also contains traces of olive oil—and most importantly, the flooring in this room was clearly torn up by human hands at some point. This also could have been the floor that was vandalized by the Barians or the Venetians. There is evidence of a fancy sacred gate, thin pillars with a decorated metal grate, which would have kept eager pilgrims at a distance from the tomb. (The altar and burial chamber at the church in Bari where Nicholas now rests are arranged similarly.)

If the Turkish team is right and the body lay here at one time, then the rooms around it were probably designed to deal with the pilgrim traffic. Room 10, for example, might have been a room where pilgrims listened to sermons. There was a platform for a speaker, and at some point, someone dragged some stadium seating from the ruined theater to this room so there was a place for people to sit. Chambers 10 and 11 might have been places where pilgrims rested and prayed. There was a belief that sleeping near the sanctified corpse of a beloved saint could bring about miraculous healing. Visitors may have slumbered here, hoping for a cure in the night.

So looking through all this evidence, where was the body? Where did the guardians of the relics draw out the myron? Where did the Barians find the sarcophagus? And where did the Venetians dig? We still don't know—and we don't even know how far we can trust the written sources. Both John the Archdeacon and Nicephorus insist that the body was buried in a sarcophagus that was under a layer of concrete under the floor. The sources also agree that it wasn't immediately obvious where the saint was buried, which is surprising. The archaeological evidence suggests that the likely spots for the tomb were surrounded by pillars and fancy metal grilles that would have made it very obvious where the saint reposed.

But we should also remember that the body might have been moved over the centuries as the church itself was damaged, rebuilt, and renovated. It could, therefore, have been in more than one location during the basilica's long history. And we should remember that the Venetians were apparently not digging in the same spot as the Barians. As we try to archaeologically reconstruct the thefts of the late eleventh century, we should be looking for two separate areas where the floor was disturbed and later repaired. Unfortunately, unlike other tombs of myroblyte saints, there would be no telltale holes used to access the blessed bodies: The Barians expressly destroyed whatever flooring lay above the tomb. Further confusing the question of the function of these various worship spaces is the fact that Saint Nicholas's corpse was not the only set of relics in the basilica. The bodies of Saint Theodore and Saint Nicholas the Uncle were also revered there and may have been housed in one of these chapels. Finally, if the Anonymous Monk of Lido wasn't lying about the Venetian heist, there still would have been relics left behind after their expedition: not just the broken casket, not just the remaining myron, not just the holy icon of the saint, but a reasonable helping of bone fragments from Nicholas's rib cage and pelvis, crushed under Matteo's knees as he fumbled around in the bath of oil. These items also could have been enshrined in some of the more richly decorated ritual spaces when the church was repaired after the Venetian assault. We know that pilgrims continued to come and pray at this basilica in the years following the thefts of 1087 and 1100.

So you're welcome to form your own opinion.

Right now, at the moment, we don't have a definitive answer for where Nicholas lay in 1087 or where the Venetians hacked away at the floor in 1100—but archaeological digs are going on in the church even as this book is being written. In a few years, we may have more clues—and more answers.

AUTHOR'S NOTE

I have been fascinated with stories of Saint Nicholas since I myself was a teenager. I was a huge music fan, and when I was in college, I ran across several classical pieces that told the strange stories of Nicholas the Wonder-Worker: Benjamin Britten's cantata *Saint Nicholas*, written specifically for school choirs and orchestras, and the four twelfth-century monastic "operas" that I mentioned in the text, the Fleury plays, which are all set to very haunting ancient melodies. Here were stories of Saint Nicholas I'd never heard before: bringing murdered kids back to life, throwing bags of gold through the windows of the house next door to save the daughters from prostitution, carrying a kid through the air by the hair to save him from slavery at the court of a despot. Here was a dynamic and surprising hero. These were things I thought could somehow be turned into a book someday.

Many years later, I idly decided to find out more about this bizarre alternative Santa Claus, and I eventually stumbled upon the most important book in English on Claus lore, Charles W. Jones's compendious, if exasperating, *Saint Nicholas of Myra, Bari, and Manhattan*. It was in reading this book that I discovered that a group of thieves had broken into Santa Claus's tomb to steal his body because it supposedly drooled a healing elixir. Now, *there* was a story.

I started to think about ways I could transform that story into a historical novel. In 2022, I had the chance to go to southern Turkey, to Demre, the town where Nicholas's basilica stood. The haunting beauty of the place and the landscape of Lycia inspired me. When I got home, I spent the next several months writing my historical novel for adults about the theft of the relics, a book that was eventually called *Nicked* (Pantheon, 2024). Of course, in that book, I changed many facts, because I was consciously trying to write a swashbuckling heist novel. I used details from several of the different "translation" narratives: Nicephorus's, John the Archdeacon's, the Anonymous Monk of Lido's, and even bits of the sunnier, more optimistic Russian version, the *Kyiv Slovo*, from which I took the idea that the whole expedition had been inspired by a dream.

The thing was, most of John the Archdeacon's text had never been translated into English. None of the Anonymous Monk of Lido's text had been. As a result, surprisingly little attention had been paid to what they actually claimed had happened during the theft of the body. As I was writing my novel, I found the original Latin texts of those accounts and commissioned English translations of both of them. (John the Archdeacon's account of the Barian heist was translated by Nicky Bangs, and the Anonymous Monk of Lido's Venetian account was translated by Dr. Thomas Moody.)

What I found when I read these heretofore untranslated accounts astounded me. There were so many details that had been overlooked! In many cases, it was too late to use these revelations in my novel, which at this point was basically written. They told a very different story than the one I had told, even if you overlooked all the Hollywood details I'd made up for my book. For example, they provided much more detail about the Turkish occupation of Myra and what that might have been like—and also, I discovered that the Venetian expedition had been completely mischaracterized. No one had talked about the anonymous monk's fused masses of glass, tar, bone, and charcoal. No one had paid attention to his claim that his sailors had not simply picked up whatever shards and fragments the Barian hooligan Matteo had left behind in the sarcophagus, but had dug up bone fragments in an inaccessible stratum under the church floor.

All of this suggested a very different story every bit as good as the one in my historical novel. I felt that the full story should to be told—but that there actually wouldn't be much overlap with my fictionalized version, because there was so much new detail to chew on.

So this book was born.

I have sought to sort out fact from fiction, dispel medieval myths, and pin down what's folklore and speculation. But what I have done here is no different than what those previous hagiographers, Symeon the Metaphrast and Michael the Archimandrite, did: retelling the anecdotes from old texts, recombining them, and as I did so, bending them, I'm sure, to my will. Each of us in turn thought we were writing the truth. But does anyone really believe that the last word on Saint Nicholas has been written here by me, M. T. the Fabulist, whose very initials seem to suggest a dispiriting void? For which, of course, in true medieval fashion, I bow farewell to you, beg you to forgive me my excesses, and to pray, as relevant, for my soul.

A FEW BIBLIOGRAPHIC NOTES

Given that almost all the quotations are translations from ancient sources, I have occasionally silently edited them for length and clarity, aiming for maximum transparency of language.

If some of the endnotes are unusually detailed, it is because there has not yet been another sustained attempt to bring together into one single narrative (1) the written *translatio* accounts, (2) the archaeological evidence from the church in Myra, and (3) the forensic evidence of the relics in Venice and Bari. The notes are therefore necessary to explain some of my own conclusions and deductions. (For those interested in exploring deeper, the notes contain some intriguing nuggets—call them Easter eggs—for which there wasn't room in the main text.) Still, not all of the mysteries can yet be solved. At the moment, Turkish archaeological teams are working on the Myra site, and I suspect that in a few years, they'll provide a few answers to some of these lingering questions.

I should say that no research on Saint Nicholas would be possible without the lifelong efforts and many profoundly thoughtful publications of Father Gerardo Cioffari. My deepest thanks to him for meeting with a random pilgrim and talking about his work. I am not the only scholar to be impressed by his wisdom, generosity, and kindness.

An indispensable online aid for those with even a passing interest in the Santa Claus story is the St. Nicholas Center site (stnicholascenter.org), which brings together an astounding array of materials for kids and adults: holiday games and songs and traditional tales from around the world, recipes, costume suggestions, icons, historical doodads, articles on archaeological finds, and yet also complete scholarly translations of several of the most important classical and medieval sources used for this book.

For those who want to read a more detailed attempt to arrive at a credible biography of Nicholas himself, I suggest Adam C. English's *The Saint Who Would Be Santa Claus: The True Life and Trials of Nicholas of Myra*.

Huge thanks to my two *translatio* translators of the accounts of John the Archdeacon (Nicky Bangs) and the Anonymous Monk of Lido (Dr. Thomas Moody). Thanks also to Dr. Angelique Corthals, Dr. Lauren Mancia, Nicole Griffin, Tina Wu, Bilge Usta, and, of course, Dr. Erin Thompson, all of whom discussed aspects of this book with me and, in the last three cases, accompanied me to the sites where the action takes place. Thanks especially to Dr. Thompson for translating Italian for me and listening to far more speculation about Anatolian burial practices than any human should have to endure. I'm grateful for all our explorations into antiquity.

Many of the sources used in this book—even the very obscure ones—are now available for free online through sites like Project Gutenberg (www.gutenberg.org), the Internet Archive (archive.org), Academia.edu, or the Fordham University Internet History Sourcebooks Project (sourcebooks.fordham.edu), and, as mentioned above, the St. Nicholas Center's website (stnicholascenter.org).

The primary documents that make up the story of the heists are the three translation accounts of Nicephorus, John the Archdeacon, and the Anonymous Monk of Lido. The full list of accounts of the Barese and Venetian expeditions to Myra is as follows:

- Nicephorus (c. 1087–89). Translated by Charles W. Jones, in *Saint Nicholas of Myra, Bari, and Manhattan*. Chicago: University of Chicago, 1988: pp. 176–193. In a slightly altered form, this translation is online at https://www.stnicholascenter.org/who-is-st-nicholas/stories-legends/classic-sources/translation-i.

- John the Archdeacon (c. 1087–89). Translated by Nicky Bangs. Online at https://mtanderson.com/nicholas-translations.

- Anonymous Monk of Lido (c. 1101-1115). Translated by Thomas W. Moody. Online at https://mtanderson.com/nicholas-translations.

- Anonymous Russian account: *Kyiv Slovo* (c. 1095). Translated by Fr. Gerardo Cioffari, in "The Ancient Russian Story on the Translation of St. Nicholas's Relics from Myra to Bari," *St. Nicholas News* 67 (May 24, 2014).

- Orderic Vitalis (1120–1140), based on John the Archdeacon. Translated by M. T. Anderson. Online at https://mtanderson.com/nicholas-translations.

- Anonymous Greek account (13th century), based on Nicephorus. Translated by J. McGinley and H. Mursurillo. Online at https://sourcebooks.fordham.edu/basis/nicholas-bari.asp.

For photographs of many of the sites featured in this book, visit https://mtanderson.com/nicholas-translations.

WORKS CITED

Akyürek, T. Engin. "Andriake: The Port of Myra in Late Antiquity." In *Trade in Byzantium: Papers from the Third International Sevgi Gönül Byzantine Studies Symposium*, eds. Paul Magdalino et al. Istanbul: ANAMED, 2016, pp. 465–487.

Akyürek, T. Engin, and Koray Durak, eds. *Bizans Dönemi'nde Anadolu [Anatolia in the Byzantine Period]*. Istanbul: Tüpraş, 2021.

Akyürek, T. Engin. "Myra, the City of St. Nicholas." In *En Orient et en Occident: le culte de saint Nicolas en Europe, Xe—XXIe siècle*, ed. Véronique Gazeau, Catherine Guyon, and Catherine Vincent. Paris: Éditions du Cerf, 2015: pp. 21–37.

Albrecht, Otto. *Four Latin Plays of St. Nicholas: From the 12th Century Fleury Playbook*. Philadelphia: University of Pennsylvania Press, 1935.

Alpaslan, Sema. "Demre'deki H. Nikolaos Kilisesi Liturjik Mekanlari." *Hacettepe Üniversitesi Edebiyat Fakültesi Dergisi*, vol. 15, no. 1: pp. 159–173.

Anichkof, Eugene. "St. Nicholas and Artemis." *Folk-Lore* V (1894): pp. 108–120.

Baker, G. P. *Constantine the Great and the Christian Revolution [1930]*. New York: Cooper Square Press, 2001.

Beihammer, Alexander, *Byzantium and the Emergence of Muslim-Turkish Anatolia, c. 1040–1130*. London: Routledge, 2017.

Bellomo, Elena. "The First Crusade and the Latin East as seen from Venice: The Account of the *Translatio sancti Nicolai*," *Early Medieval Europe*, 17 (2008): pp. 420–443.

Borchhardt, Jürgen, ed. *Myra: Eine Lykische Metropole in antiker und byzantinischer Zeit*. Berlin: Gebr. Mann, 1975.

Bremmer, Jan N. "The Vision of Constantine." In *Land of Dreams: Greek and Latin Studies in Honor of A. H. M. Kessels*, eds. A. P. M. H. Lardinois et al. Leiden: Brill, 2006: pp. 57–79.

de Ceglia, Francesco Paolo. "The Science of Santa Claus: Discussions on the Manna of Nicholas of Myra in the Modern Age." *Nuncius* 27 (2012): pp. 241–269.

Çevik, Nevzat. "Myra: The Hidden Metropolis of Lycia." *Actual Archaeology Magazine*, no. 19 (2017): pp. 39–51.

Cioffari, Gerardo. *The Basilica of St. Nicholas: A Short Historical and Artistic Guide.* Bari: Patricinio di San Nicola Basilica, undated.

Cioffari, Gerardo. "Giovanni arcidiacono: l'Historia translationis sancti Nicolai nell'Europa medievale," in *Nicolaus: Studi Storici*, issue 42/43, vol. XXII (2011): pp. 43–71.

Cioffari, Gerardo. *Saint Nicholas: His life, miracles, and legends.* Translated by Victoria Sportelli. Bari, Italy: Centro Studi Nicolaiani, 2008.

Cioffari, Gerardo. *Saint Nicholas: His Life, the Translation of His Relics, and His Basilica in Bari.* Translated by Philip L. Barnes. Bari, Italy: Centro Studi Nicolaiani, 1994.

Cioffari, Gerardo. *La traslazione di San Nicola da Mira a Bari nel 1087.* Bari: Basilica San Nicola Editore, 2021.

Cockerell, Charles. *Travels in Southern Europe and the Levant, 1810–1817.* London: Longmans, Green, and Co., 1903.

Çorağan, Nilay. "The Wall Paintings of St. Nicholas Church in Demre (Myra). Recent Discoveries 1999." In *Annali di Ca'Foscari Rivista della Facolta di Lingue e Letterature Straniere dell'Universita ca'Foscari di Venezia*, no. 38, vol. 3 (1999): pp. 87–94.

D'Andria, Francesco. "The Sanctuary of St. Philip in Hierapolis and the tombs of saints in Anatolian cities." In *Life and Death in Asia Minor in Hellenistic, Roman, and Byzantine Times: Studies in Archaeology and Bioarchaeology*, eds. J. R. Brandt et al. Oxford, UK: Oxbow Books, 2017.

D'Andria, Francesco. "Il Santuario e la Tomba dell'Apostolo Filippo a Hierapolis di Frigia." *Rendiconti della Pontificia Accademia Romana di Archeologia*, LXXXIV (2011–2012): pp. 1–52.

Doğan, Sema, and Ebru Fatma Findik. *Aziz Nikolaos Kilisesi Kazilari, 1989–2009.* Istanbul: Homer Kitabevi, 2018.

English, Adam C. *The Saint Who Would Be Santa Claus: The True Life and Trials of Nicholas of Myra.* Waco, TX: Baylor University Press, 2012.

Eusebius of Caesarea. "Ecclesiastical History." Translated by Arthur Cushman McGiffert. *The Delphi Collected Works of Eusebius.* Delphi Classics, 2019.

Fellows, Charles. *An Account of Discoveries in Lycia, Being a Journal Kept During a Second Excursion in Asia Minor.* London: John Murray, 1841.

Foss, Clive. "The Lycian Coast in the Byzantine Age." *Dumbarton Oaks Papers*, vol. 48 (1994), pp. 1–52.

Fredell, Joel. "The Three Clerks and St. Nicholas in Medieval England." *Studies in Philology*, vol. 92, no. 2 (Spring 1995): pp. 181–202.

Geary, Patrick J. *Furta Sacra: Thefts of Relics in the Central Middle Ages.* Princeton, NJ: Princeton University Press, 1978.

Grant, Alasdair C. "Byzantium's Ashes and the Bones of St. Nicholas: Two Translations as Turning Points, 1087–1100." *Trends and Turning Points: Constructing the Late Antique and Byzantine World*, eds. Matthew Kinloch and Alex MacFarlane. Brill, 2019.

Hayes, Dawn Marie. "The Cult of St. Nicholas of Myra in Norman Bari, c. 1071—c. 1111." *The Journal of Ecclesiastical History*, vol. 67 (2016): pp. 492–512.

Irving, Washington. *Knickerbocker's History of New York* [rev. 1848]. Chicago: W. B. Conkey Company, undated.

John the Deacon. *The Life of St. Nicholas of Myra* [c. 880 AD]. Translated by Roger Pearse. Online at https://www.stnicholascenter.org/who-is-st-nicholas/stories-legends/classic-sources/john-the-deacon-ca-880.

Jones, Charles Williams. *Saint Nicholas of Myra, Bari, and Manhattan: Biography of a Legend.* Chicago: U. of Chicago Press, 1988.

Jones, Charles Williams. *The Saint Nicholas Liturgy and Its Literary Relationships.* Berkeley: Univeristy of California Press, 1963.

Jordan, Paul. *The Seven Wonders of the Ancient World.* London: Routledge, 2002.

Lactantius, Lucius Caecilius Firmianus. *On the Deaths of the Persecutors.* Translated by David Dalrymple. Merchantville, NJ: Evolution Publishing, 2021.

LiDonnici, Lynn R. "The Images of Artemis Ephesia and Greco-Roman Worship: A Reconsideration." *Harvard Theological Review*, vol. 85, no. 4 (Oct. 1992): pp. 389–415.

Martino, Luigi. *Le reliquie di S. Nicola: Studio anatomo-antropologico dei resti scheletrici rinvenuti nella sua tomba in Bari.* Bari: Biblioteca di San Nicola, 1987.

Martino, Luigi. "St. Nicholas: The Great Adventure (The Story of a Man and His Remains)." Conference address, 1994. Text online at https://www.stnicholascenter.org/who-is-st-nicholas/real-face/a-history-of-the-anatomical-investigations.

Michael the Archimandrite. *Life of Saint Nicholas the Wonderworker.* Translated by John Quinn and Roger Pearse. Online at https://www.stnicholascenter.org/who-is-st-nicholas/stories-legends/classic-sources/michael-the-archimandrite.

Mougoyianni, Penelope. "Confrontation and Interchange between Byzantines and Normans in Southern Italy: the Cases of Nicholas of Myra and St. Nicholas the Pilgrim at the End of the 11th Century," in *Byzantium in Dialogue with the Mediterranean: History and Heritage.* Edited by Danielle Slootjes and Mariette Verhoeven. *The Medieval Mediterranean*, vol. 116. Leiden; Boston: Brill, 2019: pp. 109–141.

Niewöhner, Philipp. "Neues zum Grab des Hl. Nikolaus von Myra." *Jahrbuch für Antike und Christentum* 46 (2003): pp. 119–134.

Niewöhner, Philipp. "The Tomb of St. Nicholas." In *Anatolia in the Byzantine Period*, eds. Engin Akyürek and Koray Durak. Istanbul: Yapi Kredi Yayinlari/Tüpraş, 2021: pp. 188–203.

Ötüken, S. Yildiz, and Eda Armağan. "Excavations at the Church of St. Nicholas in Myra-Demre and the Conservation-Restoration and Documentation of the Wall Paintings in 2005." *Adalya* 8 (January 2005): pp. 263–285.

Özgür, M. Edip. *The Church of St. Nicholas in Myra and Environs: Andriace, Teimiussa (Ucagiz), Simena (Kale), Kekova.* Ankara: Dönmez Ofset, 2010.

Renz, Frederick, dir. *The Play of St. Nicholas: A 12th Century Liturgical Drama.* New York Ensemble for Early Music. Musical Heritage Society 523 742L. Recorded in 1981.

Roche, Jason T. "In the Wake of Mantzikert: The First Crusade and the Alexian Reconquest of Western Anatolia." *History*, vol. 94, no. 2 (314), April 2009: pp. 135–153.

Rogers, Guy MacLean. *The Mysteries of Artemis of Ephesos: Cult, Polis, and Change in the Graeco-Roman World.* New Haven, CT: Yale University Press, 2012.

Rott, Hans. *Kleinasiatische Denkmäler aus Pisidien, Pamphylien, Kappadokien, und Lykien.* Leipzig, 1908.

Ševčenko, Ihor, and Nancy P. Ševčenko, translators. *The Life of Saint Nicholas of Sion.* Brookline, MA: Hellenic College Press, 1984.

Ševčenko, Nancy P. *The Life of Saint Nicholas in Byzantine Art.* Turin: Bottego d'Erasmo, 1983.

de Voragine, Jacobus. *The Golden Legend.* Translated by Christopher Stace. London: Penguin, 1998.

Wace. *The Hagiographical Works: The* Conception Nostre Dame *and the Lives of St Margaret and St Nicholas.* Translated and edited by Jean Blacker, Glyn S. Burgess, and Amy V. Ogden. Boston: Brill, 2013.

Weiss, Peter. "The Vision of Constantine." *Journal of Roman Archaeology*, vol. 16 (2003): pp. 237–259.

Yazici, Erdal. *A Monument in Lycia: The Church of Saint Nicholas in Myra.* Istanbul: Uranus, 2019.

Yazici, Erdal. *On the Lycian Way: From Fethiye to Antalya.* Istanbul: Uranus, 2021.

NOTES

7 300 AD. . . . : I have used the abbreviations BC ("Before Christ") and AD ("Anno Domini," Year of Our Lord) instead of the more modern designations CE ("Common Era") and BCE ("Before Common Era"). This is intentional: In this story, the distance in time of events from the lifetime of Jesus Christ is highly relevant. For the people in this book, whether they were saints, soldiers, or thieves, that legendary date around the year 1 was pivotal. Their sense of history was structured by the procession of Biblical epochs. In this context, describing the growth and metamorphosis of early Christianity, the more modern designations CE and BCE just seem evasive.

11 The port city of . . . : See Foss, pp. 14–16.

11 a couple of lower legs . . . : According to the ancient geographer Strabo, an "earthquake broke the figure off at the knees and no attempt was made to restore it, in accordance with a warning oracle" (Jordan, pg. 26).

12 reputedly also the birthplace . . . : Legend ascribed the birthplace to several spots, most notably the island of Delos and the Anatolian city of Ephesus, up the coast. Tourist placards in the ruins of Patara, however, claim that the birth happened in an anomalous palm grove right near the city's Roman baths.

12 Their cults may have . . . : The story of the twin births of Apollo and Artemis on the Anatolian coast is generally considered to be a mythologized memory of their cult origins in the region. It is widely assumed that Artemis was a local fertility deity who became associated with the Roman goddess Diana. There is similarly evidence that Apollo may have been an Anatolian god who was absorbed into the pantheon of international paganism. See, for example, Edwin E. Brown, "In Search of Anatolian Apollo": *Hesperia Supplements*, vol. 33 (2004): pp. 243–257.

12 That was where Apollo supposedly . . . : Apollo in his local aspects was called Apollo Patareus (the Apollo of Patara) and Apollo Lykegenes (the Lycian-born Apollo). Yazici, *Lycian Way*, pg. 144; Cioffari, *Translation*, pg. 18.

13 Her followers said . . . : Jordan, pg. 93, for example; but see C. C. Wylie and J. R. Naiden, "The Image which Fell Down from Jupiter." *Popular Astronomy*, vol. 44 (1936): pp. 514–519.

13 Despite the fact that many Anatolian Artemis Ephesia statues quite clearly have multiple breasts—and they were called breasts by writers of late antiquity—this apparently makes some modern commentators uncomfortable, and there has recently been quite a lot of argument about whether they are actually supposed to be breasts at all. Several (male) archaeologists have doubled down and suggested that they are, believe it or not, bulls' scrota. The argument is that bulls were sacrificed to Artemis, and perhaps they were first castrated and the scrota were hung on the statue. There is no firm evidence of this practice, yet the theory (first floated by Gérard Seiterle) has gained real traction.

Lynn LiDonnici has written an excellent article in the *Harvard*

Theological Review suggesting that the popularity of the scrotum theory of Artemis Ephesia might have less to do with ancient Greco-Roman religious practice than with the way twentieth-century archaeologists understand breasts. She, for example, takes issue with the argument by one historian that these could not possibly be breasts because they are too inelegant for classical statuary: that no Greco-Roman sculptor would depict breasts as such "ugly, udder-like bags." As LiDonnici points out, udders are, well, breasts. The breasts of a nurturing mother. This may suggest more about the modern viewer's aversion to noneroticized breasts than any understanding of the votive purpose of this statue in the ancient world. We might add that if the bulges do not look like breasts, they certainly don't look like bulls' scrota.

Regardless of how those bulges originated, by the time Nicholas was born (c. 260), they were understood to be breasts. The goddess is referred to in contemporary sources as "many-breasted Artemis" (LiDonnici, pg. 392), and this is presumably how Nicholas himself understood them.

13 Supposedly, his family was rich . . . : Michael the Archimandrite (henceforward, "Michael"), chap. 3.

14 It is a heroic name . . . : Michael, chap. 3.

15 Right around the time of Nicholas's birth . . . : Most notably, Saints Paregorius and Leo. Mark Wilson, in Doğan, "Jews and Christians in Ancient Lycia: A Fresh Appraisal" pg. 21.

15 On the days when Christians . . . : Symeon the Metaphrast, in Jones, *Myra*, pg. 50; Michael, chap. 5.

15 Nicholas's early biographies take . . . : Symeon, in Jones, *Myra*, pg. 49.

16 We are told that as a boy . . . : Symeon the Metaphrast: ". . . When he reached the proper age, he was sent to the *grammaticus* for schooling." Jones, *Myra*, pg. 52; see also English, loc. 834.

18 They might have been killed by the plague . . . : English, loc. 852.

18 Next door to Nicholas . . . : I am following the account of Michael the Archimandrite here (chaps. 9–18)—the first account of this deed. In Symeon the Metaphrast's account, the father seems to be an even more canny, perhaps ruthless, opportunist (Jones, *Myra*, pp. 54–57).

19 "Show me the angel . . .": Paraphrase of Michael, chap. 15.

20 "We ought to give thanks . . .": Paraphrase of Michael, chap. 17.

20 **The poet Wace has a better explanation for the three separate bags of gold: "The first one he gave them was to relieve their poverty, the second he gave them so that the three daughters could be married, and on the third occasion he gave them the gift in the name of the Holy Trinity" (Wace, pg. 281, ll. 99–104). Unfortunately, this slightly more rational explanation wasn't taken up by anyone else.**

21 Here was a young man . . . : English, loc. 1213.

22 So Nicholas spent his youth . . . : Michael, chap. 20.

22 Myra was a good-sized city . . . : T. Engin Akyürek. "Andriake: The Port of Myra in Late Antiquity." In *Trade in Byzantium: Papers from the Third International Sevgi Gönül Byzantine Studies Symposium*, eds. Paul Magdalino et al. Istanbul: ANAMED, 2016.

22 In dark huts around the square . . . : Alfaro, Carmen and D. Mylona. "Fishing for Purple Shellfish (*Muricidae*) in Ancient Greece: Acquisition Technology and First Steps in Purple Dye Production," in *Production and Trade of Textiles and Dyes in the Roman Empire and Neighboring Regions*, eds. Carmen Alfaro, Michael Tellenbach, and Jonatan Ortiz. University of Valencia, 2014.

23 Ancient authors tell us that . . . : Borchhardt, pp. 76, 79–80.

24 "There are sea bass, bluefish . . .": Athenaios, in Borchhardt, pg. 76.

24 Down by the port . . . : Nevzat Çevik et al., "A Unique Discovery in Lycia: The Ancient Synagogue at Andriake, Port of Myra." *Adalya* 13 (2010): pp. 335–366. Cf. Wilson, in Doğan, "Jews and Christians," pg. 15.

24 And that night, one of them . . . : I follow Symeon the Metaphrast here (Jones, *Myra*, pp. 58–60); it does not differ greatly from Michael the Archimandrite's account (chaps. 21–24).

26 He wasn't even a priest . . . : The ordination of a layperson as bishop was certainly unusual in the period, but was not unheard of (Cioffari, *Translation*, pg. 24).

26 "Accept this man as our shepherd . . .": Symeon, in Jones, *Myra*, pg. 60.

27 The Tale of the Boiled Baby . . . : This story is told in the twelfth-century Anglo-Norman poet Wace's verse *Life of Saint Nicholas*. The episode does not appear in any of the earlier Greek or Latin lives, and is almost certainly something cooked up by the French. (Wace, pp. 282–285, ll. 157–194.) Cf. Fredell, pg. 200.

29 "Who would not be amazed . . .": From an eighth-century sermon by Andrew of Crete. Translation online at https://www.stnicholascenter.org/who-is-st-nicholas/stories-legends/classic-sources/andrew-crete.

30 Meanwhile, peoples of other nations . . . : Baker, loc. 414.

30 When the emperor Diocletian . . . : Lactantius, pg. 44.

31 "You shall not have other gods beside me . . .": From the Ten Commandments. Exodus 20: 3–5. *New American Bible*, revised edition.

31 This was awkward. . . . : For example, in the manifesto of Maximinus: Eusebius, loc. 1695–1696.

32 The Christians were a government . . . : Baker, loc. 1050, 1059.

32 Christian writings and scriptures were confiscated . . . : Eusebius, loc. 1605.

33 The Romans were geniuses . . . : Lactantius, pg. 62.

33 Christians were killed by leopards . . . : For example, Eusebius, loc. 1615.

33 The bodies of other Christians . . . : Eusebius, loc. 1618.

33 Instead, he had their ears . . . : Lactantius, pg. 88; cf. Eusebius, loc. 1626.

33 "At length they did expire . . .": Lactantius, pg. 62. His details are confirmed by Eusebius's description of the torture and immolation of one of the Nicomedian palace servants after the fire (Eusebius, loc. 1612).

34 Nicholas, in his church in Myra . . . : The theologian Methodius of Olympos. Wilson, in Doğan, "Jews and Christians," pg. 26; cf. English, loc. 1555.

34 "Being subjected to blows . . .": This is taken from the eleventh-century opening of *The Synaxarion of Nicholas*, online at https://www.stnicholascenter.org/who-is-st-nicholas/stories-legends/classic-sources/synaxarion.

37 "We shouldn't wonder at this pathological . . .": Martino, *Reliquie*, pg. 53.

38 More brutally, it appears . . . : The maxilla is deviated. Martino (*Reliquie*, pg. 11) appears to imply that the fracturing occurred postmortem. However, his photos seem to indicate that the sutures around the nasal cavity remain intact, suggesting the rebuild of the bone after a traumatic injury. (Interview with Dr. Angelique Corthals, December 18, 2023). Cf. Wilson,

in Doğan, "Jews and Christians," pp. 27–28. For examples of forensic reconstructions of Nicholas's face, see https://www.stnicholascenter.org/who-is-st-nicholas/real-face.

39 He called on priests to practice . . . : Eusebius, loc. 1632; Bremmer, pg. 58.

39 Meanwhile, to the north . . . : Eusebius, loc. 1819.

39 As he marched with his army . . . : There is little agreement where this vision happened. Baker claims Constantine saw the cross just outside York, England (loc. 1588), which seems to have more to do with Baker's own hearty nationalism than anything reported by Eusebius. Weiss much more convincingly argues the vision occurred near Autun, France, in 310 AD (Weiss, pp. 247–249).

39 "Constantine said that about noon . . .": Eusebius, loc. 1821.

40 "Most interesting is the idea that Constantine . . .": This theory has been advanced by several scholars, most notably Peter Weiss (2003). While this kind of scientific explanation exasperates some historians, I find Weiss's argument compelling: it actually brings into alignment the three contemporary written sources for the vision, one pagan, two Christian (which otherwise seem to be at odds), as well as the iconographic evidence of coins minted in Constantine's name.

40 This would have been particularly. . . . : Or Sol Invictus, "the Unconquered Sun." Bremmer, pp. 70–71.

41 Again, he saw the symbol . . . : Eusebius (loc. 1821 ff.) and Lactantius (pp. 99–100) both have versions of this vision, but they don't match up exactly.

42 "an infinite number of owls": pg. 44, in Zosimus. *The History of Count Zosimus*. London: W. Green and T. Chapman, 1814. Online at https://www.tertullian.org/fathers/zosimus02_book2.htm.

42 They issued a statement of religious freedom . . . : Versions of the Edict of Milan survive both in Lactantius (pp. 110–112) and Eusebius (loc. 1743 ff.).

42 "Perceiving long ago . . .": Eusebius, loc. 1744.

43 "whatever Divinity lives . . .": Eusebius, loc. 1744.

44 Nicholas would have been released . . . : Technically, if Nicholas was imprisoned in Lycia, he probably would have been released by the deathbed recantation of Emperor Maximinus Daia in 313 AD. See Lactantius, pg. 114, Eusebius, loc. 1709.

44 When every land subject . . . : Symeon, in Jones, *Myra*, pg. 19.

46 In the same year as Constantine's Edict of Milan . . . : Eusebius, loc. 1698–1699. Cf. Lactantius, pg. 37. Cioffari suggests the crisis described in the *Lives* of Nicholas was not the famine of 313, but the famine of 333 (*Translation*, pg. 35).

46 There were three ships . . . : A slight anachronism: Constantine did not declare Constantinople a capital until 330 AD. This may be why Cioffari assumes it was the later famine (see note above).

46 Nicholas begged . . . : Michael, pg. 37.

47 the granary still stands . . . : For archaeological details of the granary, see Borchhardt, pp. 66–71.

47 It was built by the emperor Hadrian . . . : Akyürek, "Andriake," pg. 469.

47 You can still see carvings . . . : Borchhardt, pg. 68.

49 In those days, three boys . . . : This retelling is based on the original Hildesheim play (Jones, *Myra*, pp. 128–133) and the slightly later Fleury play (translated in the recording notes by Renz/New York Ensemble for Early Music), which are written in verse. As discussed, the detail of the pickling tubs comes from later versions (thirteenth century)—see Jones, *Myra*, pg. 135.

49 "We have borne the burden . . .": From the Fleury play *Tres Clerici*. Renz, pg. 34.

50 "For a price . . .": For the pies, see Fredell, pg. 199.

51 In the case of this ghoulish . . . : See the discussion in Jones, *Liturgy*, pp. 90–117. Jones claims the first version was the Hildesheim play, written before 1038. Cf. Albrecht, pg. 26.

52 Modern scholars look . . . : For example, Albrecht, pp. 26–42.

52 In others, they're served . . . : Fredell, pp. 183–184.

54 The Tale of the Demon in the Temple . . . : Michael, chaps. 28–29.

54 The Myrans were very proud . . . : Çevik, pp. 44–45.

54 They would sacrifice bulls . . . : See Rogers, *passim*, which also covers the shift in ritual protocols over time.

55 Because Artemis also helped sailors . . . : LiDonnici, pg. 404, n. 63.

55 "When Nicholas launched his attack . . .": Symeon the Metaphrast, in Jones, *Myra*, pg. 20. In a similar passage in the apocryphal *Acts of John*, the evangelist destroys the temple of Artemis at Ephesus merely through prayer. He casts out the place's resident demon, at which the altar cracks, the idols collapse, and the roof falls in, killing the high priest. John subsequently resurrects the priest. It is unclear if Nicholas's biographers could have read the *Acts of John*, however, a noncanonical, even heretical, Gnostic text that wouldn't have been in wide circulation. (*Acts of John*, chaps. 37–47. *The Other Bible: Ancient Alternative Scriptures*, ed. Willis Barnstone. San Francisco: Harper, 1984, pp. 420–422.)

56 Around 330 AD . . . : English, loc. 1960.

56 "The sound of thunder was heard . . .": *Augustan History*, quoted in Rogers, pg. 251.

57 The description of Nicholas's attack . . . : Cioffari, *Miracles*, pg. 26. See Foss, pp. 9–13, for a description of Letoon and its nearby city, Xanthos.

57 The Roman poet Ovid . . . : Ovid (*The Metamorphoses*, Book 6) does not mention the specific location, simply placing the action in Lycia; Antoninus Liberalis, describing the same event in his own *Metamorphoses* (chap. 35), is more explicit and connects it to the cult site near Xanthos. Antoninus Liberalis's complete work is online at https://topostext.org/work/216. Cf. T. R. Bryce, "The Arrival of the Goddess Ledo in Lycia." *Historia: Zeitschrift für Alte Geschichte*, vol. 32, no. 1 (1983), pp. 2–4.

58 But then some great catastrophe befell Letoon . . . : Foss, pg. 12.

58 People carved crosses . . . : Foss, pg. 13.

60 The Tale of the Drowning Sailors . . . : Paraphrase of Michael, chaps. 34–36.

61 He said they shouldn't thank him . . . : Voragine, pg. 12.

61 In one variation, a fisherman's . . . : Jones, *Myra*, pg. 76.

61 In another account . . . : Jones, *Myra*, pg. 76.

62 One of the earliest biographies . . . : The ninth-century author Methodios, in Jones, *Liturgy*, pg. 42 n.

62 Sailors from Anatolia . . . : English, loc. 2162.

62 In this way, oddly . . . : There are far-fetched theories trying to connect Nicholas with various sea gods, sea monsters, and mermen as well. See Anichkof, pp.117–120.

62 "Under the cloak of religion . . .": Vigilantius to Jerome, quoted in Jones, *Myra*, pp. 10–11.

63 An old Serbian carol . . . : Anichkof, pg. 109.

64 The Tale of the Hellfire Jar . . . : This retelling blends details from Michael, chaps. 44–46, Symeon (Jones, *Myra*, pg. 22), and Voragine (pg. 13). Voragine places the episode during Nicholas's life; the earlier two accounts place it after his death, as pilgrims traveled to his tomb.

64 The demon Artemis . . . : Voragine says this is not Artemis but the Devil himself dressed as a nun—but then oddly changes his mind halfway through and says it is Diana (i.e., Artemis). Michael simply calls the figure a demon who had lived in the temple of Artemis. Cf. Anichkof, pg. 112.

65 "Rise at dawn . . .": Michael, chap. 46.

65 "The whole ship was being . . .": Michael, chap. 47.

65 "You really are he . . .": Voragine, pg. 13.

66 "Emperor Constantine recalled . . .": Bremmer, pg. 71.

68 "I will pray to . . .": English, loc. 643.

68 "He sees you when you're sleeping . . .": From Haven Gillespie and John Frederick Coots, "Santa Claus Is Coming to Town" (1934).

69 In Constantinople, the imperial capital he'd named after himself . . . : Baker, loc. 3536.

70 The Tale of the Three Generals . . . : The

following is paraphrased from the *Praxis de Stratilates*, translated in Jones, *Myra*, pp. 29–36. Cioffari believes the original might have been written as early as 350 AD (see English, locs. 2383–2402). The events are mentioned in the "Encomium" of Saint Proclus, c. 440 AD, making this the oldest surviving record of a legend of Saint Nicholas.

70 Nicholas pushed his way to the front . . . : Jones, *Myra*, pg. 31.

71 The three generals were impressed . . . . It's notable that historically, this regional governor, the *praeses*, was installed by Constantine himself, who had just separated Lycia into its own administrative district and made Myra its capital (Foss, pg. 2).

72 Then he appeared by Ablabius's bed . . . : Voragine, pg. 14.

73 They distributed gold . . . : Foss, pg. 24.

73 There really was, believe it or not . . . : Baker, loc. 3307.

73 "a band of persons addicted . . .": English, loc. 2335.

73 The story also preserves another historical fact . . . : English, loc. 2230; Cioffari, *Life*, pg. 19.

75 The day came when it was time . . . : Symeon, in Jones, *Myra*, pg. 65.

75 And so Nicholas died . . . : The late medieval tradition states that he died in 343 AD (Voragine, pg. 15); Cioffari places the death in 341–342 (*Translation*, pg. 43); English surmises a decade earlier, in 333–335 (loc. 2807). Jones discusses textual evidence for the possible dates (*Myra*, pg. 12), but reaches no conclusion.

75 We are told that "at his passing . . .": Voragine, pg. 15.

76 "His body, buried . . .": Michael, chap. 41. This tradition was therefore at least a couple of hundred years old by the time the League of Saint Nicholas set out for Myra to steal his corpse.

76 "To the spot come multitudes . . .": John the Deacon, in Jones, *Myra*, pg. 66.

77 "It is sprinkled on those who approach . . .": English, loc. 2889.

78 Even William the Conqueror . . . : According to Orderic Vitalis in Hayes, pg. 495.

79 In different versions, the boy . . . : Jones, *Myra* pg. 76. One of the monastic musicals in the Fleury plays, *Filius Getronis* ("The Son of Gethron"), is a lovely sung version of this story.

79 He whips a young poet-musician . . . : The tale of the "Widow of Bari." Jones, *Liturgy*, pp. 57–61.

80 But it's interesting that the author . . . : Stanton, Charles. *Medieval Maritime Warfare*. Barnsley, UK: Pen & Sword Maritime, 2015: pg. 47; Konstam, Angus. *Byzantine Warship vs. Arab Warship: 7th–11th Centuries*. Oxford: Osprey, 2015: pp. 38–39.

81 This was the Roman form . . . : The *annona* dole. See Michael McCormick, *Origins of the European Economy: Communications and Commerce, AD 300–900*. Cambridge, UK: Cambridge University Press, 2001: pg. 87.

81 Reliable northwest winds . . . : Foss, pp. 1, 25–26; Akyürek, pg. 467.

81 Across the river stand the ruins . . . : Foss 25.

83 The earliest mention of Nicholas . . . : Theodore the Lector. See Cioffari, *Translation*, pg. 5.

83 As a result, in 325 . . . : Baker, loc. 3142.

83 Many of them had been tortured . . . : For example, they "still showed the wounds and scars in their flesh, and especially among the bishops, such as Nicholas, Bishop of Myra, Paphnutius, and others." Xanthopoulos, *Historia Ecclesiastica*, in Cioffari, *Miracles*, pg. 17; cf. English, loc. 1185.

84 In a list of over three hundred bishops . . . : Cioffari, *Translation*, pg. 5.

84 The lists that contain around three hundred names . . . : Cioffari, *Miracles*, pg. 22, is the best summary of the documentary evidence for Nicaea.

84 The burning brick was designed to be a demonstration to Constantine of the triune nature of the Trinity: Like the Trinity, Nicholas argued, the brick is a single object, constant in its substance, that still consists of three distinct elements (water,

earth, and fire, just as God is singular, yet contains the Father, the Son, and the Holy Spirit). As he explained this to the emperor, the brick obligingly burst into flame and dripped water onto the floor. The heretic he reputedly punched at the Council of Nicaea was Arius, who preached that Jesus Christ was not coeternal with God the Father. These scenes of Nicholas at Nicaea appear, for example, painted on the ceiling of the Basilica of Saint Nicholas in Bari. (Cioffari, *Basilica*, pg. 43.)

85 We know that in the mid-sixth century . . . : Procopius, *Of the Buildings of Justinian* [c. 560]. Translated by Aubrey Stewart. London, 1888: pg. 26. Online at https://www.gutenberg.org/ebooks/65404.

85 In Myra, after an earthquake . . . : Yazici, *Monument*, pg. 11. It may also have been funded by Emperor Justinian in the wake of the 529 earthquake (Akyürek, "Myra," pg. 22).

85 On the island of Rhodes . . . : Jordan, pg. 27.

86 "Where I could not uncover a story . . .": Jones, *Myra*, pg. 48.

86 It has led some to throw up their hands . . . : Cioffari, *Translation*, pg. 7.

88 "When I speak of this . . .": Interview with the author, March 3, 2023.

88 He has cautioned people . . . : For example, Cioffari, *Translation*, pg. 87.

89 Now stories are told about how . . . : Albrecht Berger, trans. *Accounts of Medieval Constantinople: The* Patria. Cambridge: Harvard University Press, 2013: pg. 145.

89 Pilgrims come to Myra from all over . . . : Yazici *Lycian Way*, pg. 283; Akyürek, "Andriake," pg. 471; Akyürek, "Myra," pg. 37.

89 ☞ From the *Life* of Saint Nicholas of Sion, whose exploits in the sixth century were often confused with those of Saint Nicholas of Myra, our fourth-century saint. The locals complained that the tree had slain an old lumberjack. Nicholas of Sion had the tree chopped down (despite the demon's protests) and had sawyers cut the haunted cypress trunk up to make boards for a new monastery (Ševčenko, *Sion*, pp. 35–41). I wonder whether the story of the body buried in the roots of the tree did not inspire the weird story of the corpse of a later Saint Nicholas, Saint Nicholas the Younger (ninth century), being devoured by an oak tree. See Anthony Kaldellis and Ioannis Polemis, editors and translators. *Saints of Ninth- and Tenth-Century Greece.* Cambridge, MA: Harvard University Press, 2019: pp. 21, 31–33.

89 The church is burned and rebuilt . . . : The stages of destruction and reconstruction of the Basilica of Saint Nicholas at Myra can be tentatively summarized: Nicholas's own church was likely destroyed in an earthquake in 529 AD, after which a new structure was built by the emperor Justinian in the 530s. An Arab fleet attacked Myra in 789, and the church sustained considerable damage. It was rebuilt in a more modern style for the period, as a domed basilica—only to be attacked again, as mentioned below, by Humaid ibn Ma'yuf in 808. Restoration was likely carried out in the early ninth century. Pirates, either North African Zinds or Sicilians, captured and sacked Myra in 1034—but the church was swiftly repaired and enlarged by the emperor's brother Ioannis Orphanotropos after Saint Nicholas appeared to him in a dream and

offered to cure his epilepsy. This renovation was likely completed in the 1040s under the regime of Emperor Constantine IX Monomachus and his wife, Zoe, according to an inscription found locally. In the years after the Bari and Venice heists, the church was repaired again—presumably because of the considerable damage the Italian relic thieves had caused to the interior. Confusingly, each of these renovations and expansions included portions of earlier buildings, which makes the dating of any given feature difficult. See Sema Doğan, "Kaynaklar Esliginde Aziz Nikolaos Kilisesi," in Doğan, pp. 35–62.

95 "We could just snatch the body . . .": John the Archdeacon, chap. 3. This line of dialogue is a hypothetical reconstruction based on the reported discussion.

95 They would be sailing right past the port . . . : An anonymous Russian account suggests that the whole trip was planned out ahead of time specifically as a heist. In that version, an unnamed cleric of Bari has a dream in which Saint Nicholas appears to him and demands to be picked up and brought back to Italy. The voyage to Antioch to sell grain is just a ruse or a pretense. (*Kyiv Slovo*, chaps. 7–9.)

The two earliest versions both agree that the decision to rob the tomb was made on the spur of the moment while the ships were at sea. This is, without a doubt, the more likely scenario, given how unprepared the sailors themselves were to deal with the corpse and how unprepared the city of Bari was to receive it. The chaos that ensued when the League reached their home port suggests that no one knew the relics were on their way. The anonymous Russian author is simply trying to make the whole caper look more like God's will and less like a desperate stunt that happened to work out.

96 Some of them, we are told, immediately thought it was a fantastic idea . . . : John the Archdeacon, chap. 3.

96 Centuries before, when the word of the sacred healing ooze . . . : This story of the tooth, retold in John the Archdeacon (chap. 1) may be connected with a somewhat vague tradition that Emperor Basil I tried to remove the body but was, in some unspecified way, unable to get the limbs out of the basilica. (See, for example, Grant, pg. 259; Anonymous Monk of Lido, chap. 12).

96 The remains of Saint Nicholas were important to Myra . . . : Emperor Constantine VII, for example, called Myra "Thrice-blessed, myrrh-breathing city of the Lycians, where the mighty Nicholas, servant of God, spouts forth myrrh in accordance with the city's name" (Yazici, *Monument*, pg. 6).

96 **The ooze connected with Saint John the Apostle, buried at Ephesus, was a somewhat special case, because it required special assembly. On certain feast-days, Saint John would supposedly revive in his tomb sufficiently to start breathing again, and a fine powder would blow out of a grate. This was collected and mixed with either holy water or wine. The resulting paste was used for healing. See D'Andria, *Santuario*, pp. 31–33.**

97 **The Latin word used here and elsewhere for the device that draws out the myron is *peniculum*, which typically means either a sponge or a brush. Of those two options, a sponge clearly makes more sense in the context.**

The thing is, *peniculum* literally means "little penis," and I wonder whether in this case the word isn't actually referring to something like a thin glass, metal, or ceramic pipe, which was lowered through the holes in the sarcophagus to extract a sample of the myron

by stopping up one end of it. This might explain how they drew out liquid despite the narrow bore of the holes on extant sarcophagi, like the tendril sarcophagus mentioned on pages 121–122. If there was a larger aperture, a simple dipper could have been used.

98 He'd never be able to keep the stolen tooth . . . : John the Archdeacon, chap. 1.

99 Saint Nicholas got his revenge . . . : The general in question was Humaid ibn Ma'yuf, the governor of Syria. Theophanes, *The Chronicle of Theophanes Confessor*, translated by Cyril Mango and Roger Scott. Oxford, UK: Clarendon Press, 1997: pp. 663–664.

100 It had recently been invaded . . . : This account is based on A. C. S. Peacock, *The Great Seljuk Empire*. Edinburgh: Edinburgh University Press, 2015; Alexander Daniel Beihammer, *Byzantium and the Emergence of Muslim-Turkish Anatolia, ca. 1040–1130*. London: Routledge, 2017; and John Freely, *Storm on Horseback: The Seljuk Warriors of Turkey*. London: I. B. Tauris & Co., 2008.

100 Now bands of Turkish warriors . . . : Technically, the warrior-nomads who descended on Lycia were probably ethnically Turkmen, with only a nominal allegiance to the Turks of either the Great Seljuk Sultanate to the east or the newly established Sultanate of Rūm at Nicaea. See, for example, Roche, pg. 136.

102 "How solitary sits the city . . .": Lamentations 1:1, New American Bible, revised edition.

102 They had been hiding themselves there for at least two years . . . : This estimate is based on the vision of Saint Nicholas mentioned later. In general terms, the timeline of the Turkish occupation of Lycia is extremely unclear. Beihammer (pp. 205, 244) says that Byzantine sources start mentioning the Turkish occupation of Western Anatolia in 1080/1081, with an uptick in 1086, which would match this date. Cf. Roche, pp. 137–141.

102 They were probably paying the Turkish . . . : Anonymous Monk of Lido, chap. 9. The idea of some kind of tribute or payoff makes sense: elsewhere in Anatolia, the inability of the former Byzantine citizens to cultivate crops due to the violence of the Turkish incursions led to widespread famine (for example, Roche, pp. 139–140), whereas here, the population appears to have lived precariously in their fortress for at least fifteen years. There must have been some way for them to procure food.

103 The church's courtyard . . . : John the Archdeacon, chap. 3. The passage literally says that "the man in charge of that fortress [*castrum*]" had died. While one might expect this to refer to a local Byzantine official, the presence of a large crowd of Turkish mourners from surrounding territories most strongly suggests that this was a Turkish chieftain. It is not impossible that the Turks felt obliged to attend the funeral of a Christian governor, but it does seem less likely. Either way, a funeral party of Turkish horsemen at the basilica suggests an intriguing syncretism and at least a provisional cooperation between Muslims and Christians during the occupation.

103 So the Barians gave up . . . : John the Archdeacon, chap. 3.

104 Venice was an Italian city far to the north . . . : For the economic motive in the rivalry between Venice and Bari and how it spurred on the theft of Nicholas's bones, see Hayes, pp. 502–504, and Geary, pp. 101–102.

106 Rival cities. Rival merchants . . . : John the Archdeacon, chap. 3.

107 Saint Mark had been buried in Alexandria . . . : Geary, pp. 88–94.

108 Let's stop for a moment to look . . . : The full roster of the League of Saint Nicholas appears in two places: in an expense account for disbursements from the Basilica di San Nicola in 1175 and in the Beneventan recension of Nicephorus's *Translatio*. Each of these two sources lists fifty-one names in common, and eleven names that the other does not include—in Nicephorus's case, because several of them are citizens of Trani (including the three enslaved men) who were paid a flat fee, rather than being

included in the annual payouts that the rest of the crew enjoyed. This brings the total to roughly seventy-three people on the three ships. For a discussion of these rosters, see Cioffari, *Traslazione*, pp. 21, 23, 49–53; cf. Cioffari, "The Sailors Who Brought the Relics of St. Nicholas from Myra to Bari," *Saint Nicholas News*, no. 15 (April 30, 2011); and the St. Nicholas Center's "Bari Sailors—1087," online at https://www.stnicholascenter.org/who-is-st-nicholas/saint-in-bari/bari-sailors-1087.

109 The Norman dukes punished Bari . . . : Cioffari, *Traslazione*, pp. 17–18. For more on the Normans in Apulia, see the wonderful *Deeds of Robert Guiscard* by William of Apulia, translated by G. A. Loud, online at https://ims.leeds.ac.uk/wp-content/uploads/sites/29/2019/02/William-of-Apulia.pdf.

110 "ten hands of St. Prokopios . . .": Christopher of Mytiline, "To the Monk Andrew, who buys the bones of ordinary people as the relics of saints" (Poem 114), in *The Poems of Christopher of Mytiline and John Mauropous*, edited and translated by Floris Bernard and Christopher Livanos. Cambridge, MA: Harvard University Press, 2018, pg. 243.

110 If these relic specialists couldn't find bones . . . : Ibid, pg. 247.

110 So despite their enthusiasm . . . : John the Archdeacon, chap. 4.

111 On April 20, 1087 . . . : This precise date for the Barian expedition arriving in Myra is based on John the Archdeacon's account of a sailor's dream on the trip home (chap. 12), in which Nicholas promises that they will arrive home in Bari twenty days after they remove the body—and they arrived back on May 9. While Cioffari accepts this date (*Traslazione*, pg. 42), he also points out that Nicephorus is more detailed about the route home—and Nicephorus has the saint announce that they will arrive back in Bari twenty days *after the dream itself*, which happens a few days out from Myra (Nicephorus, in Jones, *Myra*, pp. 186–187). This would push the actual date of the heist about four or five days earlier.

112 They marched up from the harbor . . . : "Fortified in a battle line and provisioned as if they might meet enemies." John the Archdeacon, chap. 4.

113 They entered the church, passing from bright . . . : It seems likely these paintings were there at the time of the heist, perhaps executed during the renovation of the 1040s. Çorağan, pg. 90; cf. Doğan, in Doğan, pp. 41 and 43.

113 Over the altar was spread . . . : A ciborium. The pillars would probably not have been the four that stand there today—they appear to have been stuck on inexpertly with cement at a later date. Doğan, in Doğan, pg. 315; Borchhardt, pg. 306 n. 23.

113 An octagonal pulpit . . . : Doğan, in Doğan, pg. 322.

114 This was probably the baptistry . . . : Niewöhner ("Neues," "Tomb") argues compellingly that this room was a baptistry, analogous with the floorplans of other Lycian churches. Alpaslan (pp. 161–163) suggests that it was a place for the preparation of the bread and wine of Communion and the storage of liturgical items. Çorağan (pg. 93) speculates that the frescoes on the dome here might well have been painted in the twelfth century, so there may have been different images on the ceiling when the Barian thieves made their visit.

114 They had another body to find . . . : Doğan, in Doğan, pp. 304–306.

115 They could not wait any longer . . . : Nicephorus, in Jones, *Myra*, pg. 178.

115 ☞ **To examine the clues about the exact location, see the map on page 221.**

115 ☞ **The plate in the floor is entirely my own speculation, assuming some similarity with the system the mariners subsequently arranged in the church at Bari, and with myroblyte saints' tombs elsewhere in Anatolia. The two Barian narratives are very clear about two things:**

(1) Nicholas's sarcophagus lay under a marble floor, which was pried up and destroyed, and (2) the myron was extracted from the sarcophagus from above, presumably through a hole in a lid. We might imagine, therefore, a construction like the ones that survive elsewhere in Anatolia where a "manhole" or even terracotta pipes lead through the floor to the tomb to facilitate the production of myron and contact with entombed relics. In particular, the church of Saint Philip at Hierapolis, to the north of Myra, serves as an excellent example of the kind of arrangement we might expect, complete with a burial chamber (hypogeum) accessed by clay tubes. Francesco D'Andria has provided photos and diagrams for how the systems at Hierapolis and Ephesus worked. (See D'Andria, "Sanctuario," pp. 28–33; cf. D'Andria, "Sanctuary," 15–16.) The survival of some of this sacred plumbing elsewhere in Anatolia and around the Mediterranean makes the congruent descriptions from the two Barian narratives of the theft from Myra more credible.

The one eccentric element would be the hiding of a decorative sarcophagus, specifically, under the floor. Typically these were used for display. The floor burials that have been discovered in the church at Myra are not elaborate. This would seem to indicate a simpler box for Nicholas than the highly ornamented, repurposed tendril sarcophagus discussed on pages 121–122 (see note to pg. 121).

The Anonymous Monk of Lido's account of the Venetian heist claims that the sarcophagus the Barians broke into was standing against a wall (not under a floor) when the Venetians arrived. Laying the saint to rest in a sarcophagus in a niche above ground would not be an unusual arrangement, all other things being equal, but of the three accounts, the Anonymous Monk's seems in general to be the least reliable. The saint's sarcophagus with its remaining sacred oil and bone chips could have been moved out of its hole in the floor when the floor was repaired after the Barian heist, but that is pure speculation. It's important to note that even the Venetian thieves apparently assumed that the body would most likely be under the floor, in some kind of burial chamber—which is why they tore the floor up and found their weird bituminous mass.

As of this writing, archaeological work is going on to clarify possible sites in the church for Saint Nicholas's tomb, under the auspices of the Turkish Ministry of Culture.

Unfortunately, none of the archaeologists involved were willing to go on record when contacted. Therefore, these are entirely my own surmises.

115 "Behold the place, as it has been passed down . . .": John the Archdeacon, chap. 5.

116 "At that point they knew . . .": Nicephorus, in Jones, *Myra*, pp. 180–181.

117 "Why do you ask . . .": Nicephorus, in Jones, *Myra*, pg. 179.

117 It was time for the thieves . . . : John the Archdeacon, chap. 5.

118 Another looter added that the pope . . . : Nicephorus, in Jones, *Myra*, pg. 179.

118 The monks were horrified. . . . : Anonymous Greek account, chap. 3.

118 "The color left their faces . . .": Nicephorus, in Jones, pg. 180.

118 A young man—a hothead . . . : Cioffari, *Traslazione*, pg. 26; cf. Nicephorus, in Jones, *Myra*, pg. 181.

119 Another monk, a senior monk . . . : Nicephorus, in Jones, *Myra*, pg. 181.

119 The saintly monk continued . . . : Nicephorus, in Jones, *Myra*, pg. 181.

119 Then, surprisingly, the monk expressed . . . : Nicephorus, in Jones, *Myra*, pg. 181. This recounted vision is the only clue as to when the Seljuk Turkish invasion reached Myra. If the three citizens' vision happened a year before (1086), and involved the saint scolding the citizens for hiding out too long already in their fortress, we have to assume that they had been there for a while already—putting the original invasion around 1085 or perhaps even earlier. While there are a few scanty sources that refer to the Seljuk occupation of Lycia, there are none that give any definite date for the invasion. This somewhat shaky calculation in Nicephorus's narrative is in fact the best source for the timeline of the occupation of this whole region.

119 Two of the priests, Lupo and Grimoald . . . : John the Archdeacon, chap. 6.

121 Some archaeologists believe . . . : The whole of the following discussion is derived from Urs Peschlow's report on the sarcophagus in Borchhardt, pp. 163–186, and the lid, pp. 205–210. At the time of that survey, it was uncertain if the lid belonged to the sarcophagus, given the lack of matching marks for the hardware that attached coffin to lid. When the sarcophagus was later moved away from the wall, the corresponding indentations were found. See Niewöhner, "Neues zum Grab," pg. 120.

121 The really fascinating feature of this tendril . . . : Peschlow maintains that these funnel holes were used for the introduction and extraction of the oil. (Borschhardt, pg. 351). But Philipp Niewöhner points out, quite reasonably, that this feature is not unique. Other sarcophagi from the Byzantine littoral have these holes drilled in the lids, presumably used for funeral libations. (Niewöhner, "Neues," pg. 120; "Tomb," pp. 189–191.) In a private correspondence, he expressed doubt that the holes in the lid would be large enough to extract the myron, in the absence of any other draining mechanism (August 22, 2023). I would argue that the term for the device used to extract the myron (*peniculum*) could include either a sponge on a stem or even a glass tube which would work perfectly well with these apertures. Even if the primary function of such holes was to provide for some kind of libation (Byzantine funeral rites involved feeding the dead at certain intervals after burial), this is entirely consonant with the idea of pouring myron into and extracting myron out of this particular saint's tomb (Cf. de Ceglia, pg. 246). Even if the tendril sarcophagus is not Nicholas's—which it may well not be—the texts demand a similar plumbing arrangement anyway.

122 We are told that the priests Lupo and Grimoald . . .": Nicephorus, in Jones, *Myra*, pg. 182.

123 He later told the scholar John the Archdeacon . . . : John the Archdeacon, chap. 7.

124 Watching this awful spectacle . . . : Nicephorus, in Jones, *Myra*, pg. 183, with a few phrases from the parallel speech in the Anonymous Greek account, chap. 7.

125 Father Lupo slung the package . . . : John the Archdeacon, chap. 8.

126 The crew members who had remained . . . : Nicephorus, in Jones, *Myra*, pg. 183.

126 Finally the League made its decision . . . : Cioffari, *Traslazione*, pp. 27–28. For the roster of who sailed on which ship, so far as is recorded, see pg. 23.

126 They took the body aboard . . . : John the Archdeacon, chap. 9. Cf. Cioffari, *Traslazione*, pg. 28. Cioffari here says it was a wine barrel, which it could have been. The supposed relics of the container itself are still held in the treasury of the Basilica of Saint Nicholas in Bari. For what it's worth, they appear not to be barrel staves but pieces of a box.

127 While all this went on . . . : Nicephorus, in Jones, *Myra*, pg. 185.

128 The cause was lost . . . : Anonymous Greek account, chap. 9.

128 "The mourners cried out these things . . .": John the Archdeacon, chap. 10.

129 "Indeed there were very few . . .": Nicephorus, in Jones, *Myra*, pg. 185.

130 Having taken council . . . : *Kyiv Slovo*, chaps. 12–14.

133 Some versions of the text . . . : Orderic Vitalis, pg. 4. John the Archdeacon has "hyrondinis" but Orderic Vitalis, who generally follows John, has "irudinum." Pierre Bouet, "Orderic Vital et la translation du corps de Saint Nicolas," *Nicolaus Studi Storici*, issue 42–43, vol. 22 (2011), pg. 132, n. 17.

133 "After expending every bit of energy . . .": Nicephorus, in Jones, *Myra*, pp. 185–186.

134 They pointed fingers . . . : John the Archdeacon, chap. 11.

134 At this, a man named Romuald . . . : Cioffari, *Traslazione*, pg. 29; cf. John the Archdeacon, chap. 11.

136 "After celebrating mass, with quieted winds . . .": Nicephorus, in Jones, pg. 186.

136 But the days were apparently fair . . . : John the Archdeacon, chap. 12. Note that Nicephorus reports this slightly differently: that Nicholas promises it will take twenty days *from the time of the dream* to reach Bari (Jones, *Myra*, 186). See the discussion of the route on Cioffari, *Traslazione*, pp. 28–31, esp. 30.

136 "Therefore," we are told . . . : John the Archdeacon, chap. 12.

139 The sailor Leone Pilillo's written version of the contract with Dom Elias is extant and is reproduced in Cioffari, *Traslazione*, pp. 43–48. This is a fascinating document, a legal renunciation by Pilillo of his right to the annual income from the pilgrims, in exchange for a one-time flat fee of fifty gold pieces. It appears he needed some fast cash—and the church had convinced him that it was sinful to profit from church income anyway. In the course of the contract, the lawyer recounts all of the stipulations of the original verbal and written contracts between Abbott Elias and the sailors in 1087.

139 They drove a hard bargain . . . : The payment roster from 1175 is reproduced on Cioffari, *Traslazione*, pp. 49–51.

140 The archbishop abandoned his trip . . . : Nicephorus, in Jones, *Myra*, pg. 190.

140 "So the sailors and the Abbot Elias . . .": in Cioffari, *Traslazione*, pg. 34.

141 He was a close advisor of the Norman duke . . . : Archbishop Urso was an advisor to Duke Robert Guiscard (1015–1085); the Abbot Elias, on the other hand, was one of the last appointees of the Byzantine (Eastern Roman) administration before they were driven out by Guiscard and the Norman invaders in 1071. Nonetheless, it is clear that after the Saint Nicholas riots, Urso and Elias reached some kind of agreement, and they collaborated closely for the next two years, until Archbishop Urso's death. (Elias succeeded him as archbishop.) Though the populace might originally have rioted in opposition to "Norman" control of the Nicholas relics, once a plan was

agreed upon, the Norman rulers clearly embraced the decision to build a new basilica for the saint. Bari's Norman rulers (Bohemond and Roger Borsa) were the ones who eventually granted the city the right to build the new basilica in the old governor's palace. It seems likely this site appealed to them because, in demolishing the palace of the Eastern Roman governor, they signaled their defiance to the Eastern Roman Empire itself and the security of their own hold over Apulia.

Anyway, the precise nature of the factionalism that led to the riots remains unclear.

Mougoyianni, pp. 111, 115, 119; cf. Hayes, pg. 505.

141 In any case, rightly or wrongly . . . : Nicephorus, in Jones, *Myra*, 191.

142 Nicephorus is the one who tells us . . . : Cioffari discusses John the Archdeacon's career and particular biases in "Giovanni arcidiacono: l'Historia translationis sancti Nicolai nell'Europa medievale."

143 What was the experience of being . . . : Nicephorus, in Jones, *Myra*, 192.

144 There's one interesting detail . . . : John the Archdeacon, chap. 22.

145 We are told that the Myrans made an incense . . . : Storax in modern terminology. Andrew Dalby, *Tastes of Byzantium: The Cuisine of a Legendary Empire*. London: I. B. Tauris, 2010: pg. 45.

145 Archaeologists may even have found . . . : Ötüken, "Excavations," pg. 42; de Ceglia, pg. 246; Ötüken, in Doğan, pg. 105; but cf. pg. 106, n. 88, where he appears to express some hesitation.

145 Throughout the complex . . . : Doğan, in Doğan, pg. 302.

145 They have also found the small . . . : See B. Yelda Olcay Uçkan and Özgü Çömezoğlu Uzbek ("Glass Findings"), in Doğan, pp. 528–530.

145 Relics supposedly radiated . . . : The technical term for renewing sacred oils through contact with a corpse like this is *apomyrizein*. See de Ceglia, pg. 246.

146 By 1089 the crypt was complete . . . : Cioffari, *Traslazione*, pg. 42.

147 And at the center of the crypt . . . : Ibid.

147 It took many more years for Bari . . . : There are questions about its exact date of completion and its (very late) date of consecration. See Cioffari, *Basilica*, pg. 4; Hayes, pp. 509–510.

150 Starting in 1096 . . . : Anonymous Monk of Lido, chap. 1; cf. Bellomo, pg. 432, n. 69.

150 Many of them set out on ships . . . : Hayes, pp. 507–509.

152 "Now that our men had possession . . .": From the chronicle of Raymond of d'Aguiliers, in *Fordham University Medieval Sourcebook: The Siege and Capture of Jerusalem*. Online at https://sourcebooks.fordham.edu/source/cde-jlem.asp.

152 When Jews (who had aided . . . : Amin Maalouf, *The Crusades through Arab Eyes*. Translated by Jon Rothschild, London: Al Saqi Books, 1984: loc. 117.

152 The Crusader princes . . . : From the *Gesta Francorum*, in *Fordham University Medieval Sourcebook: The Siege and Capture of Jerusalem*. Online at https://sourcebooks.fordham.edu/source/cde-jlem.asp.

153 The Venetians did not want to join . . . : For a discussion of their reluctance, see for ex. Grant, pg. 262.

153 So what they did was wait . . . : Anonymous Monk of Lido, chap. 2.

154 They assembled a crew of soldiers . . . : Anonymous Monk of Lido, chap. 22.

154 Then "the ships . . .": Anonymous Monk of Lido, chap. 3.

155 That winter, the Eastern Roman emperor . . . : Anonymous Monk of Lido, chap. 5.

156 Why would a Christian fleet attack . . . : See Bellomo, pp. 426–427.

157 A modern historian has created . . . : Grant, pg. 258.

157 The Venetian fleet anchored . . . : Anonymous Monk of Lido, chap. 9. This is an interesting detail, given that the emperor, Alexios Komnenos, had supposedly largely reclaimed the Anatolian coast from the Turks at this point, after the campaigns of 1097–1099. This suggests that there were still active bands of Turkish /

Turkmen nomads active in the area. Given the rhythms of nomadic transhumance, they were probably difficult to hunt down. They tended to go up into the higher grazing lands in the summer and come down from their winter pasturage when the heat dissipated in October. (See Roche, pg. 142.)

158 There was no pretense that the army . . . : Anonymous Monk of Lido, chap. 10.

159 "So far we have used soft words . . .": Anonymous Monk of Lido, chap. 11.

163 Saint Nicholas the Uncle . . . : Saint Nicholas the Uncle was actually the uncle of Saint Nicholas of Sion, a sixth-century saint who had lived near Myra in the mountains of Lycia. It was very common to confuse Saint Nicholas of Myra and Saint Nicholas of Sion in the centuries that followed their deaths. The Anonymous Monk of Lido likely did believe that Saint Nicholas the Uncle was in fact Nicholas of Myra's uncle. The passage that he cites in chapter 15 to describe the uncle, however, was originally from the Life of Saint Nicholas of Sion. (See Ševčenko, *Sion*, pg. 23.) Since the eighth century, these two saints had been confused and passages from the life of the one were included in stories about the other.

163 They put together some clues . . . : Anonymous Monk of Lido, chaps. 16 and 17.

164 Inspired by the idea . . . : Anonymous Monk of Lido, chap. 17.

164 A palm tree grew . . . : The description of this peculiar detail (Lido, chapter 17) is very unclear. Dr. Angelique Corthals has pointed out to me that some early Christian burials, in imitation of Egyptian burials, included portions of palm trees to symbolize life and rebirth. This could be a confused account of that—or a fib supposed to play on that symbolic tradition. The palm tree is not native to Lycia, but there are groves of them (at Patara, for instance) which were imported from Egypt.

165 "Holiest father, Nicholas! . . .": Anonymous Monk of Lido, chap. 24.

166 "Eaten up by sadness . . .": Anonymous Monk of Lido, chap. 25.

166 "These men were either afflicted . . .": Lido, chap. 26.

167 clay bricks that were subjected to great heat . . . : For a parallel case of bricks fusing into slag, a "dark, glassy matrix," see, for example, M. J. Magee, et al. "Chemical and Archaeological Evidence for the Destruction of a Sacred Animal Necropolis at Ancient Mendes, Egypt," *Journal of Archaeological Science*, no. 23 (1996): pp. 485–492. I am indebted to Dr. Angelique Corthals for bringing this example to my attention.

167 evidence of fire . . . : There are fire layers present in the stratigraphy of portions of the church (Otüken, in Doğan, pg. 129), evidence of at least one conflagration that might have collapsed a floor-burial such as those found in several locations around the church and fused the contents into a single mass.

168 "Those who fight bravely . . .": Anonymous Monk of Lido, chap. 36.

169 "But the Christians, who were stationed . . .": Anonymous Monk of Lido, chap. 43. Cf. Bellomo, pp. 429–431.

171 When a contemporary US politician . . . : https://www.wsj.com/articles/SB1001020294332922160.

172 In a French play . . . : Jean Bodel, *Le jeu de saint Nicolas.* Edited and translated by Jean Dufournet. Paris: Editions Flammarion, 2005.

174 "O Venice, truly blessed . . .": Anonymous Monk of Lido, chap. 22. For clarity, I have here substituted "Lycia" for the original's "Greece," an inexact designation based on Latin prejudices.

174 Conveniently, Nicholas himself appeared . . . : Bellomo, pp. 424–425.

175 "A shiver of emotion . . .": Martino, *Reliquie*, 9.

176 "In those two and a half hours . . .": Martino, *Reliquie*, 9.

177 Each year, when the priest . . . : de Ceglia, pg. 250.

177 unusually pure water . . . : The Institute of General Chemistry and Hygiene was enamored with the idea of the purity of all things Italian, not just holy water. It was founded by dictator Benito Mussolini to prove the excellence of the Italian people in science so that they could "implement, in Italy's name,

that colonization and spiritual brotherhood with the neighboring nations, to which Bari now feels inevitably called." Its first president, Nicola Pende, was one of the signatories of the Manifesto of Racist Scientists (1938). See de Ceglia, pp. 241–243.

177 Martino speculates that . . . : Martino, *Reliquie*, 10.

177 They made up a legend . . . : de Ceglia, pp. 245, 247–248.

178 The crypt is extremely cool . . . : Martino, *Reliquie*, 11.

178 The examination revealed the details . . . : Martino, *Reliquie*, 58–59.

180 The Venetians had popped the top to . . . : All of the following is taken from Martino, "Adventure."

181 "The bones of the saint, preserved in Venice . . .": Martino, "Adventure."

183 "still stuck together . . .": Anonymous Monk of Lido, chap. 23.

183 I asked a forensic anthropologist . . . : Interview, December 18, 2023. Dr. Corthals also pointed out that the tar on the bones described in the source could actually have been the remains of an early Christian embalming practice. In flimsy imitation of Egyptian embalming practices, early Mediterranean Christians would sometimes use tar to seal a body's wrappings and stave off decay. It was not particularly effective. If this corpse was heated in a fire, the tar would have melted and fused onto the bones. This practice would not have been uncommon in the fourth century (during Nicholas's life), and persisted until the eighth century. Similarly, they may have used resin to embalm the body; this also would have coagulated and fused in a fire to become an extremely hard substance, as the Anonymous Monk of Lido describes it. Regardless, the tar is not difficult to explain if there was a fire in the church at some point—if this really does represent a previous stratum of church building—and if, of course, the monk's account is accurate, and not a fabrication.

183 I believe that the two churches in the two rival cities . . . : It is, of course, possible that the guardians of the Basilica of Saint Nicholas in Myra had been dousing the wrong skeleton in myron for several hundred years, and that the Venetians, by pure chance, stumbled on the real burial site, lost for centuries. It is also possible that the Anonymous Monk of Lido made up the whole laborious story of the chunks of glass and coal, and that these bone fragments really were skimmed out of the same broken sarcophagus that the Barian bones came from—that they are part of the same skeleton. Both of these scenarios seem extremely unlikely. I am inclined to credit the strange particularities in the monk's story—only because the details are so oddly specific. We can be pretty certain that the Venetians carried something away from Myra, given that this account was written about fifteen years later, when there were still probably a couple hundred people who'd been part of the Venetian expeditionary force who were alive and able to tell their stories.

184 His tomb would be . . . : We know that by the mid-sixth century, the church in Myra was famous as his martyrium, as it is mentioned several times in the *Life of St. Nicholas of Sion*, another Lycian saint.

184 He steals a lot . . . : For a chart of the shared details, see Grant, pg. 258.

185 Venice did not manage to spread . . . : Cioffari, "Giovanni arcidiacono," pg. 50.

185 As the League of Saint Nicholas grew older . . . : Cioffari, *Traslazione*, pp. 49–51.

186 Back in Lycia, in Nicholas's homeland . . . : For the difficulty of dating precisely the reconquest of western Anatolia, see Roche, *passim*.

186 They reclaimed the city . . . : The dating is not precise. The clearest indications we have are that the Venetians believed there were still at least roving bands of Turks in the area in 1100—but that by 1102, the English pilgrim Saewulf could stop off in Myra without any worry. See his account in Thomas Wright, ed. and trans. *Early Travels in Palestine, Comprising the Narratives of Arculf, Willibald, Bernard, Sæwulf, Sigurd, Benjamin of Tudela, Sir John Maundeville, de la Brocquière, and Maundrell*. London: Henry Bohn, 1848: pp. 94, 116–117.

187 There is archaeological evidence of these

repairs . . . : This is assuming that this corridor was constructed during the renovations around 1100 and not those around 1040. Çorağan, pg. 90.

187 Though Nicholas's body was gone . . . : Özgür, pg. 17; cf. Jones, *Myra*, 11–12, 28.

188 By the twelfth century . . . : Cioffari, *Life*, 83.

188 A few centuries later, reports . . . : Jones, *Myra*, 315–318.

188 Over the years, more and more professions . . . : Jones, *Myra*, 273–274.

189 The church and the city around it . . . : At one time, it was thought that a series of floods had driven people to abandon the church. It now seems certain, based on the stratigraphy of the silt, that it was a single catastrophic flood. (Niewöhner, "Neues," pg. 124.)

191 The city of Amsterdam passed laws . . . : Jones, *Myra*, 330–331.

191 By this point, Dutch children . . . : Jones, *Myra*, 317.

197 Over the next several weeks . . . : Andrew Burstein, *The Original Knickerbocker: The Life of Washington Irving*. Cambridge, MA: Basic Books, 2007; pg. 107. Cf. Elizabeth Bradley, *Knickerbocker: The Myth Behind New York*. New Brunswick, NJ: Rivergate Books, 2009, which discusses the antecedents and germination of Washington Irving's hoax in more detail, especially in its first chapter.

198 "New York had ever been called New Amsterdam . . .": Jones, *Myra*, 344.

198 The story he tells is that when a party . . . : Irving, loc. 169.

200 The Saint Nicholas that Washington Irving drew . . . : Irving, loc. 132.

200 That fortress and that church . . . : Irving, loc. 187.

200 He referred, later in the History . . . : Irving, loc. 187.

201 Irving describes him "riding . . .": Irving, loc. 216.

201 Irving's brother-in-law . . . : James Paulding, *The Book of Saint Nicholas, Translated from the Original Dutch of Dominie Nicholas Ægidius Oudenarde*. New York: Harper & Bros., 1836.

202 The one snippet from this fad . . . : Paul Hond, "The Story Behind the Most Famous Christmas Poem of All," *Columbia Magazine*, Nov. 19, 2021. Online at https://magazine.columbia.edu/article/story-behind-most-famous-christmas-poem-all.

204 At about the same time that Irving was scribbling . . . : The following is all taken from Cockerell, pp. 165–167.

206 In the summer, he was basically . . . : This is assuming that he is the same old priestly custodian encountered by another English traveler, Charles Fellows, a few years later (Fellows, pg. 200).

206 The Englishman was admiring . . . : Cockerell, pp. 166–167.

207 When a Frenchman visited . . . : Charles Texier, *Asie Mineure: Description géographique, historique, et archéologique*. Paris: Firmin Didot Frères, 1862: pg. 691. The story of the Russian theft also appears in Charles Fellows's travelogue, pg. 200.

208 When the League of Saint Nicholas stole his remains . . . : The *Kyiv Slovo*, which appears to have been written around 1095.

208 In the 1850s, during the reign . . . : Özgür, pp. 21–22; cf. Doğan, pp. 51–53, who gives the princess's name as Anna Galitsyna.

208 They seized the land back . . . : Rott, pg. 326.

209 When a German archaeologist . . . : All of the following is taken from Rott, pp. 324–342.

210 "To the north of the church . . .": Rott, pg. 327.

211 Enter advertising artist . . . : There had been a few Coca-Cola ads with Santa in the 1920s, but Sundblom's images quickly became iconic. "Haddon Sundblom and the Coca-Cola Santas," Coca-Cola Company. URL: https://www.coca-colacompany.com/about-us/history/haddon-sundblom-and-the-coca-cola-santas.

212 In 1939, an ad writer . . . : Smithsonian Snapshot: "Rudolph the Red-Nosed Reindeer," December 21, 2010. Online at https://www.si.edu/newsdesk/snapshot/rudolph-red-nosed-reindeer.

212 "He knows if you've been bad . . .": From "Santa Claus Is Coming to Town," by J. Fred Coots and Haven Gillespie (1934).

213 "Friend, don't glorify Satan . . .": "Santa Claus & Satan's Cause," Bible Baptist Publications, Martin, TN. Online at https://biblebaptistpublications.org/holidaytracts.html. Cited in Jeremy Seal, *Nicholas: The Epic Journey from Saint to Santa Claus* (New York: Bloomsbury, 2005).

221 First, let's stroll around the church . . . : Doğan, in Doğan, pg. 313.

222 For one thing, in a funeral corridor . . . : Borchhardt, Appendix I (pp. 349–351) actually concludes, on the evidence available at the time (1975), that the tomb was in this funeral corridor (3 in this map), and not in the side chapels. It was this study which I used to place the hidden sarcophagus in my own fictional treatment, *Nicked* (2024). Nowadays this theory is generally disregarded in light of more recent evidence. It seems more likely that the sarcophagus burials in this corridor were wealthy patrons who wanted to be laid to rest near their patron saint.

222 The delicate inlaid floor . . . : Doğan, pp. 145, 272.

223 One German archaeologist . . . : Philipp Niewöhner ("Neues," "Tomb") argues that the second side chapel (4 on our map) was the saint's martyrium, partially on the evidence of similar churches, and points out that much later tradition places the body here. The beautiful inlaid floor in this chapel has indeed been inexpertly and asymmetrically patched with large slabs of stone (as shown in Doğan, pg. 272). (N.b.: Niewöhner does not put credence in the *translatio* accounts and assumes that the martyrium here was an arcosolium burial—above ground, in a niche.)

I would add that the larger, cross-shaped third side chapel (5) is of potential interest: The funeral corridor with the Nicholas frescoes leads to it; it is more substantial than the other chapels; and it was apparently enlarged (its *opus sectile* floor doesn't cover all of its floor space, and clearly suggests that a smaller chamber was expanded). Archaeologists generally have dated this funeral corridor (3) and cross-shaped chapel (5) to the beginning of the twelfth century—that is to say, in the years right *after* the heist. This dating, however, is based on stylistic grounds and perhaps should not be taken for granted. If this side chapel and corridor were built during the renovations of the 1040s, the cross-shaped chapel could have been the location of Nicholas's tomb when the Barians arrived.

And if, on the other hand, these rooms were indeed built or rebuilt around 1100–1110, they could have specifically been built around some cult object left behind after the theft—like the broken sarcophagus that previously housed the saint, or the sacred icon the Barians left behind. It is even possible, if we are to believe the Anonymous Monk of Lido's story of Venetian oversight, that the sarcophagus still contained bone fragments left behind by Matteo in his haste, the shattered remains of Nicholas's rib cage and pelvis. These were supposedly ignored by the Venetians, who refused to consider the sarcophagus half-filled *with myron*. Regardless, we know that pilgrim traffic to the basilica continued after the body was stolen and widely recognized to be in Bari. Sufficient relics clearly remained to draw to the faithful to visit Myra—as, indeed, the broken sarcophagi in the church still draw Russian pilgrims to this day.

Generally, it's important to remember that the church was damaged, renovated, and reconstructed many times in its history, and it is possible that the body reposed in different places in different epochs. Furthermore, it is possible that one or more of these sacralized spots held the relics of St. Theodore and St. Nicholas the Uncle at some point—the sixth century saint whose nephew founded one of the churches Dr. Niewöhner uses as a comparison.

223 Several of those rooms . . . : Ötüken, in Doğan, pg. 105; but cf. pg. 106, n. 88.

223 It is likely that at least for a time . . . : Ötüken, in Doğan, pg. 81. I find the Turkish team's evidence and deductions very persuasive.

223 Its floor also contains traces . . . : Ötüken, in Doğan, pp. 83–87; cf. Çiğdem Alas's article on the flooring (esp. Doğan, pp. 285–286), which records numerous interesting finds and observations. Alas dates the construction of this suite of rooms to the sixth century, based on the mortar used.

223 There is evidence of a fancy sacred gate . . . : A templon. Doğan, in Doğan, pg. 308. It appears there was also a templon in the cruciform chapel (5 on our map), discussed and reconstructed on Doğan, pp. 309–311. This might suggest that at a different point, Nicholas's body was buried there—or that Theodore and Nicholas the Uncle were stored there.

(But note: The current theory is that this wing of the church was enlarged right *after* the theft of the bones, which complicates either of those suggestions—unless the stylistic dating of the renovation of the cross-shaped chapel and the burial corridor to the early twelfth century is mistaken. Otherwise, it seems more likely that the southern annex was enlarged to house whatever relics were left behind after the theft.)

224 There was a platform for a speaker . . . : Ötüken, in Doğan, pp. 74–75. I find the Turkish team's evidence and deductions very persuasive.

224 under a layer of concrete . . . : See notes to pp. 115 and 121, above, regarding the possible arrangement used to access the sarcophagus from above.

INDEX